THE COMMON MAN'S COMMENTARY SERIES®
AMERICA'S "BLUE COLLAR" BIBLE STUDY™

JESUS IS COMING BACK ANY DAY NOW

I & II THESSALONIANS
A VERSE-BY-VERSE STUDY

DAVID R. WILLIAMS, D. MIN., D.D.

FOUNDER OF THE AMERICAN CENTER FOR PACESETTING LEADERSHIP

JESUS IS COMING BACK ANY DAY NOW

I & II THESSALONIANS A VERSE-BY-VERSE STUDY

THE COMMON MAN'S COMMENTARY SERIES®
AMERICA'S BLUE-COLLAR BIBLE STUDY™

For quantity discounts visit www.DaveWilliams.com, email info@DaveWilliams.com, or write P.O. Box 80825, Lansing, MI 48908

Jesus is Coming Back Any Day Now!
Copyright © 2024 by David R. Williams
ISBN: 978162-985072-6
Editor in Chief: Joel Kilpatrick
Cover Design by: The Cloud Digital
Layout Design: Kristy Grundner
All Artistic Illustrations by Michael Tomanica

www.DaveWilliams.com

24 25 26 27 28 – 9 8 7 6 5 4 3 2 1

Printed in the United States of America

CONTENTS

Thank you ... to my wonderful wife, Mary Jo,
for helping me edit this book. I love you, MJ.

INTRODUCTION

Welcome to the Common Man's Commentary on Paul's two letters to the Church in Thessalonica!

Unlike some commentaries, which are often thick, boring, and have intimidating titles, this book is aimed squarely at the common Christian with maybe just a little academic knowledge of the Bible. I wrote the Common Man's Commentary series to draw out the practical lessons in each section of a particular book of the Bible. We don't get bogged down in Greek and Hebrew, but we dig a little deeper into each passage.

These two letters from Paul have so many answers for us today! Every lesson in this book will include principles that can advance your life. You will gain a deeper understanding that will help you each day. In this study of I and II Thessalonians you will learn:

- **How to lack nothing in life**
- **How to make a lasting impression on others**
- **How to live pure in an X-rated world**
- **How to deal with troublemakers**

And much more! We are going to take these letters and break them down into understandable bites, so we can act on what Paul teaches us. Your faith will grow! Your love will grow! I'm excited about how this study will forever impact your life, so let's start.

ACKNOWLEDGMENTS

While I cannot thank all the people who have poured into my life over the years, I'd like to acknowledge a few. The late Dr. E. Glenn Snook, taught me how to take complicated matters and simplify them to everyday language. The late Pastor Chuck Smith of Calvary Chapel regularly took us through a refreshing verse-by-verse Bible study. And how could I not mention the late Dr. J. Vernon McGee and his Through the Bible radio program? Dr. McGee kept it simple.

A special thanks to my editorial team. You guys are the best. You help me accomplish more in less time.

David R. Williams, D. Min., D.D.

HISTORY OF PAUL'S FIRST LETTER TO THE THESSALONIANS

St. Paul's first letter to the Thessalonians is St. Paul's first epistle. It is the earliest documented writing of the Christian Church.

The City of Thessalonica was the capital and largest city of the Roman province of Macedonia. The city served as a great center of trade and commerce in the Roman Empire. Today, it is known as Thessaloniki or Salonica.

Before Paul came along, the Church was quite Jewish.

Only after St. Paul arrived on the scene, did the Church begin to spread into Gentile areas. Paul was a true apostle, launching into fresh territory, preaching both to Jews and Gentiles alike, which created a certain tension. Paul could be credited with the amazing feat of transforming a temple-like religion into a faith that was taken to marketplaces of the cities.

Paul believed that faith in Jesus Christ was not meant to be locked up in a certain once-a-week experience in the place of worship, but was designed to be an every day, every moment, everywhere faith, including the streets, homes, and workplaces of every city and village. Paul's letter to the Thessalonians is Paul's first endeavor to put into words his thoughts about the Christian faith in everyday life.

He wrote this first letter about 22 years after the Death, Resurrection, and Ascension of Jesus. This would be around 52 A.D. Paul planted and established the Church at Thessalonica on his second journey (Acts 17:1-9) and wrote the letter while working in Corinth.

We can summarize the purpose of Paul's writing to the Thessalonians this way: (1) To commend them for their steadfastness and persistence, even under persecution, (2) To provide instructions on holy living, (3) To address and correct the false teachings and erroneous concepts concerning the second coming of Christ

The challenge Paul addresses strongly in both of his writings to the Thessalonians has to do primarily with rumors and false concepts of Christ's return. The Church was wondering why Christ had not yet returned and Paul attempted to clear the matter in their minds and hearts. Paul assures them that the Rapture will occur, the antichrist will come, and God will always be faithful to deliver His people.

I THESSALONIANS OUTLINE

I. Introduction
   A. Greeting (1:1-2)
II. Instructions
   A. Church Instructions (1:1-10)
      1. How to be a Model Church
      2. How to Accelerate Your Good News
      3. How to Make an Impression on Others
   B. Dealing with Deceit (2:1-8)
      1. How to Handle Opposition & Deceit
      2. How to Deal with False Prophets
   C. Matters to the Believer (2:9– 4:12)
      1. How to Encourage and Comfort Others
      2. How to Become an Established Believer
      3. How to Live Pure in a Triple X-rated World
      4. How to Lack Nothing in Your Life
III. End Times Eschatology
   A. How a Believer Approaches the Last Days (4:13-18)
      1. What Happens After Death?
      2. The Rapture
      3. Comforting the Believer
   B. How the World Will Handle the Rapture (5:1-10)
      1. Understanding the "Day of the Lord"
      2. Staying Awake and Sober
      3. God's Wrath and Our Deliverance
   C. How to Have a Happy, Healthy Church (5:11-14)
      1. Comfort in Light of Coming Events
      2. The Place of Clergy
      3. Warnings and Exhortations
IV. Paul's Concluding Remarks (5:15-28)
   A. How to Reboot Your Life

1 Thessalonians 1

1 Paul, and Silvanus, and Timotheus, unto the church of the Thessalonians which is in God the Father and in the Lord Jesus Christ: Grace be unto you, and peace, from God our Father, and the Lord Jesus Christ.

2 We give thanks to God always for you all, making mention of you in our prayers;

3 Remembering without ceasing your work of faith, and labour of love, and patience of hope in our Lord Jesus Christ, in the sight of God and our Father;

4 Knowing, brethren beloved, your election of God.

5 For our Gospel came not unto you in word only, but also in power, and in the Holy Ghost, and in much assurance; as ye know what manner of men we were among you for your sake.

6 And ye became followers of us, and of the Lord, having received the word in much affliction, with joy of the Holy Ghost.

7 So that ye were ensamples to all that believe in Macedonia and Achaia.

8 For from you sounded out the word of the Lord not only in Macedonia and Achaia, but also in every place your faith to God-ward is spread abroad; so that we need not to speak any thing.

9 For they themselves shew of us what manner of entering in we had unto you, and how ye turned to God from idols to serve the living and true God;

10 And to wait for his Son from heaven, whom he raised from the dead, even Jesus, which delivered us from the wrath to come.

LESSON 1

HOW TO BE A MODEL CHURCH

I Thessalonians 1:1-4

1 Paul, and Silvanus, and Timotheus, unto the church of the Thessalonians which is in God the Father and in the Lord Jesus Christ: Grace be unto you, and peace, from God our Father, and the Lord Jesus Christ.

2 We give thanks to God always for you all, making mention of you in our prayers;

3 Remembering without ceasing your work of faith, and labour of love, and patience of hope in our Lord Jesus Christ, in the sight of God and our Father;

4 Knowing, brethren beloved, your election of God.

We are going to learn a lot in this lesson! This is where we begin a verse-by-verse study of the wonderful books of I and II Thessalonians, which were letters the Apostle Paul wrote to Christians in a city where he had ministered. In this first chapter, we'll see what it takes to be a model church and a model Christian. The first few verses of I and II Thessalonians lay out a path for us to follow toward becoming a model church *together* and model Christians *individually*. But first a little background.

PAUL'S STRATEGY FOR SUCCESSFUL CHURCH PLANTING

Thessalonica was the capital city of Macedonia and the largest city in Macedonia. It was once named Therma for its hot springs, but the Romans changed the name to Thessalonica when they took it over. Paul went there because it was the most strategic city in that area. His ministry strategy was to go to the largest and most influential cities and establish a church. Then he would branch out to the smaller communities and cities and build churches there too.

The strategy worked pretty well: within thirty years the whole known world had heard the Gospel! That's why Mount Hope Church, where I was pastor for 31 years, used the same approach. We established a church in an influential city like Lansing, then, we went into smaller cities like Grand Blanc, Portland, Gaylord, Corunna, and Jackson. The proven most effective tool for evangelism is church planting. It's getting preachers and ministers out there and establishing churches where people can become involved. There is no more effective way to win and disciple the world than the way Paul did it.

Paul ran his tent-making business from Thessalonica, which indicates that he was there for a while. But when he started preaching the Gospel in the synagogue, there were public riots and he was forced out of town after just three weeks. Most of the Jews there had rejected the Gospel, so Paul preached to and won Gentiles to the Lord. Thus, the church of Thessalonica was made up mostly of Gentiles. But some of the Christians, such as a man named Jason, began to be harassed by authorities. The government was taking property from the Christians, holding it as bail and vowing that if Paul ever came back to town, they would take everything the Christians owned. It was preventing Paul from going back to Thessalonica to check on the church. But he loved those people; they were dear to him.

This letter that Paul wrote to them, in about 52 A.D., was his first Epistle. He wrote it while he was in Corinth.

ENEMY SMEAR CAMPAIGN

Paul's enemies had launched a smear campaign against him back in Thessalonica. Paul was troubled because his critics were determined to discredit him. As a result, Paul bared his soul to the believers in Thessalonica hoping they would not be drawn in by the slanderous misinformation campaign of his maligners. His purpose in writing this letter was to reconnect with the church that he had left behind rather quickly. He didn't want the Thessalonian Christians to think that he didn't love them or that he had abandoned them. He told them he had tried to come back to them but that Satan hindered him.

> **1 Thessalonians 2:18**
> **Wherefore we would have come unto you, even I Paul, once and again; but Satan hindered us.**

Let's focus on that for a moment, because it is one of the enemy's typical strategies, which we see at work here.

SATAN ATTACKS TO DISCREDIT PAUL

Whenever something good and godly is in its seedling stage, Satan attacks it. He knows that it's a lot easier to get a seed out of the ground than it is to bring down a mighty oak tree. The church in Thessalonica was a seedling, just taking root, beginning to bud. So, Satan took the opportunity to attack. He did it in several ways, chiefly by infiltrating the church with people who wanted to discredit Paul. There were unscrupulous people in this church who tried to profit from being antagonistic and spreading negative things about Paul, (just as there are such people in many churches today!)

These criminal infiltrators told the new Christians that Paul was nothing but a "greedy charlatan." They frightened the Thessalonians by saying there was not going to be a Rapture, as Paul claimed, but that they were going to go through the Tribulation (which, by the way, they claimed had already begun). The new believers in this fledgling church believed this because the persecution against them had increased. Not only that, they believed the lie that if somebody died before the Rapture they wouldn't make it to heaven, which of course, was another enemy tactic.

CORRECTING THEOLOGICAL AND ESCHATOLOGICAL ERRORS

They were confused by all these different false teachings that were circulating in Paul's absence, and so Paul was writing to correct these theological and eschatological errors introduced by false teachers and heretics attending the church at Thessalonica. He wrote to set this little flock's hearts at ease.

One other thing about young churches: they aren't just targets for satanic attacks, but they tend to be more enthusiastic, energetic, on fire, and even "wildfire" for God. The other side of this coin is that they also tend not to be fully instructed in the things of God. They need wisdom and guidance. That's normal.

Whenever there's a new work or a new ministry you'll find people going to a few extremes, but I'd rather have the fire of God and a few extremes than to have a church that's cold and dead. As the pastor of a church-planting church, I would much rather plant churches even though we'll have one or two that go overboard now and then. Who minds a little wildness occasionally? So what? That indicates that there's life! And where there's life, something good can grow.

The old saying goes, "I'd rather try to tame a wild horse than revive a dead one." Give me a lively church any day over a stuffy dead one. No church is perfect, and we all need instruction to learn and grow.

An example of this was a prophetic movement that swept through some churches in the 1990s. As a new emphasis, some excesses and extremes accompanied it, and this caused people who were in dead-like churches to criticize the whole movement and say it was not of God. They similarly criticized the Jesus movement in the 1960s and the charismatic movement in the 1970s by pointing to excesses and extremes. People did the same at the Pentecostal outpouring in1906, 1914, and in subsequent movements that were "wild and extreme," but gave birth to some of the greatest churches in America. I find that things have a way of working their way out if we stay in God's Word and accept God's instruction.

1 THESSALONIANS 1:1

WHAT PAUL'S GREETING MEANS

Let's dive into Paul's words.

> **[1]Paul, and Silvanus, and Timotheus, unto the church of the Thessalonians which is in God the Father and in the Lord Jesus Christ: Grace be unto you, and peace, from God our Father, and the Lord Jesus Christ.**

Notice first that Paul did not use his apostolic title in the greeting of this letter. He had a true friendship with the people of Thessalonica. He knew they understood his authority and respected his leadership. He did not need to assert his apostleship. Secondly, he introduced himself in the context of his assistants and friends who were with him. Timothy was his convert and his young son in the faith. And even though they understood Paul's authority and position, Paul counted himself as their equal. He didn't write, "From Paul the great apostle and his two minor assistants..."[1]

When people put the clergy on a pedestal, we do a disservice to the church of Jesus Christ. That's why I don't think clergymen should always wear robes or anything else that sets them apart from the people of the church (except perhaps on occasions such as ordination or official services), because we are all, according to St. Peter, "living stones, being built into a spiritual house."

We all, as followers of Christ, have different authority levels in God's Kingdom, nonetheless, we are still brothers and sisters in the Lord. I don't think we should set the clergy higher than the laity. We are all one in Jesus Christ.

Verse 1 continues...

> **...unto the church of the Thessalonians which is in God the Father and in the Lord Jesus Christ**

Paul addressed his letter to the church of the Thessalonians, which is "in God the Father and in the Lord Jesus Christ." When you accept Jesus into your life as Lord, you come into a great family. You get to know God the Father, God the Son, and God the Holy Spirit. There is no safer place to be than to be in Christ. That is where you are built into a model Christian. That's where you begin to resemble Christ.

Notice also that Paul is addressing the people in "the church of the Thessalonians." These words are not just filler. He is talking to the church, not to a bunch of individuals.

One of the worst things you can do is lead people to Christ and not steer them to a good local church. I've heard some people say they are committed to Jesus Christ but not to a specific church. Hogwash! If they are not part of a church it shows that they are not truly committed to the head of the Church, Jesus Christ.

Paul likened the church to a body, with Jesus Christ as the head. To be part of the body of Christ you have to come to the head, which is Jesus. But then you naturally and necessarily become a part of the body. It's simply impossible to be committed to the head but not to the body. No groom commits himself just to the bride's head, but to her whole body. You are in love with a whole person. Jesus is connected to His body, and His body is connected to Him. We express our connection to Him by being in a church where we partner together for the sake of missions, evangelism, and making disciples. Then we go on to the next stage of growth in the church and become a mentor, a disciple maker, and a teacher.

There is no safer place to be than to be a part of a local body of believers committed to the Lordship of Jesus Christ.

TRUTH ILLUSTRATED – PLANE WITHOUT WINGS?

While in flight school years ago, I became good friends with my flight instructor, Bill, a wonderful man, then in his seventies. He was like my adopted dad away from home. One time I went back to Tulsa to see him. We went to Tony Roma's for dinner, and as we were coming out I asked, "How are things going over at the church?" He was silent. His wife, Lois, put her hands on her hips and said, "You tell him, Bill." Bill bowed his head and softly answered, "Dave, I quit going to church. They canceled the aviation ministry because the insurance was too high. I got upset and left. But don't worry—I'm still committed to Christ."

Now it was my turn to teach him. I came back with an answer, "Suppose we wanted to fly around for a while, so we went out to the airport, opened up the hangar and there was a beautiful plane engine. It was well-oiled, the shiniest, best plane engine that you've ever seen. It had the prettiest propeller on it, but no wings, no tail, no fuselage. How high do you think we would fly?"

He responded, "I think I get your point."

You cannot simply be committed to Christ without being committed to His body, any more than you can commit to flying an airplane with just an engine and no wings, tail, or fuselage.

When we turn from sin and turn to Jesus Christ, we're born into the Church of Jesus Christ. But now we must also be committed to, and identified with, a local expression of Christ's body. Becoming rooted in a local church is a visible expression of our invisible identification with Christ.

THE KIND OF FAVOR THAT BRINGS YOU JOY

No church is perfect. I learned that a long time ago. One of the reasons no church you attend will ever be perfect—is because you're in it! As long as the church is on earth, you will never find a perfect church. But you need to find a church where Christ is exalted, the Holy Spirit has freedom, where God's Word is preached uncompromisingly, and where you can get your roots down deep.

Paul continued in verse one,

> **Grace be unto you, and peace, from God our Father, and the Lord Jesus Christ.**

The word "grace" means favor, which comes from the Greek word "charis" which is related to the word "joy" ("Chará" in Greek). So, grace is the favor that brings you great joy.

When we experience God's grace, joy is the natural result.

At our church in Lansing, I taught a verse-by-verse study in the book of Romans, and joy began to overflow in the church as we studied God's grace and re-discovered how to live by faith. We were overjoyed again about being saved not by our works but by God's grace through our faith in His Son Jesus.

Somebody wise once said that joy is the most infallible sign of God's presence in a person's life. I'm not talking about happiness, because people are not always happy. Happiness depends on happenings—notice it has the same root. If something happens that we don't like, it takes away our happiness. But joy is something different; it's something deep down, based on God's presence and grace at work in our lives. The Bible says, "In thy presence is fullness of joy" (Psalm 16:11). It's amazing how something bad can happen but you can still have joy unspeakable and full of glory which leads to peace from God our Father in the Lord Jesus Christ.

Paul also said "Peace." We tend to misunderstand this word. We think of peace as the absence of war. I'm reminded of Winston Churchill's immortal words, "We shall fight on the beaches, we shall fight on the landing grounds, we shall fight in the fields and in the streets, we shall fight in the hills." That sounds like some people's family vacation!

But what does the word "peace" literally mean? Does it only mean the absence of fighting or friction? No. Study the root of this word and you may be radically surprised.

Peace means wholeness, soundness, and prosperity in the widest sense—spiritually and materially. It is complete and total prosperity of being. Peace means living the good life! We can expect this kind of peace, this kind of prosperity when we've experienced God's grace.

1 THESSALONIANS 1:2

BEING THANKFUL FOR EVERYBODY?

Paul said a lot in that first verse! In the second verse, he went on:

> **2 We give thanks to God always for you all, making mention of you in our prayers**

I've met some pastors who don't give thanks for anybody in their church. They gripe about everybody for this or that reason. Of course, there are always some "stinkers" and "crabs" and annoying people in any church or organization. I've met plenty of them! For example, when I'm in the foyer of my church in between services, some people try to dominate my time. Invariably the same predictable people just *have* to see me every week, not thinking that there are a thousand or more other people who might like to at least shake my hand and say hello.

These inconsiderate people will complain about this and gripe about that. I've found them waiting by my car hours after a service. I used to dread leaving the building. Some nights I'd call my wife Mary Jo and say, "I'm just sleeping here tonight. They're waiting at my car for me." Some folks can be so insensitive. They seem to think they're the only people in the world.

But over the years I have learned to thank God for every one of the annoying people in my life. Friends used to tell me to quit being so patient with people. They wanted me to fight back at times instead of putting up with people's ungodly attitudes. But I just thanked God that He sent them to me. I read one paraphrase of I Corinthians 13 that says, "Love hath no bodyguards." I like that.

You, too, can be thankful for everybody who comes into your life. There are always annoying people and "sandpaper people" who rub you the wrong way, but maybe God sent them to rub off some rough spots in your life. Everybody is valuable and everybody has worth. A pastor should thank God for every soul God sends to his church—crabby ones, weak-minded ones, feeble-minded ones—because none of us is perfect and nobody grows at the same rate.

Paul even said he and his companions made mention of all those people in their prayers.

Paul must have had a long prayer list!

I've noticed that Christians often say, "I'll be praying for you!" But do they do it? I hear people say it across the foyer on Sunday morning to each other: "I'll be praying for you." It's more like a glorified "see-ya-later," than a promise. I believe if we say we're going to pray for someone, we should pray!

Often people come up to me at church and say, "Pastor, please pray for me," and then they share a need. I'm often unsure if they actually want me to pray for them, or if they're just wanting me to hear about their need. But in every case, I have a backup minister, or my wife, or somebody who's with me write the request down so I don't forget about it. I want to be a person of prayer and follow through on what I say I will do. One of the joys of my life is when I go to prayer in the morning and spread out the little blue cards with all the prayer requests I've received and pray over each one individually.

1 THESSALONIANS 1:3

THREE PILLARS OF A MODEL CHURCH

Now Paul starts describing the model church. In verse 3 he tells them why he's so thankful for them and gives three reasons why they're a great church:

> **3 Remembering without ceasing your work of faith, and labour of love, and patience of hope in our Lord Jesus Christ, in the sight of God and our Father**

Here are the three reasons Paul praises the believers in Thessalonica:

- **Their work of faith**
- **Their labor of love**
- **Their patience of hope in our Lord Jesus Christ in the sight of God our Father**

PILLAR 1 - FAITH

The first pillar that makes a model church is work produced by faith. Paul insists throughout his writings that true faith is busy, not lazy. True faith produces actions. Faith without works is dead; It doesn't accomplish anything. True faith has to be working for something to be considered faith.

I love being around an active church. I love driving into the parking lot and seeing cars everywhere. I love it when I have to ask someone what's going on today and why are there so many people here today?

TRUTH ILLUSTRATED – EFFECTIVE MINISTRY

One of the busiest and most effective churches I've ever seen is the Dream Center and Angelus Temple in Los Angeles[2]. Everywhere you go, they're busy. They're taking buses into neighborhoods to put on puppet shows for kids. They send out food trucks and other buses that pick people up on Skid Row and bring them to the church services. They bring in prostitutes in the middle of the night so they'll be safe from their pimps. That's a church with real faith.

True faith isn't going to church so you'll be blessed. It's actively becoming a blessing for others. "It is more blessed to give than to receive," Jesus said (Acts 20:35). "But without faith, it is impossible to please him," (Hebrews 11:6). True faith always includes action.

If you are going to please God you have to act on your faith.

PILLAR 2 – LOVE

The second pillar that made the Thessalonians a model church and an example to others was their labor of love. The word "labor" sounds awfully dull. It brings to mind joyless work. Labor most likely is dull if you don't love Jesus. Every bit of work you do is drudgery in that case. But when you love somebody, there is great joy in labor. A husband works hard because he loves his family. A wife loves her husband so she doesn't mind cooking a good meal. She doesn't mind picking up after him. It's a labor of love.

TRUTH ILLUSTRATED – LOVE CAN HURT

One time my family was on vacation and we were in a swimming pool. I was out in the middle and saw my young son go under the water. I swam over to him, got under him, and pushed him up with my arm, but how I pushed him made it feel like I was breaking every bone in my body. Still, I pushed because I wasn't going to let him drown. I remember pushing him up and out, and as a result, I was in pain for eight months. I went to the doctor and he said I had torn a muscle. But I wouldn't have taken back what I did. I would have ripped every muscle in my body and wouldn't have counted it a sacrifice, because I love him.

And that's what makes a model church. It labors from a heart of love.

Every morning I see people driving to work, and sitting at traffic lights, and the looks on their faces tell the whole story. They are going to jobs they hate. I have rarely, if ever, had that problem. My mother will tell you that I'm a natural worker. I enjoy labor.

When I was eight years old, I sold things door to door. At twelve years old I had a paper route. At fifteen years old I worked at the gas station, then as a dishwasher at the airport restaurant, and after that, as a security guard at the old Spartan horn factory. I was always working, always laboring.

As an adult, when I worked at the power company in the pump room, I realized I didn't enjoy it anymore. Work had become drudgery. I spent all day going around checking gauges and fine-tuning the process. Then one day I read the Scripture in Colossians that says, "Work willingly at whatever you do, as though you were working for the Lord rather than for people. Remember that the Lord will give you an inheritance as your reward and that the Master you are serving is Christ.[3]

That day I made the Lord my employer. I said out loud, "Lord, I work for You and I work with You."

My joy came back! I went around every hour checking those meters with renewed enthusiasm, and if there was a little spilled oil I'd go to the janitor's closet, find a rag, and clean it up. I had the whole area looking shiny and spotless. The next thing I knew, I got promoted, and then the guy in line for the next promotion turned it down and I got promoted again!

God rewards work. He does not reward laziness.

I knew a pastor whom I'll call Ralph who never prepared a message to preach on Sunday morning. He'd come out with a bunch of clichés, maybe yell, loosen his tie, and throw a little sweat. I think the only reason he sweated was because he didn't prepare anything. On Sunday morning Ralph never had a message and so he would pray earnestly, "Oh Lord, give me your message." He did this week after week to no avail. One Sunday he was on the platform during worship time and he prayed, "God, give me your message." Finally, the Lord spoke to him and said, "Ralph, here's my message for you. You're lazy." Try preaching that.

When you're in love with Jesus, and you love people, you can work eighty hours and it seems like ten.

D. L. Moody said, "I get weary in the work sometimes, but never weary of the work."[4]

PILLAR 3 – HOPE

The third pillar that made them a model church was their "patience of hope in our Lord Jesus Christ, in the sight of God and our Father."

Patience means perseverance.

Hope is the conviction that things will be better in the future. Hope is a vision of good up ahead.

- **Young girls hope to be brides someday.**
- **Boys hope to have great careers.**
- **We all hope for good things, promotions, better pay, and better times to come.**
- **Hope is what sustains us.**

But the hope that makes a model Christian and a model church is not hope in man, it is hope in our Lord Jesus Christ. How many times do we see groups protesting and petitioning the government to give more money for their cause? They are hoping in men and government.

Real hope is the active expectation in Jesus Christ that whatever happens, the outcome will be good and right. Hope never gives in, never gives up. Hope is having certainty in your mind and in your attitude that you expect the outcome to be right in God's sight.

1 THESSALONIANS 1:4

WHO GETS ELECTED?

The next verse is one of the most misunderstood doctrines of the Christian faith. It says,

> 4 **Knowing, brethren beloved, your election of God.**

This is what theologians call the doctrine of election. There are a lot of weird ideas surrounding these few little words. Some sincerely believe that God has elected some people to go to hell and some to go to heaven. Certain denominations don't try to evangelize anyone because they figure that certain people are elected to heaven and some are not, and there's nothing anyone can do about it.

The other extreme is universalism, which says that God has elected everybody to go to heaven no matter what religion they belong to. The result again is that evangelism seems unnecessary since they believe everybody (or almost everybody) is going to heaven anyway.

The idea of being elected to go to hell sounds absurd because the Bible says, "For God so loved the world, that he gave his only begotten Son, that whosoever believeth in him should not perish, but have everlasting life" (John 3:16).

THE DOCTRINE OF ELECTION

The doctrine of election is quite simple.

Israel was God's elected nation and still is. They were to be His witnesses, His light, and His people. They were to be under His blessing and His care if they followed His ways. If a foreigner joined Israel, they became a part of Israel and part of the elected nation. But beginning with the death and resurrection of Jesus, God elected the Church to be His witness collectively. The Church became His chief testifier in the world, His light to the nations. Yet, God is not done with Israel. The day is coming when the Jewish people will accept their true Messiah and once again be known as God's elect nation.[5]

YOU CAN CHOOSE TO BE ELECTED

If an individual chooses to join the Church by coming to Jesus Christ, they become a part of the elect. And this is the key point: You can choose to be part of the elect. It's within your control. It's not predestined for you. If you have accepted Christ as your Savior, you are part of God's elect.

So, don't let people confuse you about the doctrine of election.

SUMMING IT UP

In this lesson, we have already bit into the meat of this letter. We learned we were elected to do works of faith. We were elected to a labor of love. We were elected to expect the best from God. We were elected to have an air of certainty concerning the future.

God has a plan for you and it's a good plan. It's a plan to make you a model Christian and build a model church through you and others.

Let's now see how we can speed up the good news.

POWER PRINCIPLES:

- **We are all one in Jesus Christ. The clergy is not spiritually "higher" than the people they serve.**
- **To be fully committed to Christ, we must also be an active part of a local church.**
- **You can be thankful for everybody—even difficult people.**
- **Faith, hope, and love are the pillars of a model church.**
- **You can choose to be part of God's elect.**

LESSON 2

HOW TO ACCELERATE YOUR GOOD NEWS

I Thessalonians 1:5-6

[5] For our Gospel came not unto you in word only, but also in power, and in the Holy Ghost, and in much assurance; as ye know what manner of men we were among you for your sake.

[6] And ye became followers of us, and of the Lord, having received the word in much affliction, with joy of the Holy Ghost.

Each of us has somebody in our lives who needs a word from God. Sometimes we are called to give that word to someone. When we do, we want it to be powerful. We want it to penetrate their darkness. We deeply desire it to be used by God to bring light to the unsaved family member or colleague, or to encourage a fellow believer.

1 THESSALONIANS 1:5

FOUR KEYS TO SUCCESSFUL COMMUNICATIONS

If you have ever wanted to present the message of Christ to someone, or felt that you needed to share a word from the Lord, this verse in I Thessalonians will help you. It shows the five keys to successfully presenting the Word. Paul writes,

[5] For our Gospel came not unto you in word only, but also in power, and in the Holy Ghost, and in much assurance; as ye know what manner of men we were among you for your sake.

The reason Paul went to Thessalonica sets the stage for us to learn our first powerful lesson. Paul went to Macedonia because of a vision of a man saying, "Come over into Macedonia, and help us." (Acts 16:9) Paul responded in faith and established a church in Thessalonica by speaking the Gospel to them. Think about that. The Gospel did not come to them by an angel. It did not come via a lightning bolt. It didn't come by a spaceship from another galaxy. It didn't come by God speaking from the clouds. It came by a man who was willing to go. Paul went there, spoke the Gospel, and taught them the Word. And that's the first key to effectively presenting God's Word.

KEY NO. 1 – YOU MUST USE WORDS, AND NOT JUST ANY WORDS, BUT THE RIGHT WORDS.

Some people say to me, "I don't talk about the Gospel or about Jesus. I just let my light shine, and people around me see the Gospel in my moral living." That's good, but it's not enough. There must be words. Words form sentences and sentences create a vision of reality in our minds. Paul spoke words, but not mere words. He spoke the right words.

If you read words from a store catalog or the phone book, they may be informative but they do not bring life or have the power to transform. Only the Word of God can produce life and transform hearts.[6] His Word abides forever[7]. That's why I pray before I preach, "God, give me words; put a watch over my mouth and don't let me say any more than I have to, but nothing less than I need to."[8]

If you speak words into people's lives, they must be words of life and truth.

It's amazing how some people want to be spiritually powerful or to be seen as having spiritual authority, but they don't stay closely connected to the Word of God, the Bible. They put the Bible on the shelf and still try to act in spiritual authority.

TRUTH ILLUSTRATED – BIBLE OR CATALOG?

A pastor was visiting a house one day, and the mother wanted to impress him. So, she told her five-year-old daughter to go into the back room and bring out the book Mommy loves so much. The girl returned with the Sears catalog. I wonder what book the little girl would return with if it were you who asked her to fetch your favorite book?

To share the word effectively we must use the right words—the Words from God Himself.

WORDS WITH POWER!

Words alone are not enough to transform lives. Have you ever heard two preachers preach virtually the same sermon, and one produced a great impact, while the other did not? That's because words alone will not change anybody. Four other components must go along with the words.

1. They must be the RIGHT WORDS
2. They must be POWERFUL WORDS
3. They must be CONFIDENTLY SPOKEN WORDS
4. They must be WORDS OF INTEGRITY

Paul said he didn't want to speak with enticing words of man's wisdom but with the demonstration of the power of the Holy Spirit.

1 Corinthians 2:4
And my speech and my preaching was not with enticing words of man's wisdom, but in demonstration of the Spirit and of power

KEY NO. 2 – YOUR WORDS MUST HAVE POWER

Words alone, no matter how articulate and well-presented, cannot penetrate a person's spiritual blindness. There must be power behind those words. The Gospel we preach, which is the same as the Gospel Paul preached, is not just a presentation of ideas, a philosophy, a system, or a religion. It is the very power of God! It is the greatest power ever known in creation, a power greater than any human power could ever be.

5...but also in power, and in the Holy Ghost...

Power is a buzzword these days. There are power suits, power lunches, power talks, Power Point presentations, power exercises, and power formulas. Infomercials often use the word "power" to give their products a certain allure. It's not just a "juicer," it's a "power juicer." They promise it will give you more power and energy than you've ever had. Just send four power payments of $49.95, plus $33 shipping and handling.

Advertisers entice buyers with the idea of power, and their enticements are pretty strong. Many times, I've been tempted to pick up the phone and order the latest power product.

TRUTH ILLUSTRATED – THE MOSQUITO SEMINAR

Let me give a silly illustration of our power versus God's power. Imagine a mosquito doing a live infomercial for other mosquitoes. This mosquito says, "Gather around, and thank you all for paying your $1,559.95 to attend this power seminar. I'm now going to show you how to have greater power. You're all going to be the most powerful mosquitoes in the world. I'm going to teach you how to power talk, power walk, and power fly." Just then, a big eagle swooped down and ate the mosquito who was presenting the seminar. Every other mosquito at the seminar watched and said, "Now that's power."

That's the difference between the power of the Gospel and the power of any human system or man-made philosophy. People can go on about their mosquito philosophies, but God wants us to have eagle faith! We can mount up with wings as eagles, and see more than others can see, because Jesus, the powerful One, lives inside of us.

Paul identifies who is behind this power: The Holy Spirit. Only He can penetrate people's lives and transform them with His power. You and I have no power to affect others unless we have the power of the Holy Spirit flowing through us.

John Stott, the famous British minister, said the Word without the Spirit is powerless, but the Spirit without the Word is weaponless[9]. God has joined together His Word and His Spirit. If you want power, you must have both.

The Holy Spirit will help you to prepare a message or a word for somebody.

Many times, I've been invited to speak somewhere for a special occasion, and I prepare the message I plan to deliver. Two days before the event, the Holy Spirit speaks something else to me, and I've got to start over from scratch. I've learned that I don't preach what I want to preach, I preach what He tells me to preach. Only then does it have the power to transform people's lives. I tell preachers, don't just have a sermon in a can and think it's going to change people's lives. If the Holy Spirit says to preach it, then go ahead and preach it. But be sure to seek a specific word from the Lord for a particular event. Those specific words, in the power of the Holy Spirit, carry an amazing benefit for people's lives.

WORDS WITH CONFIDENCE!

> **5...and in much assurance...**

Even a powerful word has to be presented in a certain way.

Paul wrote, "For our Gospel came [to you] ... in much assurance."

In the Greek language, the word "assurance" means "confidence and conviction on the part of the presenter." It means he or she has heard from God and is confident in what they say.

KEY NO. 3 – SPEAK WITH CONFIDENCE

When you go to speak to a friend or relative, and you've prayed about it thoroughly, and you feel like God has given you the word, you can speak it with confidence knowing that it won't return void.

> **Isaiah 55:11**
> **So shall my word be that goeth forth out of my mouth: it shall not return unto me void, but it shall accomplish that which I please, and it shall prosper in the thing whereto I sent it.**

The confident words the Lord gives you will penetrate and do something in listeners' lives, a work of grace, a work of mercy, or a work of conviction. If a person is in sin, the only way that they are convicted is if the word has power in the Holy Spirit, and you're speaking it with confidence.

It's hard to be under conviction when a preacher gets up and says, "God says thou shall not commit adultery, but we're living in a different day, and I can understand there are a lot of people cohabitating before marriage. Who am I to judge?"

No! When you speak for God, you must present only a biblical worldview, not a modern cultural worldview.

Where is the assurance? There has to be assurance in the things we believe and preach. A messenger who lacks confidence will not be heard or respected.

WORDS WITH INTEGRITY!

Paul said,

> **5...as ye know what manner of men we were among you for your sake.**

In another letter Paul wrote, "For we are not as many, which corrupt the word of God" (II Corinthians 2:17).

He was pointing out that words have power only when the messenger has integrity.

KEY NO. 4 - INTEGRITY

There's a proverb in one of the modern Bible translations that I love.

> **Proverbs 25:19 NLT**
> **Putting confidence in an unreliable person in times of trouble is like chewing with a broken tooth or walking on a lame foot.**

It says that to rely on an unreliable person is like trying to walk with a broken foot. Who wants to listen to an unreliable messenger? Nobody. In the same way, people want messengers who are committed to obeying the messages they are speaking.

Success comes from having the right word, speaking it confidently in the power of the Holy Spirit, and being a person of integrity.

TRUTH ILLUSTRATED – LIVING IT

I knew a lady who would sit at her kitchen table smoking cigarettes and saying, "I never want to catch you kids smoking."

Another woman was giving lessons on how to have successful relationships and a happy marriage. But people came to find out she had been divorced five times and married six times. She was trying to keep that a secret from everybody.

Suppose a man sells motivational products and gives exciting speeches that move you to the core. Like other motivational speakers, imagine that he teaches you how you can lose weight, gain respect, set goals, have successful relationships, gain power, and exceed all your expectations. And then you discover that his personal life is actually in shambles. His family is a mess, his marriage is sour, and other areas of his life have crashed. He's like that mosquito. Even though he may be a likable person, is he a credible messenger? Not according to God's Word.

Some people, including a few preachers, are only concerned about how much they can get out of their undiscerning and ignorant listeners. That's corruption, not integrity. If you're going to speak something, make sure you're a credible messenger. Paul's lifestyle made him a credible messenger, and so did Silas' and Timothy's.

1 THESSALONIANS 1:6

FOLLOWING THE WORD

For your words to be effective, the hearer must trust you and be motivated to take action.

> **6 And ye became followers of us, and of the Lord, having received the word in much affliction, with joy of the Holy Ghost.**

None of us wants to be a failure. I don't ever hear anybody praying that they will fail in their new business venture or a new relationship. We naturally want to succeed.

The Thessalonians were succeeding. But what made them succeed? They became followers of their spiritual leaders. They followed the men who were credible and confident, men who had a clear word from God. They didn't follow the flashes in the pan. They followed the proven men of God, Paul, Silas, and Timothy. The word "follower" in the Greek language means "imitator or mimicker." It's okay to mimic someone else. Everybody does it. What does matter is whom it is you are imitating.

TRUTH ILLUSTRATED – IMITATING DAD

When my son was two years old, he wanted to copy everything I did. He'd do something and insist, "Dad does it this way." We must know the character of those whom we are imitating. Paul said the Thessalonians became followers, imitators, and mimickers of him and the Lord.

Many of the churches we planted from our Mount Hope Church imitated our format and ministry approach. We have more than forty daughter and branch churches, and the ones that have mimicked the mother church are the most successful. Nearly one thousand people meet in just one of our daughter churches. That pastor has modeled the church after ours, using our principles for church growth, church planting, and so on. He tells people, "I want to be like my spiritual father."

But other pastors have said things like, "I don't want to be a clone of Mount Hope Church in Lansing." Today they're out of the ministry. They didn't last. The lesson is clear: If you find somebody who is doing ministry right, follow them as they follow the Lord! I have followed many people. I've stood on an awful lot of shoulders in my life. It's no shame to follow good men and women of God.

WHAT GOOD IS A "TALKIE" WITHOUT A "WALKIE?"

Paul also wrote that the people had "received the word." It may sound obvious, but think about it: What good is a talkie without a walkie? No good at all. They go together. You can talk in a walkie-talkie all you want, but if nobody's listening on the other end, it's futile. Your hearer must become a receiver of the word. Paul said they had received it even in much affliction, meaning intense pressure.

Many people in the church in Thessalonica had left other religions to follow Christ. They had left paganism and Judaism and were being persecuted for this. Family members said things like, "You're leaving the religion of our family. We've been devoted to that synagogue for generations, and now you're shaming us by deserting our religion." But in the midst of all that, there was great joy among those who embraced the Gospel.

It seems counter-intuitive that joy and afflictions go hand in hand, but they often do. Wherever the Gospel goes, there is joy, and often persecution. When the disciples brought the Gospel to Ephesus, and a local cult was put out of business, there was great joy in the city. They burned all their religious artifacts[10]. But Christians were also persecuted as a result. When the disciples were whipped for preaching in Jesus' name, they rejoiced and considered it a great joy to suffer for Christ[11]. The world cannot put affliction and joy together, only Christians can.

> **Acts 16:16-26**
> **16 And it came to pass, as we went to prayer, a certain damsel possessed with a spirit of divination met us, which brought her masters much gain by soothsaying:**
>
> **17 The same followed Paul and us, and cried, saying, These men are the servants of the most high God, which shew unto us the way of salvation.**

18 And this did she many days. But Paul, being grieved, turned and said to the spirit, I command thee in the name of Jesus Christ to come out of her. And he came out the same hour.

19 And when her masters saw that the hope of their gains was gone, they caught Paul and Silas, and drew them into the marketplace unto the rulers,

20 And brought them to the magistrates, saying, These men, being Jews, do exceedingly trouble our city,

21 And teach customs, which are not lawful for us to receive, neither to observe, being Romans.

22 And the multitude rose up together against them: and the magistrates rent off their clothes, and commanded to beat them.

23 And when they had laid many stripes upon them, they cast them into prison, charging the jailor to keep them safely:

24 Who, having received such a charge, thrust them into the inner prison, and made their feet fast in the stocks.

25 And at midnight Paul and Silas prayed, and sang praises unto God: and the prisoners heard them.

26 And suddenly there was a great earthquake, so that the foundations of the prison were shaken: and immediately all the doors were opened, and every one's bands were loosed.

TRUTH ILLUSTRATED – POWER IN ADVERSITY

Not long ago I had one of the worst weeks in all my life. My doctor gave me something to flush out my gallbladder. I rarely get sick, but I got roaring sick this time. I was in Florida and had an awful lot of work to do, but I couldn't do anything. I couldn't even think straight. I lost my cell phone somewhere and had to buy a new one. Everything went wrong. Then I got a call from my mom, and she was crying. She said she'd had a biopsy, and it came back positive for breast cancer. I felt horrible.

I cried, "God, I know you're good and your mercy endures forever. I need a word from you. You know when I hear a report that someone has cancer, it feels like a death sentence." I was troubled until I received a word from the Lord the following Monday. I came to church and prayed, "God, I have got to have a word from you, because this is intense pressure." God began speaking to me. He gave me a plan for how to move forward. Our church held a big anointing service and prayed for many people. As a result, scores of healing testimonies were reported that night. My mom came up and was anointed with oil and prayed for. I walked her back to her seat, and she said she felt so good. She said it was the first time she ever felt so much of the power of God.

That Monday I started praying, and God gave me a whole page of prayers to pray for my mom, based on the word of God. Every paragraph was based on God's Word. Then he gave me a prayer for the grandkids to pray. And he gave me a prayer for my siblings to pray. The Lord said to anoint her with oil as often as we could, at least twice a week, and have her husband anoint her every day. I also looked into what we could do naturally with her diet and supplements. Everybody in the family had a part in this plan, and we carried it out. We prayed every day and anointed her with oil. I was filled with joy and peace after receiving the word from God, so I was able to visit my mom's house without any worry. We'd joke and goof around. And there was peace over the whole house.

She went in for surgery and we were there for hours. There was so much joy in our hearts, even though it was serious, sobering, and even scary. Still, there was that joy of the Holy Spirit, even under intense pressure. After surgery, she came wheeling by, smiling and waving at everybody. It wasn't a fun season, but still we had a great time even throughout that difficult season. That was over 30 years ago. At the time of this writing, she is 93 years old and still going strong.

FACING ADVERSITY

Whenever you face an adverse situation; a time of intense pressure, there will be a word from God to break that pressure, and it will bring you joy even in the affliction. If you look in Acts 17, you will see how much pressure the Thessalonian Christians faced when they were building that church.

> **Acts 17:5-8**
>
> **5 But the Jews, which believed not, moved with envy, took unto them certain lewd fellows of the baser sort, and gathered a company, and set all the city on an uproar, and assaulted the house of Jason, and sought to bring them out to the people.**
>
> **6 And when they found them not, they drew Jason and certain brethren unto the rulers of the city, crying, These that have turned the world upside down are come hither also;**
>
> **7 Whom Jason hath received: and these all do contrary to the decrees of Caesar, saying that there is another king, one Jesus.**
>
> **8 And they troubled the people and the rulers of the city, when they heard these things.**

When you are serving Jesus Christ and preaching his Word, some people will feel threatened by you and will respond with hostility. They will envy you for your confidence, your power, and your integrity. They may come after you the way they did to the Christians in Thessalonica. That is the time to receive God's Word and continue to walk in the joy of the Lord. Because our words come from the right source, they are given with confidence in the power of the Holy Spirit, and if we are living as we should, then our lives reflect the integrity of God's Word.

So, don't be afraid to share the Gospel or the word God has given you. Be bold! You will see great results.

POWER PRINCIPLES:

- **To effectively share the good news of the Gospel, you need to use the right words, with the power of the Holy Spirit behind them.**
- **Step out in faith and speak with confidence and integrity**

LESSON 3

HOW TO MAKE AN IMPRESSION ON OTHERS

I Thessalonians 1:7-10

[7] So that ye were ensamples to all that believe in Macedonia and Achaia.

[8] For from you sounded out the word of the Lord not only in Macedonia and Achaia, but also in every place your faith to God-ward is spread abroad; so that we need not to speak any thing.

[9] For they themselves shew of us what manner of entering in we had unto you, and how ye turned to God from idols to serve the living and true God;

[10] And to wait for his Son from heaven, whom he raised from the dead, even Jesus, which delivered us from the wrath to come.

1 Thessalonians 1:7

MAKING A LASTING IMPRESSION

Everybody wants to make a lasting, positive impression on people. When people come into your life, you naturally want their life to be better because they know you. That's what makes Paul's next statement so beautiful:

> **[7] So that ye were ensamples to all that believe in Macedonia and Achaia.**

This word "ensample" (example) comes from the Greek word "tupos" or "typos." No, this doesn't mean a mistake you made on a letter or report. Rather it means an example, a stamp, an impression[12]. Paul was saying that these Thessalonians put a stamp or a mark on people everywhere they went. They made a positive impression!

Notice the order of events. These believers:

- **Received the Word**
- **Spoke the Word**
- **Followed their godly leaders**

- **Endured opposition**
- **And then made an impression on others**

BECOME AN ENCOURAGEMENT TO OTHERS

It's useless to think of making an impression on others if you don't do the other things first. Like the Thessalonian believers, you can become an encouragement to everyone you meet. You can become a lifter, not a "put-downer," a fueler instead of a drainer.

Have you noticed that some people in life seem to fuel you up while others seem to drain you? I want to be a fueler, not a drainer. The people in Thessalonica were such fuelers that they blessed everybody everywhere they went. They were encouragers, even though they were facing intense pressure.

DRAINERS OR FUELERS?

I've had more experience with drainers than I would have liked. One casual translation of the Bible calls such people "human bloodsuckers." Some of them try to take their monkeys and put them on your back. I have had people over the years come to me and say, "Pastor Williams, God has given me a great vision and He told me to come to you for financing." I always thought, "Amazing! God gave him a vision but I am the one that is supposed to pay for it." Then I have to tell them in so many words that they could take their monkey right back to where they got it.

The Bible says a man's gift will make room for him[13]. If God has given you a gift, a vision, and a calling, He will make a way to fulfill it. People will partner with you without your having to throw your monkey on them.

Some people are such drainers that I will not put them in church leadership posts. Some will come to church wanting to be recognized as some kind of great leader, and when I tell them to take a course or wait awhile, they will often say something like this: "The reason I am not successful is that the pastor does not recognize the gift I have. He does not recognize my talent."

TRUTH ILLUSTRATED - DISCERNMENT

Frequently I will have discernment about someone and not want him in leadership. Occasionally, but not often, I even have unusual supernatural experiences. One time I was praying in my office after a service. At the time there was a couple in the church that claimed to possess some kind of prophetic gifts. But I would not elevate them as leaders. They were always trying to move into some prominent position and I was always holding them back. I did not know why I had this check in my spirit.

But while praying that day, I opened my eyes and found myself in the back seat of their car listening to their conversation. I was not really in the backseat of their car. It had to be a vision or a divine word of knowledge, but it could not have seemed more real. It was obvious to me that they could not see me. I heard them talking. They were criticizing me and other staff members, saying that we didn't recognize their gifts and all they had to offer the church. The next thing I knew I was back in my office in prayer.

At the next church service, I told the congregation about the experience, without naming the couple. After the service the husband came up to me, his face red and beaded with sweat. I shook his hand and said, "How are you doing?" He said, "Not very good after that sermon." God had pointed them out as being what they were—drainers!

DRAINERS ARE NOT SPIRITUAL GIANTS

Drainers project themselves as spiritual giants, but they suck the life out of people. They want to boss people around, telling them what God wants them to do. Nobody in the Body of Christ should be known as a drainer or blood-sucking leach. Let's put something into people's lives, not try to take something out for our own personal benefit. Let's be fuelers and life-givers like the Thessalonians were.

1 Thessalonians 1:8

HOW TO BE FAMOUS

The Church of the Thessalonians was a model church, known throughout the country.

> **8 For from you sounded out the word of the Lord not only in Macedonia and Achaia, but also in every place your faith to God-ward is spread abroad; so that we need not to speak any thing.**

Anywhere Paul and his fellow ministers went, people had already heard about this wonderful church. They had notoriety and fame.

What were they famous for? Their faith in God, their being fuelers, life-givers, and encouragers. Everywhere these believers in Thessalonica went, they were a sterling example of Christ's love.

Talk about making an impression! Notice this little phrase: "You sounded out the Word." From the Greek language, that means, "echoed with a rippling effect beyond itself." It is like thunder, or like dropping a heavy rock into the water. Paul said that was how they sounded out the Gospel. Why is that? It's because every person in the church saw themselves as missionaries. They did not see themselves as merely businessmen or traveling merchants. As their merchants went out to other cities from Thessalonica, they would say something like, "Lord, show me my mission as I go to this next city." They were not seeing their mission as getting that $15,000 deal. God would provide that, but they wanted to hear from God exactly who they were supposed to touch with the Gospel.

RECEIVING AND TRANSMITTING

The Thessalonians had gone from being receivers to being transmitters. If you only receive the Gospel and don't turn around and start transmitting it, you'll stop getting a fresh signal from God. We all need a constant, fresh flow of knowledge and spiritual revelation coming into our lives, and the only way to keep receiving is to keep transmitting what we have already received. Some people get stuck in old revelations because they don't share the revelation they have. They cannot get any more; they are blocked up with the previous. But the Thessalonians were transmitting their revelation and knowledge everywhere, leaving a powerful impression on people far and wide. I call that being a model church!

"FEED ME, FEED ME"

Some Christians only come to church to "be fed." That is utter selfishness. Sure, we all must be fed. I want to have the best-fed flock in the world. But if people come only to be fed, they'll get stopped up. We should feed on the Word of God so we can feed others with what we know. That way it multiplies way beyond ourselves—it ripples outward and touches many lives.

NO TELEVISION, RADIOS, INTERNET, OR PRINTING PRESSES

The Thessalonians did not have a television ministry, a web page, a radio ministry, a media ministry, or a book-publishing department. Yet they reached the whole known world in a way that was spontaneous and inexpensive[14]. They got people talking about Jesus, making Him the "talk of the town."

Here's an idea: instead of gossiping about each other all week, why not start talking about Jesus? Imagine how effective it would be at work, at home, at school, and at play if we used our conversation to promote Him. I've observed that over eighty percent of a church's growth comes from people talking to friends and relatives. It does not come from television, radio, or advertising. The Thessalonians mastered the concept of bragging about Jesus, and they became famous.

1 Thessalonians 1:9

MORE LESSONS FROM A MODEL CHURCH

Paul continues,

> **9 For they themselves shew of us what manner of entering in we had unto you, and how ye turned to God from idols to serve the living and true God**

A true sign of conversion is when we turn to God and leave something else behind.

Many of these people in Thessalonica, including a great number of Greeks and a great number of the chief women of the town, turned from their idols. An idol isn't just a piece of wood or cement fashioned to look like a strange creature in a Chinese restaurant. An idol is anything we substitute for God. It is the thing to which we are devoted. Education can be a God substitute. Entertainment, riches, recreation, work, and relationships all can become idols to modern man. But Jesus saved us from worshipping dead things, as Paul wrote.

1 Thessalonians 1:10

Waiting for Jesus to Come

> **10 And to wait for his Son from heaven, whom he raised from the dead, even Jesus, which delivered us from the wrath to come.**

"Jesus" is the Greek name for the Hebrew name "Joshua."[15] Joshua was the one who took the children of Israel into the Promised Land. The name means savior or deliverer. It was fitting that Jesus would also bear the name of savior and deliverer, for that's what He is. He is the only one who can take us into the Promised Land. As Paul wrote,

> **Romans 8:11**
> **But if the Spirit of him that raised up Jesus from the dead dwell in you, he that raised up Christ from the dead shall also quicken your mortal bodies by his Spirit that dwelleth in you.**

These believers were expectantly waiting for the Lord to come for them. He delivered them, and us, from the wrath to come.

God is not indifferent to sin. God is not indifferent to those who reject His Son. God is not sitting by without emotion when people reject His plan to get them into heaven and fellowship with Him. We are told in Revelation 6:17 that there is coming a day when His wrath will pour out and this world will experience a time of trouble unmatched since the beginning of all time. It will be a time of unparalleled terror on the earth.

Revelation 6:17
17 For the great day of his wrath is come; and who shall be able to stand?

We are told in 1 Corinthians 15:51-55 that in a moment, in a twinkling of an eye, we will be changed (supernaturally). We are told in the fourth chapter of 1 Thessalonians there will be a trumpet sound and God's people are going to leave Earth before His wrath pours out. You can be sure that God will keep his Word regardless of the people who deny that the day of wrath is coming. God is right and they are wrong. Wrath will strike this world.

1 Corinthians 15:52
52 In a moment, in the twinkling of an eye, at the last trump: for the trumpet shall sound, and the dead shall be raised incorruptible, and we shall be changed.

Revelation 13, for example, tells us that the antichrist, along with his promoter "the false prophet", will cause all people to receive a mark in their hand or their forehead. Nobody will be able to buy or sell unless they have the mark. The global technology is already here.

Politicians are talking about national and global identification cards and vaccine passports.

A company in Palm Beach, Florida, produced a microchip half the size of a piece of rice, that can be injected under the skin of your hand or your forehead[16]. All your information can reside on that chip— your Social Security number, credit card numbers, and vaccine and medical history. Promoters of the "chip" say it will help law enforcement track down missing children by satellite. It will stop illegal immigration and deter terrorism because they will know where everybody is at all times. You can see how persuasive these arguments could be to the global population.

I believe we may be in the final moments before Jesus comes for His Church. Notice what Paul wrote in 1 Thessalonians 1:10:

... even Jesus, which delivered us from the wrath to come.

We already have been delivered from the penalty and power of sin, thanks to Jesus.

But there will come a day when the final deliverance will take place, a trumpet will sound, and all those who have died before us in Christ will be raised from the dead and changed in a moment, in the twinkling of an eye[17]. We are going to put on incorruption and immortality. We are going to be changed into a glorified condition, lifted off this earth, and carried to a place called Heaven where we will enjoy the Marriage Supper of the Lamb[18] while the earth spirals into its unparalleled time of torment known as the Day of God's Wrath.[19]

Jesus is coming any day now. He promised the Thessalonian church deliverance, and in the Book of Revelation, He promised the Philadelphian church that He would keep them from the hour of tribulation.

> **Revelation 3:10-11**
> **[10] Because thou hast kept the word of my patience, I also will keep thee from the hour of temptation, which shall come upon all the world, to try them that dwell upon the earth.**
>
> **[11] Behold, I come quickly: hold that fast which thou hast, that no man take thy crown.**

The wrath of God is coming. But based on God's Word, I can say with confidence that as a true believer, you have been delivered from that coming hour. We are going to heaven, beloved.

But while we're here on earth, let's continue to be model Christians and a model church! Let's put our mark on others and leave an impression that lasts for eternity.

POWER PRINCIPLES:

- **Be a fueler, not a drainer.**
- **Model Christians turn their energy outward to reach the world, instead of inward to criticize.**

1 Thessalonians 2

1 For yourselves, brethren, know our entrance in unto you, that it was not in vain:

2 But even after that we had suffered before, and were shamefully entreated, as ye know, at Philippi, we were bold in our God to speak unto you the Gospel of God with much contention.

3 For our exhortation was not of deceit, nor of uncleanness, nor in guile:

4 But as we were allowed of God to be put in trust with the Gospel, even so we speak; not as pleasing men, but God, which trieth our hearts.

5 For neither at any time used we flattering words, as ye know, nor a cloke of covetousness; God is witness:

6 Nor of men sought we glory, neither of you, nor yet of others, when we might have been burdensome, as the apostles of Christ.

7 But we were gentle among you, even as a nurse cherisheth her children:

8 So being affectionately desirous of you, we were willing to have imparted unto you, not the Gospel of God only, but also our own souls, because ye were dear unto us.

9 For ye remember, brethren, our labour and travail: for labouring night and day, because we would not be chargeable unto any of you, we preached unto you the Gospel of God.

10 Ye are witnesses, and God also, how holily and justly and unblameably we behaved ourselves among you that believe:

11 As ye know how we exhorted and comforted and charged every one of you, as a father doth his children,

12 That ye would walk worthy of God, who hath called you unto his kingdom and glory.

13 For this cause also thank we God without ceasing, because, when ye received the word of God which ye heard of us, ye received it not as the word of men, but as it is in truth, the word of God, which effectually worketh also in you that believe.

14 For ye, brethren, became followers of the churches of God which in Judaea are in Christ Jesus: for ye also have suffered like things of your own countrymen, even as they have of the Jews:

15 Who both killed the Lord Jesus, and their own prophets, and have persecuted us; and they please not God, and are contrary to all men:

16 Forbidding us to speak to the Gentiles that they might be saved, to fill up their sins alway: for the wrath is come upon them to the uttermost.

17 But we, brethren, being taken from you for a short time in presence, not in heart, endeavoured the more abundantly to see your face with great desire.

18 Wherefore we would have come unto you, even I Paul, once and again; but Satan hindered us.

19 For what is our hope, or joy, or crown of rejoicing? Are not even ye in the presence of our Lord Jesus Christ at his coming?

20 For ye are our glory and joy.

LESSON 4

HOW TO HANDLE OPPOSITION AND DECEIT

I Thessalonians 2:1-4

[1] For yourselves, brethren, know our entrance in unto you, that it was not in vain:

[2] But even after that we had suffered before, and were shamefully entreated, as ye know, at Philippi, we were bold in our God to speak unto you the Gospel of God with much contention.

[3] For our exhortation was not of deceit, nor of uncleanness, nor in guile:

[4] But as we were allowed of God to be put in trust with the Gospel, even so we speak; not as pleasing men, but God, which trieth our hearts.

1 Thessalonians 2:1

FALSE CHARGES AND SLANDER

When he left the city of Thessalonica, Paul's ministry appeared to have been a failure. False charges were trumped up against him. The believers there were harassed because of him. Paul fled town and unscrupulous infiltrators came into the church and slandered him. Yet Paul had the boldness to write,

> **[1] For yourselves, brethren, know our entrance in unto you, that it was not in vain ...**

Wow! Despite outward appearances, he insisted his work there was successful. He was saying, "We achieved something among you. Our work was not a failure even though it looked like a failure." It reminds me of the Cross itself, which looked like a failure for the Son of God— but then came Easter Sunday and the greatest victory ever for humankind. Sometimes things look like a failure on the surface but deep down there is a great victory.

SOMETIMES SUCCESS LOOKS LIKE FAILURE...AT FIRST

The real failures in Thessalonica were the false teachers and philosophers roaming up and down the streets of Greece trying to gather a crowd to teach some new philosophy or new mystery. They did it for the sake of money, sex, or fame.

Their teachings caused people to wander into worthless, non-productive, empty things. That is probably why Paul said that his time was not in vain, it was not empty or worthless and did not cause people to wander on fruitless paths. He was not like one of those false teachers so prevalent in Greece at that time. Rather, he boldly affirmed that his Gospel message would yield eternal riches.

1 Thessalonians 2:2

HANDLING HOSTILITY

> **2 But even after that we had suffered before, and were shamefully entreated, as ye know, at Philippi, we were bold in our God to speak unto you the Gospel of God with much contention.**

When you speak God's Word into somebody's life, it often creates hostility at first.

TRUTH ILLUSTRATED – RELIGIOUS HOSTILITY

For example, if you tell a very religious person, who has been trying to gain favor with God through good deeds and righteous living, that you can only get to heaven through faith in the grace of Jesus Christ, their first reaction may be anger that you're accusing them of having wasted their time. They may resist the Gospel message and may give you a hostile reception.

OPPOSING FORCES

Paul's readers understood conflict and contention because Greece was the home of the first Olympics[20]. The Olympics were taking place in Greece at the time Paul was preaching. Paul used the word "contention" which is related to the word "contest," which is what the Olympics were about. Paul was conveying the idea that when you preach the Gospel there is going to be a contest between you and the forces pulling people's hearts in the opposite direction.

Paul experienced this kind of trouble wherever he went.

His persecution had started earlier in Phillipi, where he led some prominent women and men to the Lord. Then Paul spoke in the synagogue and told the Jews that God wanted to save Gentiles. Their response? They almost killed him; he had to be protected by government guards. They closed the gate and locked it so the people would not kill Paul. He and his ministry partner, Silas, were stripped, beaten, and humiliated right on the streets, then thrown into a dungeon with their feet clamped into stocks. There in the jail, Paul and Silas sang praises to the Lord at midnight, and with some angelic help[21], experienced divine deliverance from the jail and went right to Thessalonica.

What happened in Thessalonica? The same thing! You would think that because God had called Paul to preach in Macedonia the people there would have been waiting with open arms. The good news was coming! Bring out the balloons and the welcome sign, let's have a festival! But no. Paul ended up leaving in danger of his life.

CONTENTION AND HOSTILITY

In this world, the Gospel always advances against much contention and hostility.

Satan always challenges positive progress.

One of the few promises in the Bible I do not cherish is this one: "All that will live godly in Christ Jesus shall suffer persecution" (II Timothy 3:12). This promise is like a "heads-up" so we don't quit when we hit resistance.

Paul did not quit.

He did not say, "It must not have been God's will for me to preach here." Paul kept his hand on the plow and continued moving forward. He needed to be tested. He needed to be approved for his ministry. Many people let themselves be knocked out at the first sign of contention or hostility. But if Jesus was maligned, misrepresented, and accused of being a blasphemer, a drunkard, and a demon-possessed lunatic, don't you think His followers will also be ridiculed and maligned and misrepresented?

Yet Paul said his visit to Thessalonica was not in vain. It was not a failure even though they had much contention, opposition, resistance, and hostility. Sometimes things look like failure but they are not. Sometimes you feel like a failure but you are not. In Christ Jesus, you are never a failure. You and I may fail sometimes, but that does not make us failures. Indeed, our times of apparent failure may be times of actual success! The crucifixion looked like failure...until Sunday!

TRUTH ILLUSTRATED – PREDICTIONS THAT BOMBED

I once read some interesting predictions of failure[22].

- **One man sent his poems to the editor of Atlantic Monthly back in 1902. The editor said the man did not have any talent and his magazine had no room for vigorous verse. That rejected poet was Robert Frost.**
- **In 1905, the University of Burn turned down a doctoral dissertation as irrelevant and fanciful. The author of that dissertation was Albert Einstein.**
- **In 1894, an English teacher noted on a teenager's report card that this boy had a conspicuous lack of success ahead of him. The student was Winston Churchill.**

Just because there is contention and somebody misjudges or shamefully treats you, it does not mean you are a failure.

Jesus said something amazing in Mark 10:29-30:

Mark 10:29-30

29 And Jesus answered and said, Verily I say unto you, There is no man that hath left house, or brethren, or sisters, or father, or mother, or wife, or children, or lands, for my sake, and the Gospel's,

30 But he shall receive an hundredfold now in this time, houses, and brethren, and sisters, and mothers, and children, and lands, with persecutions; and in the world to come eternal life.

Notice how He added, "With persecutions." The lesson is clear: No matter what kind of positive progress you make, there will always be contention. Somebody will always oppose you. If you are the captain of a football team, they will complain about your leadership style. If you get a promotion at work, your co-workers may start sniping about you behind your back. If you have financial success, people will blame you for not doing enough for the poor.

Unfortunately, there is no way to avoid persecution as a believer. So, when God hands you the ball and you begin to run with it, watch out for tacklers! Somebody's going to try to cut you off and drive you out of bounds—anything to keep you from that goal. The devil will contend for every promise you go after.

1 Thessalonians 2:3

THREE TRAITS OF A FALSE PROPHET

Paul didn't stay silent and let his enemies have their say. He defended his ministry against the false teachers and philosophers of his day. He differentiated himself from those who promoted false theories for their personal gain. The way it is written sounds as if he was answering the critics who had accused him of wrong behavior.

3 For our exhortation was not of deceit, nor of uncleanness, nor in guile

Those are the three earmarks of a false prophet: (1) deceit, (2) guile, and (3) uncleanness. A false prophet is like a slick salesman covering up the flaws in the product that he is trying to sell.

TRUTH ILLUSTRATED – MOTORBOAT PATCH JOB

A man I once knew was on the lake in his motorboat and hit a log, putting a hole in the boat. He pulled the boat ashore, dried it off, put masking tape over the hole, and sanded down the edges of the masking tape so it blended in. Then he painted over it and sold the boat. The guy who bought it never even saw the hole. The man who told me this was laughing and enjoying what he'd gotten away with. I thought, how can you live with yourself? What if the buyer was a father who took his kids out on the boat? Suppose that masking tape wears through, the boat begins to fill with water and sinks in the middle of the lake and a young boy dies. How could you even think of doing such a thing to another human being?

TRAIT NO. 1 – DECEIT

Deception is the art of covering something up for the sake of personal gain.

I know a blind man named Steve who now runs a video game store. Can you imagine that? He used to run a record store, which he started himself from scratch. To run the cash register he kept the twenty-dollar bills in one slot, the tens in one slot, the fives in another slot, and the ones in another. But some people would come in, buy a record, hand him a dollar bill, and say it was a twenty. So, he'd put the dollar bill in the twenty pile and give the person change for a twenty. Not only did he lose the money, but he lost the record too. The people who did this to him lost something more important: their integrity.

The word deceit in the Greek language implies "wandering."[23] People who are deceived are always wandering. They tell themselves, "I have to get into this new thing over here or that new thing over there."

They wander from one deception to another.

TRUTH ILLUSTRATED – DECEPTION AFTER DECEPTION

I talked with a man one time who said, "I used to be a Christian Scientist. Then I found out that the real way is Jehovah's Witnesses." It was one thing after another with him, and not one of them could take his soul to heaven.

Even in the Church, you'll find fickle sheep who always latch onto the latest fad and are carried away. They wonder why their life seems like it is wandering. It's because deceit in the end will always leave you feeling spiritually homeless.

A boy visited a wax museum with his dad. It was full of wax statues of famous people. But after ten minutes the boy looked up and said, "Can we get out of here and go where there are real people?"

I want a church with real people. Most people are not super-saints. It's better to be transparent than to pretend. Paul was real. He said he had problems and at times thought he was a failure. But he also defended his reputation. He demonstrated strongly that he was not a deceiver or self-gratifier.

TRAIT NO. 2 – MORAL IMPURITY

Paul also mentions uncleanness, which implies moral impurity or sensuality.

Moral impurity was typical of the false teachers in Paul's day, and it's typical of false teachers today.

TRUTH ILLUSTRATED – FALSE EVANGELIST

I remember a man who would come to town and bring what looked like a great revival. Great things were happening in the services. Demons were being cast out, and there were many alleged testimonies. He would pick someone out of the crowd and say, "God has called you to be an apostle," and ordain them as an apostle right there. He was ordaining prophets and prophetesses too.

The pastor of the church where this man was preaching was getting concerned and increasingly uncomfortable, especially when this so-called evangelist announced to the congregation that God had told him to stay there for three more weeks. Everybody excitedly applauded him, but I had a creepy feeling about this guy.

He stayed around a little longer and then suddenly, without any announcement was gone from town. The church treasury was gone with him, and the car that they were letting him drive. People started talking and found out there were four women in the congregation he was having sexual relations with, convincing them that God had sent him to "make up for their husband's romantic deficiencies."

It is appalling and infuriates me when someone uses the Gospel of Jesus Christ for unclean purposes. This was the kind of thing Paul was battling. He said he had not come to the Thessalonians in uncleanness, as false prophets did.

TRAIT NO. 3 – GUILE

He also said he and his partners did not come with guile. Guile is an interesting word. In the Bible it is called wickedness. The word means the baiting of a hook designed to intentionally mislead someone.

TRUTH ILLUSTRATED – FISHING BAIT

When I was a little boy, my dad would take me fishing. He taught me how to bait a hook and told me that it was important to hide the hook once you've baited it. Like the devil, false teachers throw out their deceptive "guile bait" on a hook. Undiscerning people then get snagged when they bite the bait.

Paul told the people that he didn't bait any guile hooks. He told the truth and always acted ethically. What you see is what you get. He used no guile; no deception in his ministry; no gimmicks.

We see guile all around us. Clever accountants use it when they slice and dice the financial figures to make a company appear strong to the investing public, when in fact the company is about to go under. Only when the company collapses, leaving people who've worked there for decades without pensions or retirement funds, does everyone realize they were the victims of guile.

But even more dangerous than financial guile is spiritual guile, where ministers bait spiritual hooks to deliberately mislead people.

TRUTH ILLUSTRATED – IMMORAL "APOSTLE"

One so-called minister had a moral failure and refused any discipline. He disappeared for about two years. He was neither seen nor heard from. Then, a couple of years later, he emerged and was no longer just a preacher but claimed God had given him a revelation that he was an apostle.

He published a book that was full of guile and spiritual hooks. It stirred up people and made them dissatisfied with their churches. He claimed that believers could not grow spiritually if they had only a pastor. They needed an apostle too. His idea was for his followers to get several groups under them, and they would receive part of the tithes from those groups. And then they could be ordained as "apostles" after they enlisted a certain number of groups under them. It was sort of a multilevel apostleship, drawing people away from simple devotion to Jesus Christ.

Funny enough, the people who usually get hooked by guile are those who think they are the most spiritual. I have found that those who project themselves as being extremely spiritual almost always have a problem in their life they are trying to cover up. They are deceived in some area so they are blinded to the guile used by other precarious hucksters.

Do not misunderstand me: I believe in the ministry of the apostle. I believe in the ministry of the prophet. I know some whom I believe to be modern-day prophets and apostles, and

I respect them greatly. But there are always deceivers out there who employ guile to snag undiscerning souls into areas off-limits.

1 Thessalonians 2:4

HOW TO BE APPROVED BY GOD

Paul continued,

> **4 But as we were allowed of God to be put in trust with the Gospel, even so we speak; not as pleasing men, but God, which trieth our hearts.**

The word "allowed" means tested and approved. Paul and his ministry partners were tested and approved by God to be stewards of the Gospel of Jesus Christ.

When you are fully approved of God, it means you have been tested.

TRUTH ILLUSTRATED – REAL OR COUNTERFEIT?

There is so much counterfeiting going on in some parts of the United States that if you use a twenty-dollar bill almost anywhere, they check it to make sure it is genuine. In the same way, we all have to be tried, so our ministries are proved true before God will entrust more to us. If you are faithful in a little, He will entrust more to you. If you are not faithful with what little you have, He cannot trust you with more.[24]

Paul said he was proven. He had been through spiritual boot camp. Everything in life has a boot camp period. You have to start at the start. You can't start in the middle. Once you pass through boot camp, you get approved for your first assignment. You have to be proven in each rank before you go to the next rank. If you are going through testing it is because God wants to approve you for a higher level!

TRUTH ILLUSTRATED – START AT THE START

Years ago, in the Boston Marathon, a lady finished the race way ahead of everybody else. The lights were on, the streamers were flying, and the horns were blaring. Then somebody noticed she was not sweating very much. It turns out, she had started the race with all the others and somehow covertly snuck over to hide behind a bush near the finish line. She jumped out from behind the bush, finished the race, and claimed to have won. She was later exposed.[25]

At a regional Christian University, I used to interview Bible school students who wanted to pursue the ministry. The university leaders appreciated the way I conducted interviews, so the administration loved to have me to come and talk to the ministry students. I asked tough questions. I wanted to know their visions and their goals. Some would say, "I want to start pastoring a church of about four hundred where they pay me $150,000 a year with full benefits." I would never approve those candidates because they were not willing to pay a price. They wanted to start in the middle.

But Paul was tested and proven. He didn't quit just because there was hostility and opposition. He met the challenge and faced the struggles. So, he was trusted with the Gospel. He was made a steward.

A steward does not own what he manages. He uses everything for his master's purposes. Paul said he was not like those who handle the Word of God corruptly. He passed the test. As believers, we, too, are stewards. We don't own anything but we enjoy everything He allows us to enjoy if we maintain good stewardship over it.

I like this next part. Paul wrote,

> **... even so we speak; not as pleasing men, but God, which trieth our hearts.**

Paul was no feel-good preacher. He stayed away from ear-tickling messages and told people what they needed to hear. I sometimes get letters from people who say they were offended and will never come back to the church I was pastoring. If I were a people-pleaser, I would have been upset. But I don't care. I won't walk gingerly. I am going to preach the Gospel and tell people the truth. You do not help people by preaching to please them. You help people when you preach to please God. I am not going to give sermonettes that only help make "Christian-ettes!"

TRUTH ILLUSTRATED – A QUOTE BRINGS IRE

On one occasion, I quoted this verse from the Bible:

> **1 Corinthians 6:9-10 NLT**
> **[9] Don't you realize that those who do wrong will not inherit the Kingdom of God? Don't fool yourselves. Those who indulge in sexual sin, or who worship idols, or commit adultery, or are male prostitutes, or practice homosexuality,**
>
> **[10] or are thieves, or greedy people, or drunkards, or are abusive, or cheat people—none of these will inherit the Kingdom of God.**

After the service, a fellow walked up to me, put his hand on his hip, and said, "I do not like the way you are stereotyping gays." It had been one of those weeks for me where I could hardly take one more negative, unfair comment. He must have thought I would apologize and be a pushover. Instead, I said, "You listen to me. I preach the Word of God in this church and I quoted the Word of God." He began backing up as I spoke. I continued, "The Bible said to repent or you will perish. I am telling you that you had better repent or you are going to perish." I got louder and louder. Finally, he backed into a pew. I walked right into the pew with him and he fell over. I said, "Would you like to be saved or not?" He started crying and said, "Yes." I brought him up to the altar and prayed the prayer of salvation with him.

Too often we tiptoe around to try not to offend people when people need to hear the truth of God's Word and God's heart. Parents come for counseling sometimes and say their son or daughter is living with their lover and would like them to get married. They want me to perform the ceremony. I ask them if they will stop living together until they get married. They usually say, "No." So I tell them to go somewhere else. I do not want to marry people who are living in sin deliberately and willfully. If they are not interested in a holy relationship with God, a holy relationship with their spouse, and a holy relationship with their future, then just forget it. Why even get married? Just live together the rest of your lives and go to hell together! Don't try to use the church to validate your sin.

On the other hand, Jesus died for sinners who will recognize they are sinners and who will turn from their sins. No guile, no deceit, no uncleanness. Be a straight shooter with God and a straight shooter with people. Speak as to please God—not men. That's a great way to be a model Christian.

POWER PRINCIPLES:

- **Even when it looks like you failed—you may have succeeded.**
- **Speaking the Word into someone's life can provoke a hostile reaction.**
- **We are promised persecution—but we can persevere and overcome it every time.**
- **False prophets use deceit, guile, and uncleanness.**

LESSON 5

HOW TO DEAL WITH FALSE PROPHETS

I Thessalonians 2:5-8

[5] For neither at any time used we flattering words, as ye know, nor a cloke of covetousness; God is witness:

[6] Nor of men sought we glory, neither of you, nor yet of others, when we might have been burdensome, as the apostles of Christ.

7 But we were gentle among you, even as a nurse cherisheth her children:

[8] So being affectionately desirous of you, we were willing to have imparted unto you, not the Gospel of God only, but also our own souls, because ye were dear unto us.

I was at a prayer meeting years ago when a new guy in our church grabbed me and said, "Pastor, I have a prophecy for you." He closed his eyes and said, "Thus saith the Lord, I say unto thee, my son, I have called thee to be a captain in my earthly army, saith God. Thy church shall grow and thou shalt lead an army of 50,000, saith the Lord."

I thought that maybe he just wanted to encourage me, but I didn't feel any particular presence of God as he spoke. I went into the prayer meeting and we were all worshipping Jesus, focusing on the Lord, lifting our hands to Him, and getting into an atmosphere of praise and worship, thanksgiving and intercession. All of a sudden this new guy decided to give another prophetic word. His booming voice rang out, "Thus saith the Lord, thou thinkest thou art in the Spirit, but I say unto thee, thou art in the flesh, saith God."

It was obvious to me and almost everybody else that this was not a word from God, but was something erroneous. It's one thing when someone gives you an erroneous "word" in private, but to do it to the flock God has given me oversight of—I wasn't going to stand for it. I stopped him and said, "Let's everybody worship Jesus as loud as we can," and we drowned him right out.

After the prayer meeting, this "prophet" walked up to me and said, "How come you stopped my prophecy?"

I told him, "Because it was a false prophecy."

He went right into his super-spiritual prophecy pose and weird, spooky-sounding falsetto voice, and said, "Thus saith the Lord, I have changed my mind about that other word I gave you earlier. Now thy church shall dwindle to twelve. Thou shalt be dressed in rags and thou shalt not even be able to clothe thy children properly, saith the Lord, for thou hast not received my man as a prophet of God." He turned around, huffed off, and went to some other church.

That week the pastor of this other church called me and he said, "Pastor Williams do you know this guy?"

I said, "Yes, he was at our church but I stopped one of his prophecies the other night at a prayer meeting and he left." The pastor said, "Well, now he's at my church. Thanks a lot, Williams!" I laughed.

1 Thessalonians 2:5

That's the kind of flattery and falseness Paul wrote about in verse 5.

> **5 For neither at any time used we flattering words, as ye know, nor a cloke of covetousness; God is witness:**

I've heard it said that flattery will get you everywhere. But that's not true. Insincere flattery is nauseating. Everybody enjoys a sincere compliment, but I can't think of anyone who enjoys flowery, buttery, and insincere compliments.

False teachers are often overly "sweet and buttery"

That is the way the false teachers operated in Paul's day. They would flatter people to butter them up and then go for the kill. They wanted something for themselves and didn't care about the people they were using for their own selfish goals.

TRUTH ILLUSTRATED – INSINCERE SELF-PROMOTERS

There was one man who always wanted to have a ministry in our church. After Sunday morning services he would grab me and try to flatter me by saying things like, "I have never seen anyone so anointed as you. When you were preaching, God gave me a vision. The windows of heaven opened up and holy rain was falling all over you as you preached." All the while I was thinking, "What does this guy want?" It wasn't long before we found out. He wanted to be my paid personal assistant! Sorry – no way!

On another occasion, I was at a major meeting of pastors, missionaries, and evangelists. At such meetings, there are always certain ministers who try to schmooze the so-called big church pastors. They are quite often itinerant evangelists who want to get into the big churches so they can get a big offering.

I was walking along with my name tag that read, "Dave Williams," and suddenly a guy yelled, "Hey, Dave, it's good to see you. Oh man, I haven't seen you in so long." I was thinking, who is this guy?

He continued, "I was hoping I'd run into you here. God is doing so many things. Oh, let me just pray for you. Now, Father, I pray for Dave here, and, ah, oh, I got a prophetic word. Thus saith the Lord, I say unto thee, Dave, that thy church shall grow to 10,000, no maybe 20,000, no 30,000—who knows, saith the Lord."

I thought, "This fellow just wants to preach in my pulpit for a week so he can take an offering." He gave me a packet of materials and said, "I'll be in touch with you. What city are you in again?" I know this story may sound far-fetched, but it really happened.

Paul said he didn't use flattering words because he and his colleagues weren't trying to please people. They were seeking to please God.

THE COVETOUS PROPHET

Flattery is often used as a cover for covetousness, just as the people in the examples I gave coveted positions of power. Paul said he and his ministry partners did not use a cloak of covetousness.

> **...as ye know, nor a cloke of covetousness; God is witness:**

A cloak is something you cover up with, like a raincoat.

Paul and his group were not coming to Thessalonica to plant a church for the sake of their own honor, prestige, money, or position.

But the false teachers in Thessalonica were cloaking their true motives. I dread a lot of the meetings I have to go to for my denomination because some men behave covetously toward positions. During floor discussions and votes, they will step to the microphone and comment on the issue just to get their name out so people will remember it and vote for them when an executive position opens up. It's self-advertising. They want to ingratiate themselves into people's memories. They covet positions.

The church I pastored had the godliest group of deacons and elders I've ever known. None of them coveted their positions. They were picked by God, approved by the pastor, and ratified by the people.

But I remember a time when a certain deacon was ratified at our annual business meeting. His wife said, "I'm so happy my husband is now a deacon. I always wanted him to be on the board."

I asked her why.

"Just for the prestige of being a deacon's wife," she answered. I thought this lady had a problem. Sadly, when her husband went off the board, she left him. I guess he didn't have enough prestige anymore.

- **Paul didn't covet anything except the best for God's people**
- **He didn't change his message depending on what group he was in**
- **He didn't do any demographic studies to find out who was in the congregation so he could tailor his message**
- **He offered the same message everywhere he went—that Jesus Christ was the Son of God, that He died on the Cross, that He rose from the dead, that He ascended to heaven, that He is coming again and the wages of sin is death but the gift of God is eternal life through Jesus Christ.**

1 Thessalonians 2:6

GLORYING IN GOD ALONE

Paul continued,

> **6 Nor of men sought we glory, neither of you, nor yet of others, when we might have been burdensome, as the apostles of Christ.**

Paul did not come seeking glory or to be put on a pedestal, to be honored or recognized. He did not want to be a burden on the church. You see, this first church in Thessalonica was quite poor at the time. The Romans would come through from time to time and take the prosperity out of the city, and everyone had to start over again. Paul did not want to be a burden on this struggling new church. Rather than receiving a salary for his work, he wanted all the tithes and offerings to go back into building it up. He didn't want to be a burden.

I've learned over the years that most guest speakers came to our church to bless us. They didn't come only for the offering. They don't come for the fanfare. But, on the other hand, I've dealt with some who were a burden from the first minute they arrived. "Pastor," they told me, "I will need three eight-foot tables set up in the foyer and I'd like you to provide four volunteers to sell all my products. We are going to need to use your copy machines to make the recordings that I'll sell. Put all the money into this bag so I get it all and make sure you pick honest people. I will need lemonade in the pulpit and it has to have a touch of honey in it. And I require an extra-long bed, so please provide me with a large suite at the hotel." They run you ragged.

Almost 100 % of the guest ministers we invited to our church were godly, ethical, and a blessing to us. Unfortunately, a couple of traveling ministers I invited told me they were coming for a love offering, but from the pulpit, they announced something different to the congregation. One of them said, "Folks, let's pray because I need $20,000 to come in this offering tonight or else I'm not going to be able to make it. This trip will be in vain."

This is sad. Our church always gave generous offerings to our guest ministers. Even some nationally recognized ministers told me they received the biggest offerings ever from our church.

I've learned over the years and have stopped inviting burdensome "ministers," but just in case one should get through, I developed a signal for my congregation. When I come out to receive the offering, I'll give the people a certain signal, and they'll respond accordingly, to the dismay of the glory-seeking, burdensome minister. I never had to use that signal in my remaining 25 years as pastor.

GIMMICKS

I've received many letters that use gimmicks to get God's people to give. I've received holy shower caps in the mail before. The accompanying letter claims that if you send the holy shower cap back with your miracle offering, the "holy man" will anoint it and send it back. Then if you wear it for twenty-four hours you will get the same anointing as the "holy man."

Another ministry sent me a scarlet thread that "Rahab the prostitute used to rescue Joshua" (he said).

Others have sent me "holy spots," "miracle gloves," "holy rice" and "miracle wheat." One minister promised that if anyone sent him seven dollars a month, for the first month they would get a certificate of blessing to hang on their wall declaring God's blessing over their life. The second month they sent seven dollars they would receive a miracle wallet. That miracle wallet would have a never-ending supply. I wondered what you're probably wondering: If he had such a miracle wallet, why would he need my seven dollars?

These types of ministries are a burden on the church and a burden on God's people. Paul wanted nothing to do with this kind of behavior.

1 Thessalonians 2:7

7 But we were gentle among you, even as a nurse cherisheth her children

Imagine that—Paul, this tough apostle who stood up to near-death beatings and imprisonment, said he was like a nursing mother to them. There is something about a mother and a child that no one but a mother knows. Even a father doesn't know it to the degree that a mother does. That child depends on the mother for nine months in the womb and then to nurse him after being born.

Paul likened himself to a mother with a child. He said he wasn't just a preacher and an apostle. He was feeding them, taking care of them. The old phrase goes, "A dad's work is from sun to sun, but a mother's work is never done." But Paul was a mother and a father to the Thessalonian church.

TRUTH ILLUSTRATED – DOWN ON THE FARM

My great-grandmother had a farm that I loved visiting because there were chickens and other farm animals. One rooster didn't like me, and he would chase me all over the barnyard. I would cry and run, and my Gramma would go out with a broom and chase the rooster away. She protected me and Paul had a heart to protect the Church.

On Grandma's farm, when it rained, the mother hen would gather up all her little chicks and put them under her wings so the rain wouldn't bother them. Paul was like that mother hen to these believers.

Mothers don't seem to get bothered by the annoying things kids can do. They cry in the middle of the night and Mom gets up and takes care of it with hardly a complaint.

My wife and I were riding the transit system in Washington, D.C. with our friends, going to a prayer event on the National Mall outside the Capitol Building. A fussing baby was sitting right in front of us being held by his mother. But the crying and fussing didn't bother the mother. Then the baby got a funny look on his face and I started smelling something. It wasn't good. It was bad; really bad! We started pointing the finger of blame at each other, just for fun, but we knew who it was. It was that baby. But the mother didn't even blink. It was as if she didn't smell a thing. I would have gotten off immediately or put the kid in a plastic bag up to its head (not really), but her tolerance was a tad higher than mine.

1 Thessalonians 2:8

Paul was like that with the Thessalonians. He was tolerant of their imperfections. He changed their spiritual dirty diapers.

He went on,

> **8 So being affectionately desirous of you, we were willing to have imparted unto you, not the Gospel of God only, but also our own souls, because ye were dear unto us.**

Paul gave his very life to people who were less than perfect. Having pastored a church for more than thirty years, I know what it is like for people to become dear to me, even people who at one point irritated me.

TRUTH ILLUSTRATED – THE OLD ANNOYING VETERAN

There was a man who I hated talking to. He was a nice guy, but he was always talking about his medical problems and what tests they ran on him that week. That was all he could talk about. "The nurse said this, the doctor did this," he would rant on and on.

I didn't enjoy hearing the details of his various medical sagas, but one day I was driving to Detroit for a meeting and my mind was full and heavy. As I was driving down the freeway, organizing my thoughts on the way, I passed a Disabled American Veterans van. I looked in and there was that guy. He was waving at me; they were taking him over to Veterans Hospital. While I was at my meeting in Detroit he called my wife and said that he saw me on the road and I looked troubled so he immediately started praying for me that God would give me peace. That kind of experience makes being a pastor worthwhile. None of us are perfect people, but we better not be counterfeits.

Paul was not a charlatan like many in his day who used flattery to mask their covetousness. Rather, he fed, cherished, and gave his very soul and life to the Thessalonians, like a mother.

Next, we will see that he also described himself as a father to them.

POWER PRINCIPLES:

- **False prophets use flattery to try to ingratiate themselves into positions of power.**
- **Ministry should be about blessing others and glorifying God, not serving or glorying in yourself.**
- **Part of pastoral ministry is nurturing people as a mother nurtures her children.**

God wants each of us to be encouragers, to be like a father who encourages his children, especially when they feel weak and worthless. There's enough discouragement in life and everyone will eventually let you down. We all need encouragers who remind us to keep moving ahead in God.

LESSON 6

HOW TO ENCOURAGE AND COMFORT OTHERS

I Thessalonians 2:9-20

9 For ye remember, brethren, our labour and travail: for labouring night and day, because
we would not be chargeable unto any of you, we preached unto you the Gospel of God.

10 Ye are witnesses, and God also, how holily and justly and unblameably we behaved
ourselves among you that believe:

11 As ye know how we exhorted and comforted and charged every one of you, as a father
doth his children,

12 That ye would walk worthy of God, who hath called you unto his kingdom and glory.

13 For this cause also thank we God without ceasing, because, when ye received the word
of God which ye heard of us, ye received it not as the word of men, but as it is in truth,
the word of God, which effectually worketh also in you that believe.

14 For ye, brethren, became followers of the churches of God which in Judaea are in
Christ Jesus: for ye also have suffered like things of your own countrymen, even as they
have of the Jews:

15 Who both killed the Lord Jesus, and their own prophets, and have persecuted us; and
they please not God, and are contrary to all men:

16 Forbidding us to speak to the Gentiles that they might be saved, to fill up their sins
alway: for the wrath is come upon them to the uttermost.

17 But we, brethren, being taken from you for a short time in presence, not in heart,
endeavoured the more abundantly to see your face with great desire.

18 Wherefore we would have come unto you, even I Paul, once and again; but Satan
hindered us.

19 For what is our hope, or joy, or crown of rejoicing? Are not even ye in the presence of
our Lord Jesus Christ at his coming?

20 For ye are our glory and joy.

1 Thessalonians 2:9-10

In the early days of the Thessalonian church, the people didn't have much money. Many had lost jobs and positions in society because they began to follow Christ. Others lost their wealth and wealth-making ability to the Romans, who would come through this important city and take over the means of prosperity, leaving the people of Thessalonica with whatever was left over. And thus the church was poor and in its infant stages, so Paul decided that rather than take money from the church, he was going to work night and day to support himself so that the church wouldn't have the burden of supporting him.

He wrote,

> **9 For ye remember, brethren, our labour and travail: for labouring night and day, because we would not be chargeable unto any of you, we preached unto you the Gospel of God.**
>
> **10 Ye are witnesses, and God also, how holily and justly and unblameably we behaved ourselves among you that believe. (1 Thessalonians 2:9-10)**

I think this is a noble attitude about the ministry; not worrying about being paid for every little thing you do. We, as ministers, must look to God as our Source of supply; not man. On the other hand, if a church doesn't take good care of its full-time pastors, God may move them to a place that will treat them properly. (Please get a copy of my books, *How to Help Your Pastor Succeed* and *The Pastor's Pay*.)

Some people today want to be paid by the church for everything. They don't consider that the money could go toward ministry. Paul had a right to receive pay from the church, especially when it grew. The Bible says,

> **Deuteronomy 25:4**
>
> **"Thou shalt not muzzle the ox when he treadeth out the corn."**

That means to let him eat some of the corn to help him keep strong and healthy. In other circumstances, Paul wrote in favor of paying your ministers, but there are times that the minister needs to either reduce his pay or stop his pay altogether and go to work. This was one of those times and situations.

TRUTH ILLUSTRATED – MINISTRY FOR MONEY?

When I entered full-time ministry the people of the church paid me a small amount, but for two years we lived off the money we had saved from working the previous seven years. I didn't mind the minuscule pay; it was a joy to minister for the sake of seeing changed lives and for the privilege of serving the Lord. I remember receiving my first paycheck at Mount Hope Church. The treasurer brought me the check and handed it to me folded over and said, "I don't know why we need to pay you." It was $25 for my first week of work. I was paid $25 per week for the next six weeks.

I couldn't survive on that, but Mary Jo and I had made a sincere commitment. We were going to work with God to build a great church. Only Jesus can build a church, and we made ourselves completely available to Him. We were willing to make tents for a living or live in a tent, if necessary, but we were going to serve God wholeheartedly no matter what.

That's why to this day I don't sympathize with people who say, "I'd like to work for God, but someone will have to pay me this much money." We had a bookkeeper's position open one time and one candidate said something like this: "If you can't pay me $80,000 a year with full benefits, I don't want it."

Well, we didn't hire that candidate. Yet there are people on my staff that took huge pay cuts to leave the secular workforce, just for the privilege of serving the Lord. And God has blessed them.

Paul felt privileged to impart God's Word to the Thessalonian church and was willing to work secularly for a season to support himself in tent making. Each one of us should be willing to do the same. If my church fell into a situation where I had to work another job to keep it going, I would gladly do it. I will not step out of God's will and plan because of a change in my paycheck. I plan to remain firmly in His will. It is the safest place in the world. And the result of your work, as Paul said, is that "your labor is not in vain in the Lord." (I Corinthians 15:58) That means your work will not be empty or fruitless, like the hireling's or false teacher's work. When you leave this life and come before the judgment seat of Christ, you will be glad you served the Lord willingly in any circumstance.

1 Thessalonians 2:11

THE FATHER'S HEART

> **11 As ye know how we exhorted and comforted and charged every one of you, as a father doth his children**

Previously we saw Paul's nurturing side, like a mother nursing them, cherishing them, changing their spiritual diapers, and feeding them. Now he describes himself as a father of these precious converts in Thessalonica.

And what does a father do?

- **He exhorts**
- **He comforts**
- **He charges (disciplines)**

A HEART TO ENCOURAGE

Exhort simply means to "encourage." One of the most important roles of a father is to encourage. That is also true of leaders who are in "fatherly" positions, such as a pastor. A big part of our job description is to encourage people. It was said concerning Jesus, "A bruised reed shall he not break" (Matthew 12:20). He will not discourage somebody who is hurting. If you are hurting and you become discouraged, know with confidence that the discouragement is not from God. He cares for you and He wants you to be always encouraged. Some people feel worthless at times. Too many people come along and try to discourage them further! I am amazed when I hear people ignore the ninety-nine good things about a person and focus on the one bad thing. That is not the Father's heart.

Paul understood that. He reminded the readers of this letter, "I encouraged you." Some people are good at encouraging.

I have a friend who has a gift of encouragement. He'll send notes to people to encourage them. He'll send me encouraging notes when we are building a new facility, or right before I go out for some speaking engagement. Little things like that matter. I got back from a trip recently and found balloons and a new coffee pot with a timer on it from the woman who keeps the office wing clean. She always leaves me a little encouraging note on my computer when she cleans the office that says something like, "Have a glorious day, Pastor Dave. Thanks for your teaching!"

God wants each of us to be encouragers, to be like a father who encourages his children, especially when they feel weak and worthless. There's enough discouragement in life and everyone will eventually let you down. We all need encouragers who remind us to keep moving ahead in God.

A HEART TO COMFORT

Paul also said he comforted them.

The word "comfort" is interesting because it doesn't mean exactly what you might think. It means, "to strengthen, to train, to make strong."

TRUTH ILLUSTRATED – STRENGTH TRAINING

Comforting is like starting a weight lifting regimen by lifting 3-pound weights, then progressing the next week to five pounds, then to seven pounds, and then to ten pounds over time. That's called strength training. Paul was strengthening the church in Thessalonica spiritually when he was there. You strengthen people by letting them test their wings. Everybody needs training and encouragement to build up their strength in the areas of God's calling on their lives. Paul showed the Thessalonians how to minister and then he let them minister. This was like giving them heavier weights to lift.

Some people get upset when I let others preach at our church, especially young ministers who have not had much practice. People gripe, "I'm not going to church if that other guy is preaching." Some people call the church to ask who is preaching this week. They only come to church if their preferred preacher is in the pulpit. By doing that they are undermining the work of strengthening.

I remember my mom and dad sitting down with me and teaching me to tie my shoes. It seemed to take forever. I would practice, and my mom would pull my crazy knots out of my shoelaces. They had to be patient with me. They didn't say, "You idiot! You should know how to do this by now." They strengthened me.

My daughter learned to crochet at the age of two. She would crochet blankets and mittens. I would say, "Trina Lee, you are so smart!" And, she would say, "Don't tell anybody I know how to do this because I don't want them to feel bad if they don't know how!" How did my daughter, Trina Lee learn? Mary Jo, my wife taught her how. My wife and I then strengthened her with our words. Everything you ever learn or do is because someone strengthens you and shows you how to do it.

Tom Monaghan, who used to own Domino's Pizza, said that Domino's Pizza went from a debt-ridden pizza joint to a billion-dollar company by one thing, and it wasn't fancy cheese, better sauce, or fast delivery. It was by strengthening the people who worked for the company. Some managers of Domino's Pizza stores started as delivery boys and rose to make six figures a year because Tom Monaghan believed in strengthening the people who worked for him.

THE HEART TO DISCIPLINE

The third thing Paul would do as their father figure was to charge them. This doesn't mean charging them money; rather, he disciplined them. In other words, he had to lay the law down sometimes. When they were naughty and not behaving, he had to act like a father and discipline them. Mothers sometimes say, "Wait 'til your father gets home!" Paul was the father and "mother" of the Thessalonian church. He administered discipline and did it in love, never in anger. He had incredible patience for the people of God.

We should always show God's mercy in all of our discipline.

TRUTH ILLUSTRATED – LATE FOR DINNER

One boy was perpetually late for dinner, and always dilly-dallying around after school. His mother finally said, "If you are late for dinner one more time, all you'll get is bread and water." The boy came home late again and on his plate was nothing but bread and in his glass was nothing but water. There were his parents and sister sitting there with full plates of food. Dad said, "Son, you messed up, and your punishment is bread and water." But then his dad did something unexpected - he took his own plate and put it in front of the boy, and took the bread and water and said, "I'll take your punishment for you." The dad ate the bread and drank the water. The son was never late for supper again.

That's a picture of what God did for us in His loving discipline. He said, "You're the one who messed up, but I'm going to take the rap for you." That's the kind of discipline Paul was talking about when he said, "I charged you."

1 Thessalonians 2:12

WALKING WORTHY OF GOD

Why did Paul do all this? He had a very good reason.

> **12 That ye would walk worthy of God, who hath called you unto his kingdom and glory.**

Paul wanted all these new Christians to walk worthy of God.

Think about it: when you walk, you're moving somewhere.

Nobody in the Christian faith has a right to sit. Paul didn't say, "sit worthy of God." He didn't say, "Lay down worthy of God." He said to walk worthy of God. That means making progress in a forward direction. Keep moving, taking on another challenge and then another challenge, pushing yourself, trusting God, lifting your faith, and putting it on the line so that you walk worthy of God.

1 Thessalonians 2:13

> **13 For this cause also thank we God without ceasing, because, when ye received the word of God which ye heard of us, ye received it not as the word of men, but as it is in truth, the word of God, which effectually worketh also in you that believe.**

Why is it that the Word of God seems to work in some people and doesn't seem to work in others? There's a simple explanation. It works for those who believe and act on it! Some people come to church and say, "I wonder what Pastor Dave's going to say today?" That's the wrong way to come to church. The right way is to come saying, "I wonder what the Lord's going to speak to my heart about today?" Then it doesn't matter who is preaching, because you're looking to the Lord for a word from his heart.

1 Thessalonians 2:14

Then Paul made some scathing remarks about men who were not walking worthy of God—certain Jews and religious leaders. He wrote,

> **[14] For ye, brethren, became followers of the churches of God which in Judaea are in Christ Jesus: for ye also have suffered like things of your own countrymen, even as they have of the Jews**

1 Thessalonians 2:15

The churches in Judea were mostly made up of converted Jews, and the Jewish religious leaders were persecuting them. The general makeup of the church in Thessalonica was Gentile, and it was the government that was persecuting them. Paul was saying the same thing was happening to both churches (Jewish and Gentile) though from different sources. Paul himself was a former high-ranking Jewish religious leader, but now he described his feelings toward his former colleagues:

> **[15] Who both killed the Lord Jesus, and their own prophets, and have persecuted us; and they please not God, and are contrary to all men**

1 Thessalonians 2:16

Have you ever known someone who is contrary to all men? I have. If you say the light's going to stay green, they say, "Nah, it'll turn red." If you wear black pants, they'll tell you brown would have looked better. In the same way, whatever Paul said, the Jews opposed him. For example,

> **[16] Forbidding us to speak to the Gentiles that they might be saved,**

They were preventing people from coming to Christ. In so doing, Paul said, they would

> **... to fill up their sins alway: for the wrath is come upon them to the uttermost.**

The New Living Translation puts it this way:

> **1 Thessalonians 2:16 NLT**
> **" ... as they try to keep us from preaching the Good News of salvation to the Gentiles. By doing this, they continue to pile up their sins. But the anger of God has caught up with them at last."**

WRATH OFTEN COMES TO THOSE WHO HINDER THE GOSPEL

There comes a time when God's patience comes to an end and the wrath pours out. God permits sin to run its course, but once it piles up too high, judgment falls, and when it falls, it falls hard.

A few years after Paul wrote this, an unprecedented famine struck Judea and people saw their children starve to death. Two years after that, there was a brutal massacre of Jews throughout the temple precincts at Passover time. That same year, Emperor Claudius expelled all the Jews from Rome. They lost everything they had worked for all their lives. And, of course, in 70 A.D., Titus and his Roman armies came into Jerusalem and slaughtered one million people in the destruction of Jerusalem. So the judgment came and came hard. Paul was not anti-Semitic or against Jews. He was himself Jewish, but he was against false Judaism. His argument with the Jews was not racial but theological.

Let's not miss the lesson here. Jesus came to seek and save the lost, and those who try to hinder God's work in the earth will face judgment. That judgment is like a huge tank rolling down the road. It never seems to be moving as fast as we'd like it to move, but it's unstoppable. You can't stop the work of God or His judgment. Jesus said, "I will build my church" (Matthew 16:18). You can either get on board or get run over.

TRUTH ILLUSTRATED – A SORCERER GETS SOCKED

There was a sorcerer in the New Testament who was interfering as Paul shared about Christ with an important government official. Paul finally turned to him and said, "O full of all subtilty and all mischief, thou child of the devil, thou enemy of all righteousness, wilt thou not cease to pervert the right ways of the Lord? And now, behold, the hand of the Lord is upon thee, and thou shalt be blind, not seeing the sun for a season. And immediately there fell on him a mist and a darkness, and he went about seeking some to lead him by the hand" (Acts 13:10-11).

The sorcerer went blind and had to have someone lead him around for a season because of judgment. Why did this judgment come? Because he was trying to interfere with spreading the Gospel.

One time the City Council of Lansing, where my church is located, tried to prevent us from opening a Mount Hope Church downtown. One of them even said, "We don't want another monstrosity in Lansing like Mount Hope Church." Within two months there was a scandal and every one of them that opposed our new Mount Hope Church downtown was swept off that council, even though some had been on that council for many years.

When we were getting ready to build the main Mount Hope Church in Lansing, there was a woman on the City Planning Commission who refused to allow us to build if we didn't make the entry road into the church like an arch or a hill. That would have made it almost impossible to get into the church in the winter because it was like a roller coaster. No other businesses or buildings had hilly entrances, but she insisted that ours should. She allegedly hated our church and any church, I later learned. We put the project on hold and that woman dropped dead in her 40's. The person who took her place in the engineering department looked at her proposal and said, "What was she thinking?" Her idea of a hill was ridiculous. I don't know, but I have often wondered if she suffered swift judgment for her actions against the church.

That's not the only story like that I know of. A young man in Washington, D.C., was appointed by a Senate committee to investigate pastors of larger ministries. The young appointee decided to stir up serious trouble against television evangelists and pastors in the mid-70s. He stated he wanted to investigate all the television ministries and allegedly said he wanted to get them off the air. Some of the key television ministers of the day, including Rex Humbard, had to go before Senate subcommittees and explain why they were preaching the Gospel on television and defend themselves against accusations of being cult leaders and charlatans.

After the hearing, the Senators had gone and that young appointee arrogantly got in Rex Humbard's face and said, "Humbard, you just wait, I'm getting all you evangelists off television for good!" Rex stood up and said, "Sir, you're forgetting one thing—God!" That afternoon that young man went to the dentist for simple dental work. He was given an anesthetic, had an allergic reaction, and died in the dental chair. This horrible event was told to me by Don Humbard, Rex's son.

WHY DO ENEMIES FIGHT SO HARD?

Why do the enemies of God fight so hard? It's because the church of Jesus Christ is succeeding. We are growing incredibly fast around the world.

I heard about a village in Indonesia where every Muslim man had the same dream one night about Jesus.[26] They were afraid to talk about it directly so they got together and one of them said, "Did you dream anything last night?" and another said, "Yes, I had a very troubling dream." Soon it came out that they had the same dream. They talked to their friend, and he'd had the same dream. All the men in the town had the same dream and they realized that it was a sign from God that Jesus really is Lord. Nearly that whole town in one day came to Jesus Christ. You can't stop the church of Jesus Christ!

1 Thessalonians 2:17-18

In verse 17, Paul's tone went from fatherly to brotherly:

> [17] **But we, brethren, being taken from you for a short time in presence, not in heart, endeavoured the more abundantly to see your face with great desire.**

Paul made repeated efforts to return to Thessalonica, but he said in verse 18,

> [18] **Wherefore we would have come unto you, even I Paul, once and again; but Satan hindered us.**

The word "hindered" means thwarted or impeded.[27] The Greek word picture is "to break up a road to make it impassable." This is what happened to Paul. Repeatedly he tried to get back to those people he loved in that church he had established. But something always came up that stopped him. It was Satan.

How did Satan hinder Paul from going? There were three ways.

- **First, Satan used the legal system to tie up all the Christians' property and threaten to keep it if Paul ever came back to town**
- **Second, the Jews were constantly stirring up trouble for Paul everywhere he went**
- **And third, Paul had to travel to Corinth where Satan had tempted one of the members into sin.**

1 Thessalonians 2:19-20

Paul was fighting a multi-front battle. But he wrote something beautiful:

> [19] **For what is our hope, or joy, or crown of rejoicing? Are not even ye in the presence of our Lord Jesus Christ at his coming?**
>
> [20] **For ye are our glory and joy.**

Paul was promising that at the coming of Jesus, they would all stand together. "You are our glory," he wrote. In other words, "You are my pride and joy!" Sometimes people show me their car, boat, or workshop and say, "This is my pride and joy." Those things don't impress me. Your real pride and joy should be the people you invest in whom you will see in heaven.

TRUTH ILLUSTRATED – THE HIPPIE GIRL

In my early days of ministry, I led a weekly Bible study at my house, and a barefoot hippie guy attended regularly. He was hitchhiking to Bible study one night and this girl pulled over and offered him a ride...and some marijuana. He said, "No, thanks. I'm a servant of Jesus Christ and I'm on my way to Bible study." She got curious and came along. She wore short shorts and a little skimpy T-shirt with nothing under it. Talk about a distracting Bible study! But that night she said she wanted to get saved, so I prayed the prayer of salvation with her. We were happy for her, but I honestly wondered if it would stick.

A few months later she was passing through Lansing and stopped by the church. A beautiful lady walked up to me and said, "Hi, Dave!" Her hair was neat. She had on a dress, high heels, and makeup. She said, "Do you remember me?" I said, "No." She said, "I'm the one who got saved at your Bible study." I was stunned! She looked different. She was different, both inside and out.

People like that should bring us great joy!

Life is about the people we influence, comfort, and encourage. Nobody will take boats, cars, or homes to Heaven, but we can take people with us by sharing the Gospel with them.

One time a visiting minister was at our church and wanted to see the sanctuary, so I flipped on the lights and he said, "Boy, what a beautiful church."

I told him, "Yes, but the people are a lot more beautiful." That's how Paul felt toward the churches he founded, and how we should feel about each other.

POWER PRINCIPLES:

- **Ministry should be about what we can give—not what we can get.**
- **Model Christians encourage and strengthen each other like a father does his children.**
- **The Christian life is a walk—not a sit or even a sprint. It requires consistent action.**
- **Those who oppose God's work will eventually face judgment.**

I Thessalonians 3

1 Wherefore when we could no longer forbear, we thought it good to be left at Athens alone;

2 And sent Timotheus, our brother, and minister of God, and our fellowlabourer in the Gospel of Christ, to establish you, and to comfort you concerning your faith:

3 That no man should be moved by these afflictions: for yourselves know that we are appointed thereunto.

4 For verily, when we were with you, we told you before that we should suffer tribulation; even as it came to pass, and ye know.

5 For this cause, when I could no longer forbear, I sent to know your faith, lest by some means the tempter have tempted you, and our labour be in vain.

6 But now when Timotheus came from you unto us, and brought us good tidings of your faith and charity, and that ye have good remembrance of us always, desiring greatly to see us, as we also to see you:

7 Therefore, brethren, we were comforted over you in all our affliction and distress by your faith:

8 For now we live, if ye stand fast in the Lord.

9 For what thanks can we render to God again for you, for all the joy wherewith we joy for your sakes before our God;

10 Night and day praying exceedingly that we might see your face, and might perfect that which is lacking in your faith?

11 Now God himself and our Father, and our Lord Jesus Christ, direct our way unto you.

12 And the Lord make you to increase and abound in love one toward another, and toward all men, even as we do toward you:

13 To the end he may stablish your hearts unblameable in holiness before God, even our Father, at the coming of our Lord Jesus Christ with all his saints

LESSON 7

HOW TO BECOME AN ESTABLISHED BELIEVER

I Thessalonians 3:1-13
1 Wherefore when we could no longer forbear, we thought it good to be left at Athens
alone;

2 And sent Timotheus, our brother, and minister of God, and our fellow labourer in the
Gospel of Christ, to establish you, and to comfort you concerning your faith:

3 That no man should be moved by these afflictions: for yourselves know that we are
appointed thereunto.

4 For verily, when we were with you, we told you before that we should suffer tribulation; even as it came to pass, and ye know.

5 For this cause, when I could no longer forbear, I sent to know your faith, lest by some
means the tempter have tempted you, and our labour be in vain.

6 But now when Timotheus came from you unto us, and brought us good tidings of
your faith and charity, and that ye have good remembrance of us always, desiring greatly to see us, as we also to see you:

7 Therefore, brethren, we were comforted over you in all our affliction and distress by
your faith:

8 For now we live, if ye stand fast in the Lord.

9 For what thanks can we render to God again for you, for all the joy wherewith we joy
for your sakes before our God;

10 Night and day praying exceedingly that we might see your face, and might perfect
that which is lacking in your faith?

11 Now God himself and our Father, and our Lord Jesus Christ, direct our way unto you.

12 And the Lord make you to increase and abound in love one toward another, and
toward all men, even as we do toward you:

13 To the end he may stablish your hearts unblameable in holiness before God, even our
Father, at the coming of our Lord Jesus Christ with all his saints.

1 Thessalonians 3:1-3

So far we have seen Paul the evangelist and church planter, Paul the pastor, Paul the mother, Paul the father, and Paul the brother. Now we see Paul as the bereaved friend. Chapter 3 starts,

> **1 Wherefore when we could no longer forbear, we thought it good to be left at Athens alone;**
>
> **2 And sent Timotheus, our brother, and minister of God, and our fellow labourer in the Gospel of Christ, to establish you, and to comfort you concerning your faith:**
>
> **3 That no man should be moved by these afflictions: for yourselves know that we are appointed thereunto.**

Paul was frustrated at not being able to return to visit his friends. He was saying, "I couldn't take it anymore. It was too much." Sometimes things seem more than you can bear. You face times when you can't take one more thing—not one more phone call, not one more piece of bad news.

But there is a solution, and Paul found the solution in his time of frustration. He sent Timothy to Thessalonica because there was no warrant for his arrest there. Timothy could check on the church. Paul also sent a letter to the church with Timothy, to convey Paul's feelings of love and devotion to them and their future in the Gospel. And Paul prayed for them.

Even though Paul was prohibited from returning, he did things to keep the relationship strong. That shows us there is a solution to every problem we face in life!

But sometimes the best solution is not our first choice.

LEFT ALONE

Paul said he was going to be left alone in Athens. The word "left" means "to be bereaved, as if somebody died." When Paul left Thessalonica it was like a death to him. Now Timothy, his young son in the faith, his co-laborer in the things of God, was going to leave Paul bereaved again. It was like another death to Paul. No wonder he said, "I die daily" (I Corinthians 15:31). He had to sacrifice friends and companionship so the Gospel would take root in Thessalonica.

It can be hard to let people go. Every time our church sent out a pastor to establish a new daughter church, it was hard for me to let them go, yet necessary to expand Christ's work. I only did it for the sake of establishing godly churches in every community in Michigan, which was our goal. And when those churches grew and bore much fruit, then I was glad

I sent the pastor out. But it was always difficult at first. Paul, too, was sending Timothy to establish the people, strengthen them, and encourage them in their faith so they would bear fruit.

I had a young girl tell me one time, "My parents are good Christians. They have been members of seven different churches in town, but every time they start a business, it always fails. What's the problem?"

The problem probably is that they never got established in the things of God, since they often jumped from church to church. They uprooted themselves each time a problem came and never became strengthened in a local church. That's why Paul sent Timothy back to Thessalonica, so the church members there would not become failures or Christian has-beens but, instead, would become strong in the faith.

KEEPING THE MAIN THING, THE MAIN THING

There is something about Timothy—he always seemed to stay within the scope of his present task. He was a true minister, which simply means "servant." He was a team player; he didn't need to run the show. When he was sent to Thessalonica, he stayed under Paul's leadership and authority. He didn't try to take over leadership of that church. As a result of this faithfulness, the day came when Timothy became the pastor and bishop of the church at Ephesus, a church that eventually exceeded an estimated 30,000 members. This was the church the apostle John attended after he returned from exile on the Isle of Patmos.

What was Timothy's scope of mission in this instance? Paul said: "He's our fellow laborer in the Gospel of Christ."

Nothing more and nothing less than the Gospel.

In the same way, your main objective as a model Christian, and our main objective together as members of model churches, is to advance the Gospel of Jesus Christ. Sometimes people have criticized me for not being more involved in social and political action. But I have found that when you help to transform people's lives with the power of the Gospel, many of the social ills and harmful behaviors take care of themselves.

Somebody called me one Sunday and said, "Are you going to participate in the march against abortion this afternoon?"

I answered, "No. I have a service on Sunday night and I'm going to be praying all afternoon that the Word of God will go forth and people's lives will be transformed."

The person on the phone retorted, "You can't be a Christian if you won't march with us against abortion."

Imagine that! I was supposed to drop my calling as a minister of the Gospel to go help him march around town with sandwich signs and banners. Now, understand, I'm totally against the detestable practice of killing babies in their mother's womb. It is murder; nothing less than a horrible offense to God and His creation. However, I'm not going to stop everything God has called me to do, to jump into a spur-of-the-moment event, sponsored by some guy I didn't know.

You see, I could start a group against abortion and then a group against drinking and so on. But to be truly effective, I should continue to preach the Gospel because when Jesus Christ gets hold of people's lives they no longer want to live immorally. Believe it or not, the week after the abortion march, the man who had called me came to our church parking lot with a megaphone and said, "Don't go to this church. Your pastor is pro-abortion because he would not march in our abortion protest last week." Honestly. While I agree with this fellow's stance on abortion, I don't want to show support for or identify with a person like that.

I simply refuse to be involved in social action apart from the Gospel of Jesus Christ. My church used to regularly contribute heavily to a food bank in town. Then we found out that they're no longer giving out the Gospel with the food because they can't get a federal grant if they do. So, we no longer support them.

I'm less concerned with people getting temporary assistance than I am with them getting the Gospel of Jesus Christ, which gives eternal help.

Timothy's scope of ministry wasn't to feed physical food to the Thessalonian church. It wasn't to raise money for the Thessalonian church. It was to labor for the Gospel of Jesus Christ. Wherever the Gospel of Jesus Christ has been received, hospitals go up, healing centers are established,[28] hungry people are fed and many are delivered from bad lives.

TEEN CHALLENGE OR "REPRODUCTIVE RIGHTS?"

Teen Challenge is a great example of that. Teen Challenge doesn't get people off heroin only to put them on methadone—as if that were a solution. They get the Gospel of Jesus Christ in their hearts and then get them off drugs completely! Any social program that does not have Jesus Christ at its core will probably end up promoting immorality and recklessness. Think of the secular government-funded pregnancy group that offers solutions to teen pregnancies, including abortions and free condoms. Does that encourage morality or moral recklessness? You decide!

Timothy's goal was to establish and strengthen the church concerning their faith. The word, "establish" means "to build up properly." It's not enough just to receive Christ. I see people at the altar Sunday after Sunday making decisions to follow Christ. But the Gospel must take root in their lives and they must become disciples of Jesus Christ if they are to become model Christians. "Establish" means also to "lay a good foundation." In your spiritual life you must put the framework in properly, then build the rooms, then do the detail work, the painting, the sanding, and the caulking, and only then will you have a beautiful building that will withstand the storms.

TRUTH ILLUSTRATED – BUILT TO STAND

Years ago, I was in Long Beach, California, with an elderly man named Mr. Schuler who built and owned the Schuler Hotel. He felt a little tremor one day and Mr. Schuler just stood there and yelled, "Bring it on, bring it on!" He knew that his hotel was built to withstand an earthquake. He had built the foundation properly.

How do Christians get established? By being part of a church and benefiting from the work of apostles, prophets, evangelists, pastors, and teachers. God gave local churches to do the finishing work on your spiritual structure. Sometimes the finishing work requires the pastor to put a nail in or hammer a bit but some people say, "Ouch, I'm leaving!" They don't stick around to get built properly.

We probably all know some folks who never got established in genuine faith, and yet they think they are spiritual giants. I get many little notes that sound so spiritual. "Dear Pastor, I've seen some issues and concerns in the church that are not being addressed and I just feel the Holy Spirit moving me now to attend a place where I'm going to be better fed." Those notes are usually from spiritual infants who think they are spiritual giants. They act like a grown-up Christian, but they are immature and need grounding.

Some people claim that their "church" is Christian television. I wonder how that works when they are sick in the hospital, or when it's time for their funeral. Who will visit? Who will attend? Other viewers? I appreciate Christian television. My program, The Pacesetter's Path, was on all over the world for 19 years via satellite and syndicated stations. But I can't be a pastor to people in Hong Kong, the Philippines, Japan, and China. Christian television supplements local ministry, but it cannot, by any stretch of the imagination, take the place of a local church.

A local church helps you get your roots down and become established. When tensions, pressures, and afflictions come, you will not be like a reed blowing in the wind. Rather you will be like a tree planted by the water (Psalm 1:3). Your spiritual building will be strong, like Mr. Schuler's hotel.

A PROMISE I DON'T LIKE

The next verse is one I wish I could omit from the Bible, but I don't have that option. It says,

> **3 That no man should be moved by these afflictions: for yourselves know that we are appointed thereunto.**

It's uncomfortable but true: some storms of life are not accidents, but appointments!

The word "affliction" means, "intense pressure," or "tensions," times when it seems like things aren't working out right. Some of those times are appointments designed for our advancement and the development of our character. Our character is developed in times of affliction. Paul said we were appointed to some of these hard times. I don't like that at all because it means when pressure comes into my life, it is probably not an accident. It is probably an opportunity for me to grow and advance.

ORGANIZED RELIGIOUS CRIME AND EXTORTION

The Thessalonians were going through storms, just as we all do. Paul tells us that the religious Jews were the source of it all. Please understand, that the Jewish people of that day were beautiful, wonderful people. But the Jewish religious leaders were no better than common criminals.

In Thessalonica when Paul started preaching the Gospel and dozens of Gentiles started coming to Christ, the Jewish religious leaders found some "worthless Gentiles" to stir up trouble and spread lies about Paul to all the other Gentiles. When Paul was finally run out of town, these religious Jews came to the new Christians and said, "If you renounce Christianity, all your persecution will stop." So, the evil band of Gentiles was not only lying about the Christians, they were persecuting them because the religious Jewish leaders were paying them to do so. It is the definition of organized crime and extortion. You might say that many churches have a certain type of "mafia," controllers who know how to keep a pastor under their thumbs.

Though none of us like being appointed for afflictions, there are two things we can do in response.

- **First, be of good cheer. Jesus said in this world we would have tribulation, but that we should be of good cheer for He has overcome this world (John 16:33).**

- **Second, speak your faith to the storm. When Jesus was in the middle of the sea with the disciples and a storm came up, the disciples started talking about the storm. "Oh boy, this is a bad storm!" "Oh, the boats are filling up!" "We're going to die!" But Jesus stood up and spoke to the storm, saying, "Peace, be still" (Mark 4:39). If you want miracles in your life, quit talking about the storms and start talking to the storms.**

NEVER MAKE A PERMANENT DECISION BASED ON A TEMPORARY CIRCUMSTANCE

Every storm a believer faces is temporary. That's why I tell people never to make a permanent decision based on a temporary circumstance. You'll end up being sorry! Every storm is meant to advance you and is meant to be temporary. When Jesus spoke to the storm while they were in the middle of the Sea of Galilee, immediately the boat was at the other side. They were supernaturally transported. To speed up the miracle process in your life, start speaking to the storm instead of about the storm and you will get better results.

A pastor was having a service one night and he said, "I'd like people to share their favorite Scriptures." An old guy got up and said, "My favorite Scripture is the one that says, 'and it came to pass.' Because whenever I get in trouble I read that Scripture and I know that my trouble came to pass, not to stay!"

When you face afflictions, pressures, tensions, and troubles, they haven't come to stay, they have come to pass! These afflictions would pass in Thessalonica, and their character would be developed so they would become a model church.

1 Thessalonians 3:4-5

A GOOD REPORT

> **4 For verily, when we were with you, we told you before that we should suffer tribulation; even as it came to pass, and ye know.**
>
> **5 For this cause, when I could no longer forbear, I sent to know your faith, lest by some means the tempter have tempted you, and our labour be in vain.**

1 Thessalonians 3:6-8

TRUE BELIEVERS SHINE THROUGH AFFLICTION, WHILE COUNTERFEITS FLAKE OFF

Paul was concerned that the devil had weakened the Thessalonians' faith. But true believers shine through affliction, while counterfeits always flake off. The same is true with ministers. Jesus said the Good Shepherd gives his life for the sheep, but the hireling runs away when the wolf comes (John 10:11).

> **6 But now when Timotheus came from you unto us, and brought us good tidings of your faith and charity, and that ye have good remembrance of us always, desiring greatly to see us, as we also to see you:**
>
> **7 Therefore, brethren, we were comforted over you in all our affliction and distress by your faith:**
>
> **8 For now we live, if ye stand fast in the Lord.**

Paul was saying, "Ah! Now I can sleep at night. Now I can rest. Now I can enjoy life to the fullest knowing what's going on in Thessalonica."

Timothy had reported that:

- **Their faith was solid**
- **Their doctrine was sound**
- **Their character was impeccable**
- **They hadn't believed any of the lies that were spread about Paul**
- **They loved Paul and couldn't wait to see him again.**

What a relief! It was like getting good tidings from an old friend when you are fearing the worst.

Sometimes it's easy to fear the worst when you shouldn't.

TRUTH ILLUSTRATED – THE BOOMERANG NEWS ARTICLE

One time in the history of my ministry in Lansing, a big newspaper ran a front-page article about me that was not entirely positive. It included a picture of me holding up my Bible with my mouth open in a weird pose. The caption accused me of offering "Bible-thumping glitz."[29] I thought it was kind of funny, but my friends were upset about it. Yet the next week our attendance was so high we could barely fit all the people in the church, and we had 3000 seats with three Sunday morning services!

It's awful when people spread lies about you. But it's a relief when people don't believe it.

Another time a tabloid television program[30] did a nasty piece on Drs. Jack and Rexella Van Impe, friends of mine, asserting, "They make big bucks by scaring the hell out people!" The show reported Jack and Rexella personally pulled in $350,000 a year. But Jack called me and told me it wasn't true. Furthermore, he was greatly concerned that his partners would believe it. He said, "We don't make that kind of money! I would never do that!"

What had happened was the ministry owned the parsonage where Jack and Rexella lived. The board got together and said, "Dr. Van Impe is getting up there in years now, so we should probably donate that house to him so if God takes him home, Rexella will have a place to live."

So, the ministry donated the parsonage to Jack and Rexella, and he had to claim that as income on his taxes that year, so it looked like they made a lot of money. I think they deserved a lot more, but I told him, "Jack, the best thing to do is just forget it." (Jack has since gone to heaven and Rexella still lives in that house. But now it's easily worth at least five times more than it was 30 years ago.)

A lot of times when you strike back at those unfair attacks, they just seem to grow larger. The truth is, probably 90 percent of the people won't even hear about the lie unless you mention it. That's what happened with Jack and Rexella. Their partners either didn't hear about the story, or they didn't believe it. It was just like the Thessalonians with Paul—they didn't believe the rumors.

1 Thessalonians 3:9-10

Paul continued,

> **9 For what thanks can we render to God again for you, for all the joy wherewith we joy for your sakes before our God;**
>
> **10 Night and day praying exceedingly that we might see your face, and might perfect that which is lacking in your faith?**

The word "perfect" is the same Greek word as "net mend."

We all have nets in life; in a sense, we're all fishermen fishing for souls. If we have holes in our nets, the fish slip out. It is like the little girl who told me that her parents were never successful in business. Their nets were full of big holes and all the fish got out. That's why you need to be established. Paul was telling the Thessalonians to mend their nets.

1 Thessalonians 3:11-12

> **11 Now God himself and our Father, and our Lord Jesus Christ, direct our way unto you.**
>
> **12 And the Lord make you to increase and abound in love one toward another, and toward all men, even as we do toward you:**

In this brief passage, Paul emphasized the deity of Christ, which is what most cults dismiss to this day. He also said God wants us to abound and increase in love, and that we are all His saints. Saints are just ordinary people who have put their faith in Jesus Christ and have started following him to the best of their ability.

1 Thessalonians 3:13

[13] To the end he may stablish your hearts unblameable in holiness before God, even our Father, at the coming of our Lord Jesus Christ with all his saints.

Paul here uses the word "coming." There are three words for this in the Greek language.

- **One is the root of our word "epiphany," which relates to the first coming of God in the flesh— Jesus being born in Bethlehem. That's why we call the Christmas season the season of Epiphany.**
- **Another word for coming is "apocalypse," which means "revelation." That is when Jesus will come the second time in His glory and be revealed to every person in this world, even those who pierced Him. It will be the revelation of Jesus Christ when he comes at Armageddon with His saints.**
- **And the third word for coming in the Greek is "parousia," which means "presence and alongside." This means that believers and followers of Jesus Christ actually come into His presence alongside Him. This is speaking of a totally different event than the Epiphany or the apocalypse.**

The word Paul uses here can only mean one thing: "Parousia." It can only be the coming of Christ for His Church before the revelation of the antichrist on the earth. It happens sometime before the world plummets into its deepest and most supreme hour of terror.

Jesus Christ is coming in the "parousia." He is coming in the clouds and the dead in Christ are going to rise and we which are alive, in a twinkling of an eye, shall be changed and caught up to meet them in the air (1 Corinthians 15:51-55 and 1 Thessalonians 4:13-18). We will be alongside Jesus forevermore. We will go to Heaven while the worst tribulation ever hits this earth. We will attend the marriage supper of the lamb, and the Judgment Seat of Christ to determine our rewards, and we will have made it to our eternal goal. That is the "Parousia," – the coming of Christ for His Church. Hallelujah!

Even though we face affliction and pressures, bereavement, and unfair treatment, these things don't come to stay; they come to pass. But when Jesus comes, His comfort and joy will be forever! Jesus is coming...Any Day Now!

POWER PRINCIPLES:

- The main thing is not social work or good deeds for their own sake, but the spread of the Gospel for Christ's sake.
- All Christians are appointed unto afflictions—but those afflictions are temporary and offer opportunities to grow.

1 Thessalonians 4

1 Furthermore then we beseech you, brethren, and exhort you by the Lord Jesus, that as ye have received of us how ye ought to walk and to please God, so ye would abound more and more.

2 For ye know what commandments we gave you by the Lord Jesus.

3 For this is the will of God, even your sanctification, that ye should abstain from fornication:

4 That every one of you should know how to possess his vessel in sanctification and honour;

5 Not in the lust of concupiscence, even as the Gentiles which know not God:

6 That no man go beyond and defraud his brother in any matter: because that the Lord is the avenger of all such, as we also have forewarned you and testified.

7 For God hath not called us unto uncleanness, but unto holiness.

8 He therefore that despiseth, despiseth not man, but God, who hath also given unto us his holy Spirit.

9 But as touching brotherly love ye need not that I write unto you: for ye yourselves are taught of God to love one another.

10 And indeed ye do it toward all the brethren which are in all Macedonia: but we beseech you, brethren, that ye increase more and more;

11 And that ye study to be quiet, and to do your own business, and to work with your own hands, as we commanded you;

12 That ye may walk honestly toward them that are without, and that ye may have lack of nothing.

13 But I would not have you to be ignorant, brethren, concerning them which are asleep, that ye sorrow not, even as others which have no hope.

14 For if we believe that Jesus died and rose again, even so them also which sleep in Jesus will God bring with him.

15 For this we say unto you by the word of the Lord, that we which are alive and remain unto the coming of the Lord shall not prevent them which are asleep.

16 For the Lord himself shall descend from heaven with a shout, with the voice of the archangel, and with the trump of God: and the dead in Christ shall rise first:

17 Then we which are alive and remain shall be caught up together with them in the clouds, to meet the Lord in the air: and so shall we ever be with the Lord.

18 Wherefore comfort one another with these words.

LESSON 8

HOW TO LIVE PURE IN A TRIPLE X-RATED WORLD

I Thessalonians 4:1-8

[1] Furthermore then we beseech you, brethren, and exhort you by the Lord Jesus, that as ye have received of us how ye ought to walk and to please God, so ye would abound more and more.

[2] For ye know what commandments we gave you by the Lord Jesus.

[3] For this is the will of God, even your sanctification, that ye should abstain from fornication:

[4] That every one of you should know how to possess his vessel in sanctification and honour;

[5] Not in the lust of concupiscence, even as the Gentiles which know not God:

[6] That no man go beyond and defraud his brother in any matter: because that the Lord is the avenger of all such, as we also have forewarned you and testified.

[7] For God hath not called us unto uncleanness, but unto holiness.

[8] He therefore that despiseth, despiseth not man, but God, who hath also given unto us his Holy Spirit.

In Paul's day, Thessalonica was a sex-crazed city. Good morals were rare. A man was thought to be moral even if he had a mistress. The chief Greek philosopher of that day, Demosthenes,[31] wrote, "We keep prostitutes for our pleasure, mistresses for our day-to-day needs, and wives for the begetting of our legitimate children and faithful guardianship of our homes."

Some family values!

1 Thessalonians 4:1

NEW TESTAMENT PORTRAIT OF "NORMAL"

But the New Testament paints a different portrait of "normal." Twice it says, "Don't be deceived...adulterers, fornicators, murderers, homosexuals, have no part in the kingdom of God." (1 Corinthians 6:9: 1 Timothy 1:10; Galatians 5:19-21)

Then, as today, many people thought you could live any way you wanted without inviting moral consequences. But Paul said that's not the way it is. There are moral absolutes. It's imperative that we follow those moral absolutes or we will share the judgment this world receives.

> **1 Furthermore then we beseech you, brethren, and exhort you by the Lord Jesus, that as ye have received of us how ye ought to walk and to please God, so ye would abound more and more.**

Paul started chapter 4 with the words, "Furthermore, then," which means, "I covered the main points I wanted to talk to you about, and now I've got some other important things to mention."

> **... exhort you by the Lord Jesus, that as ye have received of us how ye ought to walk and to please God.**

Paul is speaking not his own ideas or opinions, but commandments from the Lord Jesus.

This is like a military command. He was saying that as part of God's army, these commands come from the Commander-in-Chief Himself. We don't have the option of disobeying these orders. But he adds an amazing promise if we do obey:

> **... so ye would abound more and more.**

Some commentators say that means to abound more and more in holiness or love. But Paul left it blank on purpose, I believe. He is saying that if you want to come into an abundance of any kind, whether it's love, holiness, closeness to God, good family relationships, or more, then there are two keys:

- **One is to walk, which implies you're making progress.**
- **The second is to do things that please God.**

KEY TO ABOUNDING - WALKING

Let's look at the first one, walking. We noted before that walking means you're moving. The Bible talks a lot about walking: walking in the light (John 8:12), walking in love (Ephesians 5:2), walking not as the Gentiles walked (Ephesians 4:17), walking not by sight but by faith (II Corinthians 5:7).

This Christian life is a walk. That means we should be constantly walking closer to and becoming more like Jesus, from day to day and glory to glory, year to year, decade to decade. We should always be progressing in our Christian faith. If you ever find yourself saying, "I'm not abounding more. Why does the faith walk not work for me?" Maybe you are not walking. Maybe you are just sitting in the pew. Maybe you are asking to be spoon-fed all the time.

The writer of the book of Hebrews said there comes a time when you, as a Christian, need to grow up. You should be teaching others by now; but instead, you need the fundamental, foundational, rudimentary principles taught to you all over again (Hebrews 5:12).

> **Hebrews 5:12**
> **[12] You have been believers so long now that you ought to be teaching others. Instead, you need someone to teach you again the basic things about God's Word. You are like babies who need milk and cannot eat solid food.**

Walking is not found only in the Bible, it is a popular exercise nowadays. You can go to the mall and see "mall walkers." You can go through your neighborhood and see people walking. Some people have little weights on their wrists. We're told that a half hour a day of walking will bring your cholesterol to a better level and give you healthier blood pressure and weight. Walking is a great exercise. You don't even have to do it all at once. It can be five minutes here, ten minutes there. Anybody who says they don't have time to walk is making an excuse.

It is the same way in our spiritual lives. Moving ahead in our walk with God doesn't require training for a marathon. It just requires persistent, daily activity.

When I was pastoring Mount Hope Church, I felt that even though we were planting a lot of daughter churches, and they were planting our granddaughter churches, some people were only visiting our churches but never moving up to the next level of commitment. It seemed some were not growing spiritually, even though they had been visiting the church for two or more years.

I shared this with our staff and the pastors of our daughter churches and we came up with a plan to encourage people to walk into more responsibility and more personal growth. We call it WEBS, which stands for Win, Establish, Build and Send. That's what we do for people. Win then, establish them, build them, and send them (into some manner of ministry). I want everyone to get "caught" in one of our churches' WEBS! I want to see all of us making progress so we abound more and more in every arena of life.

KEY TO ABOUNDING - PLEASING GOD

The second key to abounding is to please God. When we come to Christ, we no longer belong to ourselves but to God. We are here for his pleasure.

You cannot live the way that just pleases you. You have to live in a way that pleases God. In everything we do and say, we should ask, "Is this going to please God? Is there a Scripture that can tell me something about whether or not it will please God?"

The Bible is crystal clear about what pleases God - faith! Without faith, it is impossible to please God (Hebrews 11:6). Faith is the substance of things hoped for, and the evidence of things not seen. (Hebrews 11:1) Faith is believing God's Word, speaking God's Word, and acting on God's Word.

If you want to abound, always stay prepared to come up to another level. Find out what pleases God and make that the main motivation of your life.

1 Thessalonians 4:2-3

WHAT SANCTIFICATION MEANS

> [2] **For ye know what commandments we gave you by the Lord Jesus.**
>
> [3] **For this is the will of God, even your sanctification, that ye should abstain from fornication:**

Sanctification means to be separated from evil and set apart for God.

There are three kinds of sanctification.

- **Positional Sanctification**
- **Practical Sanctification**
- **Total Sanctification**

POSITIONAL SANCTIFICATION

Positional sanctification is because of what Jesus did for you. You can't be any more saved than you were the day you accepted Christ as your Savior. You are positionally sanctified. You are holy. You are made a saint the minute you come to Christ.

PRACTICAL SANCTIFICATION

The Bible also talks about practical sanctification, which is yielding to the Holy Spirit and being conformed to the image of Christ. It's a day-by-day, practical process. When you're driving 80 miles an hour down the highway the Holy Spirit nudges your spirit and says, "The speed limit is 70," and you respond by slowing down to 70. That's sanctification. It is obeying the rules of God and man. It is yielding in an area where the Holy Spirit guides you or corrects you. There is no condemnation in this at all. It is simply practical sanctification, being conformed to Christ's image.

TOTAL SANCTIFICATION

Then there's total sanctification—but don't worry. We don't have to even think about that one too much right now. It will not happen until Jesus comes for us. Then we will be transformed into his likeness—completely sanctified once and for all!

TRUTH ILLUSTRATED – TABERNACLE UTENSILS

The Old Testament gives a beautiful picture of sanctification. The tabernacle utensils such as bowls and tools were set apart, or sanctified, for God's service. After a few decades, these utensils were pretty dinged up. They had traveled forty years in the wilderness with the children of Israel. They were used every day. They had dents and some of them were probably discolored, but God still said, "I'm going to use them for my service." It wasn't the instrument that made itself sanctified for God's service. Rather, sanctification happened when the priests, following God's instruction, set apart those instruments for use in the Tabernacle. After that, they could never be used again for common things.

In the same way, a lot of us were dinged up by sin before we became sanctified. I don't know how you were when you came to Christ, but I was pretty dinged up and discolored. I'm pretty sure I had at least 75 million sins on my record. But God sanctified me. I'm not the man I will be tomorrow, but thank God I'm not the man I was yesterday. Sanctification means no matter how far you've gone, or how messed up you've become, God can use you in his service and worship. By using some of the most dinged-up people, God shows His sanctifying power in us.

INSTRUCTIONS ON SEX

Now Paul gets to one of the big issues in Thessalonica: sex. The first part of their sanctification was

> **... that ye should abstain from fornication**

The word "abstain" means to cut off completely.

Fornication comes from the Greek word "porneía"[32] where we get our English word "pornography." It's the umbrella word that covers every sexual sin: premarital sex, extramarital sex, adultery, homosexuality, bestiality, pedophilia, pornography, incest, and more.

God said clearly in Leviticus 18 that these sins damn the soul.

The Bible says, "Don't you realize that those who do wrong will not inherit the Kingdom of God? Don't fool yourselves. Those who indulge in sexual sin, or who worship idols, or commit adultery, or are male prostitutes, or practice homosexuality, or are thieves, or greedy people, or drunkards, or are abusive, or cheat people—none of these will inherit the Kingdom of God." (1 Corinthians 6:9-10 NLT).

DON'T LET THIS WORLD SHAPE YOU INTO ITS MORALITY

There is no such thing as a little fornication problem. If you do it repeatedly, you are not part of God's family or kingdom. That's why Paul said, "And be not conformed to this world: but be ye transformed by the renewing of your mind" (Romans 12:2). Don't let this world shape you into its morality. Don't let your moral standards be set by modern media personalities. Listen to Paul's words!

I read Gibbon's famous book *The Decline and Fall of the Roman Empire.*[33] It is interesting and alarming to discover that there was a high rate of divorce, low family values, and open tolerance of sexual perversion in the empire's latter days. There was sex entertainment in every city, particularly Thessalonica and Corinth, which were the sex industry hubs of that day.

We see the same things in America today. An article in a local paper recently ran an article headlined, "Pornography goes mainstream."[34] A two-page article said some of the big-name movie producers, names that you would recognize, are now investing in pornography because it is a hugely profitable industry. You can get it on cable television and in just about every hotel room. The annual "adult film" convention now gives awards to their porn actors and actresses and is held at mainstream classy resorts instead of in the seedy section of town.

If we believers are not careful, we will become desensitized to the filth in our culture. We might not be shocked anymore when somebody commits adultery. We might call it "just a little tryst," or "a quick affair, just a little encounter." When somebody says, "I'm coming out of the closet," people might say, "Praise the Lord, you've finally found yourself." But no matter how sex crazy we become there is still a distinction between honorable sex and dishonorable sex. Honorable sex involves a married man and woman in a monogamous relationship. Anything else is very serious sin.

1 Thessalonians 4:4-6

> **4 That every one of you should know how to possess his vessel in sanctification and honour...**

Your vessel is your body, the instrument that contains your soul and spirit.

> **5 Not in the lust of concupiscence, even as the Gentiles which know not God:**

The long word "concupiscence" means "stirring up forbidden passions."

Stirring up forbidden passions is what people do who don't know God. Paul is again saying, "We don't take our cues from Hollywood. Moral standards come from God, and if we are going to be followers of God, we're going to walk in sanctification and cut off all manner of sexual sin."

[6] That no man go beyond and defraud his brother in any matter: because that the Lord is the avenger of all such, as we also have forewarned you and testified.

The Lord himself is the avenger of people who take advantage of other people, specifically sexually, but also generally. If a young woman gives her virginity to some fellow in a moment of passion, she has cheated her future husband and defrauded him! God will be the avenger.

TRUTH ILLUSTRATED – A HOUSE OF SPIDERS

Sexual sin is like finding yourself in a dark, musty old run-down house that's full of brown recluse spiders. Brown recluse spider venom eats your flesh. I know a lady who was bitten by a brown recluse spider and part of her leg is gone where the toxins killed the tissues. That's what adultery is like—a poison that eats away at you. Solomon put it this way: "Can a man take fire in his bosom, and his clothes not be burned?" (Proverbs 6:27) No, because God is the avenger of all such things. King David committed adultery and confessed his sin, yet he still suffered the consequences. He lost his son, and his family became full of violence. He had put fire to his chest and was burned.

1 Thessalonians 4:7-8

Paul continued,

[7] For God hath not called us unto uncleanness, but unto holiness.

[8] He therefore that despiseth, despiseth not man, but God, who hath also given unto us his Holy Spirit.

To treat God's commandments lightly is to invite the judgment of God. I sure don't want thirty minutes or an hour of physical pleasure to ruin my whole future. Let's live to please God so we can abound more and more as models of the Gospel and Christ's Kingdom. Keep walking with, and making progress in the Lord.

If you've had a failure in this area, repent now and allow the mercy of God to pour over your life and over your future. Remember, and apply, 1 John 1:9:

> **9 If we confess our sins, he is faithful and just to forgive us our sins, and to cleanse us from all unrighteousness.**

POWER PRINCIPLES:

- **Moving ahead in God requires persistent, daily activity.**
- **Believers have been sanctified, or set apart, to serve God and please Him.**
- **We can live holy even in a sex-saturated society.**

LESSON 9

HOW TO LACK NOTHING IN YOUR LIFE

I Thessalonians 4:9-12

9 But as touching brotherly love ye need not that I write unto you: for ye yourselves are taught of God to love one another.

10 And indeed ye do it toward all the brethren which are in all Macedonia: but we beseech you, brethren, that ye increase more and more;

11 And that ye study to be quiet, and to do your own business, and to work with your own hands, as we commanded you;

12 That ye may walk honestly toward them that are without, and that ye may have lack of nothing.

1 Thessalonians 4:9-12

Paul described the Thessalonian church as a body that worked together, loved each other, and was growing into greater trust and relationship than ever before. See if this describes you or your church:

9 But as touching brotherly love ye need not that I write unto you: for ye yourselves are taught of God to love one another.

10 And indeed ye do it toward all the brethren which are in all Macedonia: but we beseech you, brethren, that ye increase more and more;

11 And that ye study to be quiet, and to do your own business, and to work with your own hands, as we commanded you;

12 That ye may walk honestly toward them that are without, and that ye may have lack of nothing.

GOD WANTS US TO LACK NOTHING

This passage pairs well with a passage from Paul's letters to the Romans 12:4-6, which says:

Romans 12:4-6 MSG

4-6 In this way we are like the various parts of a human body. Each part gets its meaning from the body as a whole, not the other way around. The body we're talking about is Christ's body of chosen people. Each of us finds our meaning and function as a part of his body. But as a chopped-off finger or cut-off toe we wouldn't amount to much,

> **would we? So since we find ourselves fashioned into all these excellently formed and marvelously functioning parts in Christ's body, let's just go ahead and be what we were made to be, without enviously or pridefully comparing ourselves with each other, or trying to be something we aren't.**

Is that the way your church is? Do these passages describe your experience as part of the family of God? If not, how do we, as model Christians, grow together as the Body of Christ? How do we move beyond being isolated individual worshipers and learners to be that effective, loving, united body of believers?

> **... that ye increase more and more (v.10)**

As a pastor for over 30 years, I have identified ten levels of involvement in a church. As you read through them, try to decide which level you are in at your own church:

- **Level 1 – The fields (People who are just visiting a church)**
- **Level 2 - The crowds (people who are just part of the crowd)**
- **Level 3 - The casuals (once-in-awhile attendees who have a casual relationship with God and the church)**
- **Level 4 - The converts (people who have come to Jesus Christ)**
- **Level 5 - The regulars (people who attend often)**
- **Level 6 - The members (people who have made the initial commitment to officially belong to the church)**
- **Level 7 – The involved members**
- **Level 8 – The members who are becoming stronger disciples of Jesus**
- **Level 9 - The inner circle**
- **Level 10 - The sent ones— those who are active in ministry in the church or out of it**

My goal for people at every level is the same, to get them always to be moving up a notch. If you are a regular attendee, maybe it's time to move up a notch and become a member. Each stage allows for growth in relationships and trust. Nobody becomes part of the inner circle instantly, just as Jesus didn't choose Peter, James, and John to be part of His inner circle rashly and without consideration.

When a person is born again and baptized into the body of Christ, he now has an invisible connection to all fellow believers around the world.[35] But God expects us also to visibly identify and associate with a local expression of His universal body—a local church. That's why Paul went around and set up churches from city to city, town to town.

Belonging to a church identifies us as genuine believers. Belonging to a church provides a spiritual family of support and encouragement. It gives us a place to develop our gifts and talents. There is safety in being under the authority and spiritual protection of a godly local church. It also gives us accountability which all of us need for true spiritual growth.

Paul described the Thessalonian church as a group working together in a coordinated effort to achieve something greater than themselves, and as a result, they, as individuals were being blessed as they worked. But imagine if someone in that church kept a stand-offish attitude because they were afraid of commitment. The body would begin to break down. Just imagine your finger refusing to commit to your hand, or your hand to your arm. The image of a body shows us that commitment is essential to function. Each part is committed to the others, and all members benefit. Commitment is a two-way street of blessing.

Church members (Levels 6 and 7) are committed and connected to the local body. They are the lifeblood of the church. By contrast, attendees are more like earrings, necklaces, and other jewelry: they adorn the body but they haven't chosen to become part of the body. I agree it is better to be a piece of jewelry than nothing, but it's even better to become an official member and representative of a church.

At our church, I defined a member as a radically committed disciple of the Lord Jesus Christ, passionate about reaching lost and hurting souls in this world.

A GOOD WORD FOR ALL CHURCH MEMBERS EVERYWHERE

This is what I would tell new members when I was pastor (You are welcome to insert your church name to this and use it):

> A Mount Hope Church member is dedicated to walking through life under the Lordship of Jesus. A Mount Hope Church member is not perfect but is yielding to the Holy Spirit day-by-day, to be changed into the image of Christ, from one glorious change to the next. A Mount Hope Church member is sometimes shy, sometimes bold, but never ashamed of the Gospel of Jesus Christ. A Mount Hope Church member is joined together with a team of other Mount Hope members to make disciples of every ethnic group. A Mount Hope Church member is generous beyond the call of duty, goes the extra mile, is involved in working to make a mark on this generation, and leaves a legacy for the next. A Mount Hope Church member is sold out, to go all out, to reach out, and to pull out souls from hell's grip. A Mount Hope Church member is a representative of Jesus Christ, the pastor, and our church.

THE BODY IS ORGANIZED

I've heard many people say, "I don't believe in organized religion." I want to ask them, "Do you believe in organized automobiles?" Anything with value is organized. You can't just have an assemblage of parts sitting in a heap. An unorganized church has little value to the world, just as a pile of car doors, engine parts, and wheels would not have value unless we assembled them.

TRUTH ILLUSTRATED – ORGANIZED RELIGION?

Your physical body is complex and intricately organized. It is natural to expect the Body of Christ to have organization as well. People who don't want organized religion are asking for trouble. They act like God is a god of disorder. Imagine if the sun came up at random times, depending on God's mood. Imagine never knowing how long a day would last. We couldn't rely on anything. Our lives would be random and hectic. As it is, we can plan on when the sun is coming up and when it's going down. There is order in the universe because God is the God of order. In the same way, there has to be organization in a church.

To organize anything, you have to first know what the purpose of it is. Cars are organized for transportation. That's why they put the wheels on the bottom. In a church, the purpose is three-fold:

- **To provide a corporate place of worshiping God**
- **To evangelize the lost**
- **To build the saints for the work of the ministry.**

The first focus is upward, the second outward, and the third inward. We build and organize the church based on that threefold purpose.

A DISORGANIZED CHURCH

Moses faced the problem of a disorganized "church" when he led the people of Israel. There were two million people in his congregation and many of them wanted to speak with Moses personally for guidance, advice, or arbitration of a disagreement. That was a physical impossibility, but the people weren't willing to go to anyone else. They wanted face time with 'Pastor Mo.' Moses tried to go along and thought he was being a good pastor by seeing everyone and hearing their cases, but it was wearing him out.

BRINGING ORDER OUT OF CHAOS

He cried, "God, why did you give me these people? They're a bunch of whining brats." He started hating the people he was overseeing because he lacked proper organization. He was on the verge of a nervous breakdown and said, "God, please just kill me. It would be kinder than leaving me here to do a job I can't do."

God answered his prayer—but not by killing him. Rather, He gave wisdom to Moses' father-in-law Jethro who came to Moses and said, "You think you're being a good pastor, trying to hear everybody's case, day in and day out, but what you are doing is not good. Select some people who are full of the Holy Spirit, and pray that God will put some of your anointing on them. Put some over ten, some over a hundred, and some over a thousand." In our day this might translate to, "Set up some trained leaders, assistant pastors, and associate pastors. When people have a problem, they can go to the lay ministers or somebody in charge of their fellowship group. If that doesn't solve it, they can go to their assistant pastor, and if their assistant pastor can't handle it they can go to the associate pastor." As a last resort, take it to the pastor for a resolution.

Sometimes people don't like this system because it keeps them from getting to the pastor or someone else. I've heard people say, "Nobody at that church is available for me," but what that usually means is that the person they wanted to see wasn't available. But the one you want to see may be different from the one God has in mind.

One time a blind lady came up for prayer after a service. She wanted a specific person to pray for her, but instead, a little obscure lady who was a part of our prayer team prayed for her. The blind lady may have been disappointed at first, but she left that service seeing, and her doctor sent me a letter saying it was impossible; a miracle. God used the person He wanted to use.

HOW TO KEEP THE PASTOR FROM HAVING A "NERVOUS BREAK-DOWN"

Moses implemented Jethro's advice and several things happened.

1. The people quit complaining because all their needs were getting met.
2. Others got to use their gifts.
3. The ministry of Moses was multiplied.
4. And Moses lived and led them for a long time because he didn't have a nervous breakdown.[36]

When a church loves each other and works together in unity, everybody has room to grow as God wants them to. Early in the New Testament, the church ran into the same problem Moses had. In Acts chapter 6 the widows wanted the apostles to come over and bring them a meal or solve their problem. The apostles were getting tied up in so many things that they finally came to their senses and said, "Look, this isn't right. We're supposed to be praying and studying the Word, but instead, we're out helping everyone." So, they selected seven men full of the Spirit and wisdom and appointed them over those matters. Stephen, Phillip, and other laypeople became leaders in the church.[37]

At Mount Hope Church, I quit trying to counsel people. We had a trained counseling ministry that helped people. I never knew what people's personal problems were. I'm glad for that because I could preach freely, and if God spoke to somebody through my message, they knew it was from the Holy Spirit speaking to them, not from a counseling session with me. A man recently came up and grabbed me and said, "You've been reading my mail." He meant that I was preaching right to his problem or area of need. I said, "I haven't been reading your mail, but I have been listening to the Holy Spirit."

When Mount Hope Church was first considering making me the pastor (four decades ago +), the board asked me if I would go visit everybody in the church as the previous pastor did. I said I would not. First, most people don't want to be visited anymore. They're so busy that they don't appreciate the pastor barging in to have coffee (or fried chicken). But I also wanted to be a pastor, not a politician. I told the board I wasn't going to worry about winning the people over or getting a vote of confidence from them periodically so they wouldn't boot me out. I wasn't going to try to ingratiate myself with every big giver and big tither in the church. Rather, I was going to stay on my face before God, in God's Word, and prayer, and bring the people something of value in my sermons.

While some other pastors were out playing basketball on Saturday, I was on my face before God. While other people were out socializing, I was studying and praying because I wouldn't trade the anointing for anything else in the world. When I preach on Sunday I don't care if I make ninety-eight percent of the people mad, as long as I do what the Holy Spirit tells me to do. Having that as your purpose sets you free.

Our church was highly organized, although it sometimes did not appear that way. We had eight ministry departments with leaders and workers in each. When every part of the body is functioning properly, it works like nothing else on earth. I was coming back from a minister's conference in Traverse City one time and the roads had been salted because of the snow. Every time a car would pass me, my windshield would get all white from that salt. Just at that time, my windshield washer fluid pump broke. I pulled the lever and nothing shot out. The windshield wiper would scrape across and smear the white stuff around so I couldn't see. I had to pull off to the side of the road to dump water over the windshield and run the wipers before it froze. I had to stop at almost every other exit to clean the windshield. A three-and-a-half-hour drive took six hours! All because of one small part of the car that wasn't working.

In the same way, when one little part of the Body stops functioning properly, it can slow everybody down. If you're called to be a finger, be a good finger. If you're an eye, see. If you're an ear, hear. If you're a nose, smell. Do what you're called to do because even the smallest member—like my windshield washer fluid pump—can create a slowdown if not working.

DEFENDING THE BODY

As a spiritual body, churches have immune systems as well. When there's a sickness in the physical body, the immune system identifies the invader and helps repair the afflicted part. In churches, when one part rebels or becomes sick, it takes spiritual discernment to decide if the part can be restored or needs to be removed like a foreign invader. The hardest part of being a pastor is when I have to say goodbye to certain members who have gone bad. It's much better to restore someone, if possible. But it is not always possible.

I'm reminded of a time when my tooth was hurting terribly. I didn't call the dentist. I just took some aspirin. But the next day it was still throbbing. I couldn't get any relief from it. I saw my dentist and he told me my tooth was cracked and I needed a root canal. I took his advice and felt such great relief when the root canal was done. I was out of pain. I could study Saturday, and I could preach on Sunday. That little tooth had caused my whole body to malfunction.

But what if that tooth turned out to be unfixable? The dentist would have had to extract it because it was causing my body so much pain. That's the choice we face in the spiritual body at times. If one part is causing a lot of pain we have to discern if it can be repaired and healed or if it will only harm the rest of the body unless we cut it off.

TRUTH ILLUSTRATED – GANGRENE

I knew a lady who developed gangrene on the tip of her toe. She was a diabetic and had a small wound that didn't heal. She didn't deal with it immediately, and by the time she went to the hospital she had to have her whole leg cut off to protect the rest of her body. In the same way, if you don't cut a harmful person off from a church quickly enough, he or she can do great damage.

I was in my office one afternoon when the elders were dealing with somebody who they were asking to leave the church and never to come back. He was a predator who was trying to seduce women. He would look for a single woman in the congregation, sit by her, and strike up a conversation. Next thing you knew he was dating this lonely person and sucking the money right out of her bank account. We had three or four women say he was hitting on them, even married women whose husbands weren't there. We confronted him and he vehemently refused any discipline. "You can't tell me what I can do and what I can't do!" he yelled. "Who do you think you are?" His attitude was like a spiritual cancer.

If a cell in your body refuses to cooperate with the rest of the body, you call it cancer. It's the same way in a church. If it's not curable it has to be cut out.

The beautiful thing is that in the body of Christ, miracles still happen. Even a part that is cut off can be restored to the body. Jesus is merciful. One time a lady left our church with a group of disgruntled people. About seven years later I saw her in the back of our worship center. She came up, grabbed onto me as tight as she could, and said, "Pastor Dave, I'm so sorry I left with those people. Will you take me back?" I said, "Welcome home." God can take even a gangrenous finger that's been cut off and restore it if that part wants to be restored.

PAUL'S CLEAR TIPS SO YOU'LL LACK NOTHING

Paul encouraged the Thessalonians to remain in love. He also encouraged them to practice being quiet, not always chitter-chattering. He gave us some clear tips in Verses 9-12 to increasing more and more and lacking nothing:

- **Love one another**
- **Study to be quiet**
- **Do your own business (and mind your own business)**
- **Be a worker**
- **Walk honestly, so unbelievers will trust you**

He said he didn't even need to instruct them in this, but then he did anyway. He hoped they would grow even closer and more effective as parts of the same local body. I pray the same thing for every reader and every person in the Body of Christ.

POWER PRINCIPLES:

- **The church is a body and each of us is part. The body does not function well unless it has all its parts!**
- **The local church exists to provide a corporate place of worshiping God, to evangelize the lost and to build the saints for the work of the ministry.**
- **You should always be moving from the outer circles to the inner circles of ministry and service at your church.**
- **A good church is highly organized and knows how to deal with potential problems.**

LESSON 10

HOW A BELIEVER APPROACHES THE LAST DAYS

I Thessalonians 4:13-18

13 But I would not have you to be ignorant, brethren, concerning them which are asleep, that ye sorrow not, even as others which have no hope.

14 For if we believe that Jesus died and rose again, even so them also which sleep in Jesus will God bring with him.

15 For this we say unto you by the word of the Lord, that we which are alive and remain unto the coming of the Lord shall not prevent them which are asleep.

16 For the Lord himself shall descend from heaven with a shout, with the voice of the archangel, and with the trump of God: and the dead in Christ shall rise first:

17 Then we which are alive and remain shall be caught up together with them in the clouds, to meet the Lord in the air: and so shall we ever be with the Lord.

18 Wherefore comfort one another with these words.

AN AMAZING EVENT LIES JUST AHEAD

I spent a recent July 4th in Florida and saw an amazing display of fireworks. From where I was staying I could see fireworks in several different cities, including St. Petersburg, Clearwater, Gulfport, St. Pete Beach, and Tampa, all at one time. What a show!

But nothing compares to the amazing spectacle that will take place when the trumpet of God sounds and the dead in Christ rise. Paul was anticipating that day, and now we come to what he wrote concerning the last days and those who have died in Christ.

In verses 13-18, he introduces the subject of the Greek word, "Harpazo." In the Latin Vulgate, the word is "Rapiemur," where we get the English word, "Rapture." In both the Greek and the Latin Vulgate, it describes a sudden (rapid) "catching away." In a picture, it's sort of like a steel ball suddenly, with great force, being snatched upward when an overhead electromagnet is activated.

The Bible speaks of a coming seven-year period of great trouble, "such as the world has never seen before."[38]

Almost one-third of the Bible is prophecy. There is more prophecy in the Bible about this final seven-year period of time than practically any other single subject, except for the Millennial Reign of Jesus Christ. Jeremiah called these seven years a time of "Jacob's trouble" (Jeremiah 30:7). Daniel called it a time of trouble such as was not since the beginning of man (Daniel 12:1). Jesus called it a time of great tribulation (Matthew 24:21) and John the Revelator called it the hour of temptation that shall try the entire world (Revelation 3:10).

They were all speaking of the final seven years of human government on earth. A Satanic leader will rule during the final 42 months of that seven years, the currency will be digital (cashless), and everyone will be required to take a mark on their right hand or forehead to do any business in the "New World Order." Deception will be everywhere. Political deception, medical deception, religious deception, social deception, and the list goes on and on. It's all leading to an inescapably strong delusion to all who possess no discernment.

TORMENT AND TERROR

I believe that very shortly the world will reel into its deepest hour of torment and terror. Our world right now is in a death dive, plunging rapidly toward this time of trouble. We are in route now to a mad, fatal plunge into that horrible period spoken of by the ancient prophets.

Ominous storm clouds are gathering over the nations of the world. Frightful times are looming. Soon we will begin hearing news reports of terrifying events. A time of major chaos will come upon the inhabitants of the earth.

We are right now moving rapidly toward the climax of the ages. A devastating judgment will pour on this earth with horror, terror, destruction, and devastation.

The suffering this world is about to experience will be rapid and relentless. But just before that period (spoken of by the prophets), Jesus announced a plan of escape. In Luke 21, He said to watch and pray always that you may be counted worthy to escape all these things (Luke 21:36). The escape is available to those who are ready. That is good news for those of us who believe!

Luke 21:36

36 Watch ye therefore, and pray always, that ye may be accounted worthy to escape all these things that shall come to pass, and to stand before the Son of man.

The people in Thessalonica were, like people of today, concerned that their loved ones would escape the time of trouble. What would happen to them in the last days? The problem was that the Thessalonians had not yet been taught about the resurrection or had been taught falsely.

They knew about the resurrection of Jesus but they did not understand the resurrection (Rapture) of believers. Some false teachers and Greek philosophers at the time had been teaching that once a person is dead there is no hope of resurrection. False teaching was going around that asserted that if you died before Jesus returned, you could not be a part of the resurrection. (Does that even make any sense?)

1 Thessalonians 4:13

Paul cleared it up for them beginning in verse 13:

13 But I would not have you to be ignorant, brethren, concerning them which are asleep, that ye sorrow not, even as others which have no hope.

The term "asleep" is the Christian way of saying "dead."

When the little girl died and Jesus went in to heal her, He said, "She is only asleep" (Matthew 9:24). That meant that she was already in Paradise. The Bible says that to be absent from the body is to be present with the Lord (II Corinthians 5:8). As soon as the spirit leaves your body, it will go to be with the Lord if you are in Christ Jesus. Paul was implying that death to a believer is an easy thing. We fight it because it is an enemy, but it is really like going to sleep.

TRUTH ILLUSTRATED – WHAT IS IT LIKE TO DIE?

One daughter asked her mother, "Mommy, what is it like to die?" Her mother said, "You know when you fall asleep in the back seat of the car and you wake up in the morning in your bed? That's what death is like to a Christian. You go to sleep here and you wake up somewhere else. It's like when daddy carries you out of the car while you are sleeping and tucks you into bed."

If a person dies without having accepted Jesus Christ, there is no hope. But it is not always possible to know who has and who has not accepted the Gospel in those final moments. If you are praying for your loved ones who aren't yet saved, and they die without showing any physical evidence that they were saved, I know that Jesus can still save them before they take their last breath, if they put their faith in Him.

I remember a preacher who was worried because his son had backslidden into drugs, drinking, and wild living. He showed every evidence of being on the road to hell. It was such a burden on this father's heart. One day the son was drunk and tried to outrun a train. He lost. The train hit the car and he lived for just a few moments after he got to the hospital. When his parents arrived he was already dead. They were tormented, thinking that their son was now residing in the regions of the damned, awaiting the Great White Throne Judgment. There was nothing they could do. They felt hopeless and anguished. Then the surgeon said, "I don't know if this means anything to you, but before your son died he kept calling out the name of Jesus and then he started speaking in a foreign language. Was he bilingual?"

The son not only got saved but was filled with the Holy Spirit and spoke in supernatural tongues just before he left Earth! He made it to heaven, if just barely.

As believers, we have hope, even for loved ones who appear to be lost.

1 Thessalonians 4:14

WHAT HAPPENS AFTER WE DIE?

In verse 14, Paul wrote,

> **14 For if we believe that Jesus died and rose again, even so them also which sleep in Jesus will God bring with him.**

To be saved, we have to believe that Jesus died for our sins. His death is the guarantee of our salvation. His resurrection is our guarantee that if we die before Jesus comes, we too are going to be resurrected. It's proof. Read 1 Corinthians 15 where he says that those who sleep in Jesus, God will resurrect.

> **I Corinthians 15:51-58 NLT**
> **51 But let me reveal to you a wonderful secret. We will not all die, but we will all be transformed!**
>
> **52 It will happen in a moment, in the blink of an eye, when the last trumpet is blown. For when the trumpet sounds, those who have died will be raised to live forever. And we who are living will also be transformed.**
>
> **53 For our dying bodies must be transformed into bodies that will never die; our mortal bodies must be transformed into immortal bodies.**
>
> **54 Then, when our dying bodies have been transformed into bodies that will never die, this Scripture will be fulfilled: "Death is swallowed up in victory.**

> **55 O death, where is your victory? O death, where is your sting?"**
>
> **56 For sin is the sting that results in death, and the law gives sin its power.**
>
> **57 But thank God! He gives us victory over sin and death through our Lord Jesus Christ.**
>
> **58 So, my dear brothers and sisters, be strong and immovable. Always work enthusiastically for the Lord, for you know that nothing you do for the Lord is ever useless.**

You might ask, where are the believers now who have already died?

Are they in some sort of holding tank or "soul sleep"? No, not at all.

To be absent from the body is to be present with the Lord.[39] They are in heaven enjoying the pleasures, wonders, foods, and opulence of heaven. They would not want to come back even if we had the power to call them back. But when it is time, Jesus will come back in the clouds and all the spirits of our loved ones will reunite with their bodies, wherever their grave, urn, or remains are located.

According to 1 Corinthians 15:52, at the resurrection, in a moment, in the twinkling of an eye, the spirit of the Christian will reunite with his or her body. At that moment, the decaying body will supernaturally take on incorruption. The mortal body that was subject to sickness and death will put on immortality. The ashes of those who were cremated will be reassembled.

This event will be part of the First Resurrection. Paul wanted everybody to know this was not just him talking, but was the "word of the Lord."

1 Thessalonians 4:15-16

He wrote in verse 15,

> **15 For this we say unto you by the word of the Lord, that we which are alive and remain unto the coming of the Lord shall not prevent them which are asleep.**

In other words, those who died in Christ have an advantage. They're going to have their glorified bodies a little while before we will—about one-fifth of a second!

He goes on,

> **16 For the Lord himself shall descend from heaven with a shout, with the voice of the archangel, and with the trump of God: and the dead in Christ shall rise first**

In the Greek language, this gives us the picture of a military command, like Jesus shouted when Lazarus was in the tomb: "Lazarus come forth" (John 11:43).

The dead can no longer stay dead when Jesus says to come forth. He won't send a delegate, either. Angels will not be gathering people up at this point (they will gather people in a later end-time event, but not now); the Lord himself will do it. The dead in Christ are going to come out of their graves with immortal bodies fit for universal travel. Those who never taste death will be changed in a moment, in a twinkling of an eye.

It will be like something from Star Trek—instant transformation. All the men will look like bodybuilders and the women will be beauty queens. Nobody will need to work out at some gym or drink nutritional shakes anymore. We'll be perfected!

1 Thessalonians 4:17-18

> **[17] Then we which are alive and remain shall be caught up together with them in the clouds, to meet the Lord in the air: and so shall we ever be with the Lord.**

This is markedly different than the final phase of the Second Coming of Christ. Here is the order of what will happen.

We believers will be caught up in an instant. The picture is almost like a giant electromagnet passing over a pile of nails mixed with a bunch of wood toothpicks. They may all look similar in size or even shape, but the electromagnet will only pull up the nails.

The Holy Spirit has sealed us Jesus lovers and made us ready for that divine electromagnet. It will be an irresistible force. Where are we going? It says,

> **... and so shall we ever be with the Lord.**
>
> **[18] Wherefore comfort one another with these words.**

How do I know that we are going to be in Heaven during the time of the Tribulation on the earth? Because, we read the Book of Revelation, and 2 Corinthians, Christians are depicted at the Judgment Seat of Christ receiving our rewards while the Final Tribulation is in full force on the earth. We will hear the Lord say to us, "Thank you for the job you did while you were on earth."

> **2 Corinthians 5:10**
> **For we must all appear before the judgment seat of Christ; that every one may receive the things done in his body, according to that he hath done, whether it be good or bad.**

There is no fear for us standing before the Judgment Seat of Christ because that is when we will receive our rewards and crowns. The Lord himself, Paul tells us, will say thanks to us for our labor for him on earth. Then we'll go to the Marriage Supper of the Lamb. Wow! I can hardly wait.

Revelation 19:9
Blessed are they which are called unto the marriage supper of the Lamb. And he saith unto me, These are the true sayings of God.

THE TRIBULATION

Meanwhile, the Tribulation will be taking place on the earth. Those who come to Christ after the Rapture of the Church and those who follow Christ during the Tribulation period will be hunted down like animals. The Antichrist forces are going to slay many of them.

Death camps will be reinstituted. It will be a time of terror unlike any other.

That magnetic leader, the antichrist, will move his image into the holy temple after three and a half years. From then it will be 1,290 days until Jesus comes back, and at that time he won't come back in the clouds but at the head of a heavenly army.

Daniel 12:11 MSG
11 "From the time that the daily worship is banished from the Temple and the obscene desecration is set up in its place, there will be 1,290 days.

ARMAGEDDON ON THE HORIZON

Representatives from the armies of the world will gather in the Valley of Megiddo[40] to annihilate Israel (blaming God's people for all the world's problems), but suddenly they will see a spot in the sky becoming larger and larger. As Jude wrote in his letter, there will be an innumerable number of his saints (Jude 1:14), all riding white supernatural heavenly horses and coming down from the sky (Revelation 19:14).

People will look through their binoculars and see the One at the head of the pack is riding a huge white steed and across his chest will be written, "KING OF KINGS, AND LORD OF LORDS" (Revelation 19:16).

Jesus will no longer be a baby in Bethlehem, but now the Judge of the World, riding down with His saints to stop humanity from destroying itself. The armies of the earth will turn their weapons to fight against the Son of God and His armies, but we will have our glorified bodies and will not be able to die anymore. Those who fight against Jesus Christ will be slain by the sword of his mouth, which is the Word of God.[41] The antichrist and his promoter, the false prophet, will be thrown into hell, the lake of fire, the garbage dump of all creation, to live there forever.[42] And all who took the mark of the beast, giving loyalty to this world leader, will be thrown into hell with them.

Jesus will land on Mount Olives and step off of his horse, and an earthquake will crack the mountain east to west and go right down to the Eastern Gate.[43]

Today's Jewish people that I talked to in Jerusalem, told me that if any man walks through the Eastern Gate they will anoint him as Messiah. Jesus will indeed descend the Mount of Olives, cross the Kidron Valley, and walk right through the Eastern Gate, showing that he is the Messiah of the Jews, and for forty-five days believers will judge the earth with Jesus.

There will be some Tribulation survivors on the earth; those who made it through the Tribulation. They will not have glorified bodies and will still be procreating. The devil will be bound for a thousand years.[44]

Later a new earth with new heavens will be established, and the heavenly city, New Jerusalem will slowly come down to earth[45]. Then Earth will become Heaven's annex. This 1,400-mile-high city will touch Earth and touch Heaven. Amazing!

All of this teaching about the end times and the Rapture is found in the writings of Paul and the words of Jesus. (For a more detailed look at the end times and what's ahead, get my book, *Hope in the Last Days* published by Charisma Media on Frontline books).

Jesus said, "Watch ye therefore, and pray always, that ye may be accounted worthy to escape all these things that shall come to pass and to stand before the Son of man" (Luke 21:36).

Jesus promised the Church of Philadelphia, "I also will keep thee from the hour of temptation, which shall come upon all the world, to try them that dwell upon the earth" (Revelation 3:10).

The writings of the church fathers talk about these same events. One excerpt reads, "All the saints and elect of God are gathered together before the Tribulation which is to come and are taken to the Lord so that they may not see at any time the confusion which overwhelms the world because of sin."

You can read it in the writings of the Early Church Fathers[46]. The church fathers like Barnabus and Clemens talked about the catching away of the Church. Tertullian in 155-245 AD wrote about Christ coming for his church.

The doctrine of the Rapture of the Church was not created recently. It was a part of St. Paul's life and teachings, and the teachings of the Church for nearly four centuries before the corruption crept in. Indeed, it is how God has done things for His people throughout time. He took Lot and his family out of Sodom and Gomorrah before the judgment fell. He took Enoch out of the world before the flood came. He put Noah in the ark which kept him and his family lifted up safely from the devastating flood.

I believe this present believing generation is like Enoch. He was caught up to heaven without dying. (Genesis 5:23-24; Hebrews 11:5). We are the ones who are going to be kept from the final tragic and cataclysmic events, called the Great Tribulation.

One preacher went around preaching the sermon, "Millions Now Living Will Never Die." So, another preacher came into town and called his sermon, "Millions Now Living Are Already Dead." Both are true. People who are not alive in Christ are the living dead. But if you are alive in Christ at His coming, you will be translated into His presence in the ride of your life.

READY OR NOT, HERE HE COMES!

Every person on earth is either ready or not ready.

> **Matthew 25:11-12 NLT**
> **'Lord! Lord! Open the door for us!'"But he called back, 'Believe me, I don't know you!'**

Yes, there is a great time of trouble just ahead. But there is a way of escape: The Rapture —Christ coming for His Church. It will happen suddenly, in the twinkling of an eye. Meanwhile, let's continue to become model Christians and a model church so that we will be ready on that most glorious day of His coming.

POWER PRINCIPLES:

- **The world is moving toward its final moment of deep darkness, torment and destruction.**
- **The Bible tells us clearly what will happen for believers and unbelievers in the last days.**

1 Thessalonians 5

1 But of the times and the seasons, brethren, ye have no need that I write unto you.

2 For yourselves know perfectly that the Day of the Lord so cometh as a thief in the night.

3 For when they shall say, Peace and safety; then sudden destruction cometh upon
them, as travail upon a woman with child; and they shall not escape.

4 But ye, brethren, are not in darkness, that that day should overtake you as a thief.

5 Ye are all the children of light, and the children of the day: we are not of the night, nor
of darkness.

6 Therefore let us not sleep, as do others; but let us watch and be sober.

7 For they that sleep sleep in the night; and they that be drunken are drunken in the night.

8 But let us, who are of the day, be sober, putting on the breastplate of faith and love;
and for an helmet, the hope of salvation.

9 For God hath not appointed us to wrath, but to obtain salvation by our Lord Jesus Christ,

10 Who died for us, that, whether we wake or sleep, we should live together with him.

11 Wherefore comfort yourselves together, and edify one another, even as also ye do.

12 And we beseech you, brethren, to know them which labour among you, and are over
you in the Lord, and admonish you;

13 And to esteem them very highly in love for their work's sake. And be at peace among
yourselves.

14 Now we exhort you, brethren, warn them that are unruly, comfort the feebleminded,
support the weak, be patient toward all men.

15 See that none render evil for evil unto any man; but ever follow that which is good,
both among yourselves, and to all men.

16 Rejoice evermore.

17 Pray without ceasing.

18 In every thing give thanks: for this is the will of God in Christ Jesus concerning you.

19 Quench not the Spirit.

20 Despise not prophesyings.

21 Prove all things; hold fast that which is good.

22 Abstain from all appearance of evil.

23 And the very God of peace sanctify you wholly; and I pray God your whole spirit and
soul and body be preserved blameless unto the coming of our Lord Jesus Christ.

24 Faithful is he that calleth you, who also will do it.

25 Brethren, pray for us.

26 Greet all the brethren with an holy kiss.

27 I charge you by the Lord that this epistle be read unto all the holy brethren.

28 The grace of our Lord Jesus Christ be with you. Amen.

LESSON 11

HOW THE WORLD WILL HANDLE THE RAPTURE

I Thessalonians 5:1-10

[1] But of the times and the seasons, brethren, ye have no need that I write unto you.

[2] For yourselves know perfectly that the Day of the Lord so cometh as a thief in the night.

[3] For when they shall say, Peace and safety; then sudden destruction cometh upon them, as travail upon a woman with child; and they shall not escape.

[4] But ye, brethren, are not in darkness, that that day should overtake you as a thief.

[5] Ye are all the children of light, and the children of the day: we are not of the night, nor of darkness.

[6] Therefore let us not sleep, as do others; but let us watch and be sober.

[7] For they that sleep sleep in the night; and they that be drunken are drunken in the night.

[8] But let us, who are of the day, be sober, putting on the breastplate of faith and love; and for an helmet, the hope of salvation.

[9] For God hath not appointed us to wrath, but to obtain salvation by our Lord Jesus Christ,

[10] Who died for us, that, whether we wake or sleep, we should live together with him.

SEPTEMBER 11, 2001

Many of us remember September 11, 2001, when thousands of people showed up for work at the World Trade Center and the Pentagon with absolutely no clue as to what would happen that day.[47] Terrorists using commercial jets as missiles slammed into the World Trade Center and the Pentagon, slaughtering thousands of innocent people. On television screens across America, viewers saw mothers and fathers, still confused over the events, holding up pictures of their missing sons and daughters, wives holding up pictures of their husbands, and so on. We saw the horror on people's faces as they waited to learn whether or not their loved ones had been found alive.

The catching away of the Church, the Rapture, will bring chaos similar to what America experienced on that day, but on a much greater, global scale, and no amount of intelligence gathering will help people avoid the calamities, catastrophes, and judgments that will soon be sweeping down on them. The Rapture will be the largest "missing persons" event in all of history.

1 Thessalonians 5:1

Chapter Five of this letter to the Thessalonians begins with the word "but," which means that Paul is taking a turn here. He is staying on the same subject but coming at it from a different perspective. Chapter Four was mostly from the perspective of the Church and what will happen to those who are alive at Christ's coming and those who have died before Christ's coming. Now he takes it from the view of what it will be like on the earth after that event.

> [1] **But of the times and the seasons, brethren, ye have no need that I write unto you.**

Notice first of all that Paul, by his use of the term "brethren," is talking about Christians.

The Thessalonians, like most Christians today, wanted to circle a date on their calendar when the Lord was coming for His Church. People have been trying to figure out the day or hour of His coming for years.

TRUTH ILLUSTRATED - FINDING THE DATE?

Back in 1987, a NASA scientist said he had mathematically figured out when the Lord was coming: September 1988. He had it down to the day and so he wrote the book, *88 Reasons Why Jesus Will Return In 1988.*[48]

But 1988 passed, and so did hundreds of other predicted times before him and after him. Choosing dates is a waste of time. If we stay ready, why does it matter when the Lord returns? Our task is the same: to do His work, stay close to Him, walk with the Holy Spirit and carry out the Great Commission. In fact, the whole purpose of prophecies in most cases is to draw us into holiness and deeper godliness, so that whenever Jesus comes, we will be ready. I am convinced that if we did by chance guess the right date, God would change it, because He promised it would be at an hour that nobody knew.

> **Matthew 24:36 NLT**
> [36] **"However, no one knows the day or hour when these things will happen, not even the angels in heaven or the Son himself. Only the Father knows.**

Persecution was so heated in Thessalonica against the believers, they wondered if they were already in the Great Tribulation, about to experience God's rapid-fire wrath over the earth.

1 Thessalonians 5:2-3

[2] For yourselves know perfectly that the Day of the Lord so cometh as a thief in the night.

[3] For when they shall say, Peace and safety; then sudden destruction cometh upon them, as travail upon a woman with child; and they shall not escape.

THE DAY OF THE LORD

What does Paul mean by "the Day of the Lord?" It is mentioned twenty-five times throughout the Bible. It is not referring to a 24-hour period but rather an era of time. It begins with the catching away of the Church. Concerning the Day of the Lord, we read in Scripture,

Joel 1:15
Alas For the day! for the Day of the Lord is at hand, and as a destruction from the Almighty shall it come.

Joel 2:1-4
[1] Blow ye the trumpet in Zion, and sound an alarm in my holy mountain: let all the inhabitants of the land tremble: for the Day of the Lord cometh, for it is nigh at hand;

[2] A day of darkness and of gloominess, a day of clouds and of thick darkness, as the morning spread upon the mountains: a great people and a strong; there hath not been ever the like, neither shall be any more after it, even to the years of many generations.

[3] A fire devoureth before them; and behind them a flame burneth: the land is as the garden of Eden before them, and behind them a desolate wilderness; yea, and nothing shall escape them.

[4] The appearance of them is as the appearance of horses; and as horsemen, so shall they run.

Notice how these words from the Old Testament line up with the words of the New Testament in describing these end-time events.

Joel talks about a trumpet, and then about the Day of the Lord being a day of terrible judgment gloominess, darkness, and terror. Then he talks about the appearance of the horseman, which sounds a lot like what we read in the book of Revelation after the Church is gone and the horsemen of the Apocalypse are loosed upon the earth. Somebody once said it sounds like a Nintendo interactive video game or a first-class horror movie. It does—but it will be all too real.

Zephaniah 1:15-16 describes the Day of the Lord:

Zephaniah 1:15-16 NLT
[15] It will be a day when the Lord's anger is poured out - a day of terrible distress and anguish, a day of ruin and desolation, a day of darkness and gloom, a day of clouds and blackness,[16] a day of trumpet calls and battle cries. Down go the walled cities and the strongest battlements!

And he says in verses 17 and 18,

Zephaniah 1:17-18 NLT
[17] "Because you have sinned against the Lord, I will make you grope around like the blind. Your blood will be poured into the dust, and your bodies will lie rotting on the ground."

[18] Your silver and gold will not save you on that Day of the Lord's anger. For the whole land will be devoured by the fire of his jealousy. He will make a terrifying end of all the people on earth.

Amos 5:18-20 reads,

Amos 5:18-20 MSG
[18-20] Woe to all of you who want God's Judgment Day! Why would you want to see God, want him to come? When God comes, it will be bad news before it's good news, the worst of times, not the best of times. Here's what it's like: A man runs from a lion right into the jaws of a bear. A woman goes home after a hard day's work and is raped by a neighbor. At God's coming we face hard reality, not fantasy - a black cloud with no silver lining.

NO ESCAPE AFTER THE RAPTURE

This indicates there will be no escape from trouble. A man will run from a lion, as it were, only to see a bear coming at him.

In the Day of the Lord, God will act directly and unmistakably in the affairs of the earth. He will deal dramatically and directly in fearful judgment with all who refused to receive Christ before the Church was taken.

If you are not a Christian at the time the Day of the Lord begins, you are going to wish you were somewhere else. You may wish you had never been born. Those who have failed to make proper preparations will be in for the shock of their lives. Today mockers say, "You are preaching scare tactics. You are using an ancient book to scare people into a certain behavior. Where is the Day of the Lord? I have heard this all my life, and it is just a bunch of nonsense."

2 Peter 3:2-4
[2] I want you to remember what the holy prophets said long ago and what our Lord and Savior commanded through your apostles.

[3] Most importantly, I want to remind you that in the last days scoffers will come, mocking the truth and following their own desires.

[4] They will say, "What happened to the promise that Jesus is coming again? From before the times of our ancestors, everything has remained the same since the world was first created."

THE MOCKING WILL BE SILENCED

The Bible said there would be such mockers in the last days, and we hear them already. But, terribly for them, they will be proven wrong, their taunts will be silenced and they will experience unnecessary agony on the Day of the Lord.

THE RAPTURE OF THE CHURCH

The Day of the Lord will begin with the removal of all true followers of Jesus Christ from this earth. Matthew 24:40-42 gives an important message.

Matthew 24:40-42 NLT
[40] "Two men will be working together in the field; one will be taken, the other left. [41] Two women will be grinding flour at the mill; one will be taken, the other left. [42] "So you, too, must keep watch! For you don't know what day your Lord is coming."

In Luke, Jesus amplifies that by saying,

Luke 17:34
[34] That night two people will be asleep in one bed; one will be taken, the other left.

Jesus said his coming for his people would be like in the days of Noah, business as usual. People will be marrying and being given in marriage, eating, drinking, and being merry. Most everybody will be involved in some sort of self-indulgence and gratification.

The Day of the Lord will likely come at the same moment around the globe. Some will be sleeping and some will be working. There will be no warning. Jesus said,

Matthew 24:43
43 But understand this: If the owner of the house had known at what time of night the thief was coming, he would have kept watch and would not have let his house be broken into.

The Day of the Lord begins when the Church is Raptured out of this world to heaven. It will continue into the Tribulation which will begin when the world leader (the antichrist) brokers or confirms a seven-year covenant between Israel and a third party, which many believe will be Islamic nations. The Day of the Lord will continue through the entire seven-year Tribulation, with the final three and a half years, being known as the Great Tribulation.

The disappearance of the Church will grip people with fear at first. Every unbeliever will be struck with a maddening terror that will not abate. Paul describes the Day of the Lord as sudden, unexpected, terrible, and irreversible. He says there will be no way out for those who did not follow the Lord, no more than a woman who starts having labor pains can get out of delivery. Once true labor pains start, there is no turning back.

Once the Church is gone, there will be no way out. This earth will be committed to the judgment of God for all those who rejected Christ. It will happen like a thief in the night.[49]

Those who are left behind will be unconvinced that it has conclusively happened.

WILLFULLY IGNORANT

In Noah's day, the population didn't believe a flood was coming until it had arrived. Noah had preached about it for more than a century before it happened. But they were willfully ignorant of the judgment of God about to hit the planet.

Matthew 24:37-39 AMPL
37 As were the days of Noah, so will be the coming of the Son of Man.

38 For just as in those days before the flood they were eating and drinking, [men] marrying and [women] being given in marriage, until the [very] day when Noah went into the ark,

39 And they did not know or understand until the flood came and swept them all away-- so will be the coming of the Son of Man.

TRUTH ILLUSTRATED – THIEVES DON'T CALL AHEAD

Have you noticed that thieves don't call ahead and let you know they are coming? You don't get a message on your answering machine saying, "Hi! This is big Al and I will be busting into your house tonight and taking your big screen Smart TV. Just leave the doors open so we don't have to use our screwdriver or wreck your door."

No, thieves come when you are least expecting them. So, Jesus is going to come when this earth is not ready. He is not a thief, but He is going to come like a thief on that day, like a stealth bomber who nobody picked up on their radar screens.

He said it would be a time when the cry on people's lips would be, "Peace and safety." Everyone will be talking about peace and security. They will be talking about the peace process, the road map to peace, airport security, job security, medical security, and security of all types. Then sudden destruction will come.[50]

The Church will disappear and chaos will envelop the world. People will be holding pictures of their sons and daughters on television saying, "Has anybody seen this person?" Wives will be missing their husbands, husbands will be missing their wives, one will be taken, one will be left, one was ready, one was not, and those who are left will be like a punch-drunk boxer wondering what happened. Computer systems will break down, people will lose their retirement accounts, their pensions, their 401k's, their IRAs, and all their investments. Everything will fall into utter, massive confusion around this world, and nobody will know what to do.

Some people say if you believe in the Rapture you embrace an "escape theology." Call it what you want, but it will happen whether people believe it or not.

THE ANTICHRIST

A man will come to power, most likely out of the old Roman Empire nations, a man of lawlessness but with a magnetic, charming personality. The Antichrist will unify the world under one single government during the Tribulation. This global leader will appear on the scene as an angel of light, a man with a plan to the rescue. He will have a solution to the chaos. He will pledge to make everything right if the world accepts his system, and the governments of the world will lay down their autonomy and turn it over to him.[51] He may even convince those who missed the Rapture that it was UFOs that took loved ones to be re-educated for the harmony of the New World Order, and then they'll be allowed to return.

The world leader at that time will, for a short season, bring peace to the Middle East between Jews and Muslims. He will bring a pseudo-peace to this earth and restore financial markets for a short season. And just when everyone is accepting and espousing his lies, the Great Day of the Lord will intensify and people will be trapped on earth like Jewish people became trapped in Hitler's hell. Three and a half years or more after the Church is taken, (halfway into the seven-year tribulation) the judgment will heighten significantly and pound the earth relentlessly. The Bible describes it as an utter and hopeless ruin.

THE WORLD IS PREGNANT WITH DESTRUCTION

People will think, "I've got my investments and my savings account, so I'll be okay. The world leader knows where my loved one is." Antichrist has a plausible explanation for the disappearance of millions. People will have a feeling of security once again, but then destruction will come, hopeless ruin, a loss of everything. We'll discuss this more in 2 Thessalonians.

The world right now is pregnant with the destruction that lies just ahead. The Thessalonians understood what Paul was talking about because back in the days of Roman power, the Roman government would go to certain villages and cities and say, "Allow us to put a garrison in your city and we will give you peace and security." Antichrist forces will do the same.

1 Thessalonians 5:4-8

Paul was saying that in the time of the Lord's return, the government will not be able to guarantee you anything.

> **4 But ye, brethren, are not in darkness, that that day should overtake you as a thief.**
>
> **5 Ye are all the children of light, and the children of the day: we are not of the night, nor of darkness.**
>
> **6 Therefore let us not sleep, as do others; but let us watch and be sober.**
>
> **7 For they that sleep sleep in the night; and they that be drunken are drunken in the night.**
>
> **8 But let us, who are of the day, be sober, putting on the breastplate of faith and love; and for an helmet, the hope of salvation.**

Jesus said, "he that followeth me shall not walk in darkness, but shall have the light of life" (John 8:12). Peter said, "But ye are a chosen generation, a royal priesthood, a holy nation, a peculiar people; that ye should shew forth the praises of him who hath called you out of darkness into his marvelous light" (I Peter 2:9).

The darkness spoken of in verse five is a metaphor for a lack of direction, moral aimlessness, lacking moral standards, and having no regard for God's warnings. Those walking in darkness will be expecting peace and security, but instead sudden, relentless devastation will strike. Those refusing God's message will perish from the darkness of judgment.

Jesus said in John 3:19, "This is the verdict: Light has come into the world, but men loved darkness instead of light because their deeds were evil." They would rather ignore God and remain in moral darkness because their deeds are evil. "Everyone who does evil hates the light, and will not come into the light for fear that his deeds will be exposed. But whoever lives by the truth comes into the light, so that it may be seen plainly that what he has done has been done through God" (John 3:20-21).

> **[6] Therefore let us not sleep, as do others; but let us watch and be sober.**

Paul says, "Don't let us sleep as others do." This word "sleep" is different from the sleep we read about in chapter four.

SOME ARE CONSTANTLY FOLLOWING A MIRAGE

This sleep refers to spiritual insensitivity, carnality, and a hardness of heart toward God's message. It characterizes people who say, "If I go to church, fine. If I don't, fine. It doesn't really matter. If I read God's Word or pray, fine. If I don't, what's the difference?" It's like sleeping on the job. Not caring. It's even like being drunk. You can be drunk in lust for money and other things. There are fame drunks, money drunks, and people pursuing dreams and fantasies of self-indulgence without seeking first the kingdom of God.[52] They become drunk, deluded, and deceived, constantly following a mirage and never reaching a level of contentment.

Paul says rather, "Stay awake and be sober."

- **That doesn't mean be humorless, but rather don't become insensitive or dull to the Spirit of God.**
- **Don't live only for fun and self-fulfillment, but seek first the kingdom of God. Live for His purposes.**
- **Don't dream the way the world dreams.**
- **Don't fall into the fantasies of gaining wealth or fame apart from seeking first the kingdom of God.**
- **The purpose of our lives is to glorify God and to bring pleasure to Him, to use all our abilities to promote His kingdom for His glory and honor.**
- **God wants us to find adventure and excitement in Him instead of wasting time and talent on frivolous pursuits that won't count for eternity.**

> **[7] For they that sleep sleep in the night; and they that be drunken are drunken in the night.**
>
> **[8] But let us, who are of the day, be sober, putting on the breastplate of faith and love; and for an helmet, the hope of salvation.**

Paul then says it is not sufficient just to be awake, watching, and sober. We must also be armed with the breastplate. His readers understood this metaphor because they commonly saw Roman soldiers with breastplates from their necks to their thighs, to cover and protect their vital organs, especially their heart area. Paul was telling them to put on spiritual armor to protect their hearts, that very center of life.

Armor isn't comfortable at times, but it protects us. An unarmed soldier is useless in battle. A helmet protects our mind, so Paul was saying to watch out for your thought life. He wrote elsewhere, "But I am afraid that, as the serpent deceived Eve by his craftiness, your minds will be led astray from the simplicity and purity of devotion to Christ" (2 Corinthians 11:3). Satan tries to pull us off target. He will not always deceive you into deliberate sin but will try to get you off target from God's plan just enough to cause you harm.

1 Thessalonians 5:9-10

9 For God hath not appointed us to wrath, but to obtain salvation by our Lord Jesus Christ,

10 Who died for us, that, whether we wake or sleep, we should live together with him.

The word picture is that of a rescue. We have not been ordained or destined for this time of wrath spoken of as the Day of the Lord – the Day of Great Judgment. God hasn't destined you for that, but has instead destined you for a rescue by the Lord Jesus Christ himself. That's why Jesus said, "Be always on the watch, and pray that you may be able to escape all that is about to happen and that you may be able to stand before the Son of Man" (Luke 21:36).

JESUS COMES TO RESCUE YOU, THE BELIEVER

The whole nature of God expressed from the earliest writings is to deliver his people before judgment. When the sins of Sodom reached heaven as a foul smell, God sent two angels to destroy Sodom and Gomorrah. But first he rescued Lot and his family. Be assured we followers of Christ will be removed before the judgment of God pours out. The picture of salvation by our Lord Jesus Christ is a picture of deliverance. That will be the day when the words of Jesus are fulfilled:

John 14:1-3

Let not your heart be troubled: ye believe in God, believe also in me. In my Father's house are many mansions: if it were not so, I would have told you. I go to prepare a place for you. And if I go and prepare a place for you, I will come again, and receive you unto myself; that where I am, there ye may be also.

He died so we could live. He died so we could be rescued. He died so we could have fellowship with the Father. He died so we don't have to face God's wrath and judgment when it comes to this earth. Our judgment was taken by Jesus Christ when He hung on the cross. Paul wrote,

> **10 Who died for us, that, whether we wake or sleep, we should live together with him.**

Today it is exactly as the ancient prophets predicted it would be in the final countdown just before the Day of the Lord.

All of the nations are lined up exactly the way the prophets said they would be. All the conditions and signs and rumblings are now here.

TRUTH ILLUSTRATED - MOUNT VESUVIUS

In National Geographic Magazine a few years ago there was an article about two Roman cities near Mount Vesuvius.[53] When Mount Vesuvius first started rumbling, the people of the cities were frightened. But over time they got used to the rumblings and ignored them. Then that volcano exploded with such a force that the lava rained down on these cities, stopping people right where they stood. Archaeologists dug them up and found people who were working in the fields, frozen in the very condition in which they had died. People instantly became statues. Living individuals who were going about their day-to-day business were frozen in time. It happened so suddenly that nobody had a chance to move.

But nobody had to die. If they had paid attention to the rumblings, even two days before it exploded, they could have escaped. They saw the ominous plume of smoke days before, showing that the pressure was building, but they thought it was no big deal.

RUMBLINGS OF A DIFFERENT KIND TODAY

Today we hear rumblings of a different kind. It is a warning to come to the Lord Jesus in faith and bring as many as you can while there is still time. Let's not ignore this wonderful opportunity!

POWER PRINCIPLES:

- **Nobody knows the day and time of Christ's Second Coming - except the Father.**
- **The Old Testament and New Testament agree on what the end times will be like.**

- **The Church will be taken from the earth before this time of ultimate terror begins.**
- **We must remain awake and sober, not distracted by worldly desires or fantasies so that we can be ready when the Lord comes.**

LESSON 12

HOW TO HAVE A HAPPY AND HEALTHY CHURCH

I Thessalonians 5:11-14

11 Wherefore comfort yourselves together, and edify one another, even as also ye do.

12 And we beseech you, brethren, to know them which labour among you, and are over you in the Lord, and admonish you;

13 And to esteem them very highly in love for their work's sake. And be at peace among yourselves.

14 Now we exhort you, brethren, warn them that are unruly, comfort the feebleminded, support the weak, be patient toward all men.

The Church is not a building, a machine or a social organization. It is a community of born-again people who support one another in the love that Christ has put in their hearts. "By this shall all men know that ye are my disciples, if ye have love one to another," Jesus said in John 13:35. Sixty times in Paul's writings he refers to the church as "brethren." Twenty-seven times in 1 Thessalonians and 2 Thessalonians he uses the term. This tells us again that we are all brothers and sisters, if we have made Jesus Lord of our lives.

The Church is a living organism on the earth, made up of diverse people who have laid down their own ways and asked Jesus to be their Master. There are microcosms or fellowships of the church in cities around the world. These are the local churches. This is where we live out the "one another" experience that characterizes Kingdom living. We help one another, encourage one another, exhort one another, and strengthen one another. As Paul wrote,

11 Wherefore comfort yourselves together, and edify one another, even as also ye do.

Paul said the Thessalonians were already doing these things, and he wanted them to do them even more.

- **To comfort, you'll recall from our previous study, means to strengthen and encourage each other.**
- **To edify means to build up one another. Paul cherished this high ideal for the Christian Church, that it would live in community with one another.**

These days automation and technology let us live independently of each other, causing people to slip into loneliness, isolation, idleness and unhealthy independence.

More and more, people think they are growing spiritually by watching Christian television or regularly visiting a Christian web page without the support of a local church. But without the support of a Bible-teaching, Spirit-led local church, a Christian will spiritually die.

Jesus said, "I will build my Church" (Matthew 16:18). By this He did not mean a disconnected group of believers, but a well-connected group of believers. All through the Book of Acts, we find the apostles establishing churches from city to city. These churches were local families of believers.

TRUTH ILLUSTRATED – A CHILD WITHOUT A FAMILY

Think of it: If a child is left without a family, that child will suffer and probably die. The same is true with young believers without a family caring for them and encouraging them. It is sad, even tragic when believers neglect or ignore the local church.

You see, the local church is supposed to be a community of genuine love. We are chosen and loved by God and we draw our life from Him. This is not about socializing or networking. No, it's about accomplishing something eternal.

A happy, healthy church has the very life of God within it. People who are apathetic, indifferent, and complacent toward the church do not realize the damage they are doing to themselves and to the Kingdom. They are robbing the Body of Christ of their active involvement, and they miss out on the life of the church.

God meant for the local church to be a place of mutual community support. That is why Paul said to comfort and edify one another.

The world can be cruel and cause great pain. We need each other for comfort and edification.

TRUTH ILLUSTRATED – A RIP-OFF

A young man in my congregation shared with me that he was struggling with a situation at his job where he was paid on commission. Every time he got a paycheck he would get a list of all the sales and commissions he made. Soon he was selling two to three times more than anyone else in the store. But his paycheck did not go up and he was no longer getting a list of his sales. He found out that his manager was withholding the report because the manager was skimming money from his commissions. He called me to ask me to pray for him and to get advice on how to deal with it. I gave him some advice. I wished I could be there to settle it for him. But many of us face similar situations of unfairness and people tearing us down. We need each other's support to deal with these types of challenges.

Notice Paul said to "comfort yourselves together, and edify one another." That means we are to never leave the care, encouragement, comfort, and counsel up to an elite group of professional clergymen. Oftentimes we look to the wrong place to receive comfort. We say, "If only this pastor could pray with me, then I know God would hear," as if the pastor has a greater inside connection with God than other believers. Not so!

An elderly woman in our church got a call from her granddaughter who had lumps on both of her arms. The doctor was sending her to a specialist to find out what they were. She was scared, but this grandmother said, "Honey, you drive over to Mount Hope Church at 9:30 on Sunday and we will gather a group to pray for you." The granddaughter showed up and the grandmother grabbed some ordinary, non-clergy people to pray for her. They gathered around her and began to pray. The moment of divine connection was so powerful that people could hardly stand as the prayer was going up. The granddaughter kept the appointment with the specialist, and by the time she got to his office, the lumps had disappeared. That's the power of a believing community!

1 Thessalonians 5:12-13

THE PLACE OF CLERGY IN THE CHURCH

Then Paul talks about the relationship of a church to its clergy:

> [12] And we beseech you, brethren, to know them which labour among you, and are over you in the Lord, and admonish you;
>
> [13] And to esteem them very highly in love for their work's sake. And be at peace among yourselves.

The word "know," in the Greek language means "honor and respect" and it also carries the idea of acceptance.

God placed apostles, prophets, evangelists, pastors, and teachers in the Church. Sometimes they are called different things, depending on the city and the type of church. They might be called elders, overseers, shepherds, pastors, or bishops. But it all refers to the leaders God has given the church.

Pastors in particular have a unique responsibility. They are among a congregation, but they are also over its people in authority.

- **They are not on a pedestal, but they have a special responsibility**
- **That is why a pastor can warn his people**
- **That is why he should discipline people**
- **He has been given the high responsibility of watching over people's souls**
- **He warns the community of wolves in sheep's clothing**
- **He warns of immorality and dangerous practices that will hurt believers and their relationship with God**
- **A pastor is not a celebrity, a prince, or a king. But neither is he the buddy of everyone in the church because he bears unique responsibilities**
- **Pastors must perform a balancing act. They have to be among the people, but also over the people.**

Pastors have limitations. As a pastor, I well understood that I was not the Holy Spirit. That's obvious to anyone who knows me! It relieves a lot of pressure when a pastor stops trying to be the Holy Spirit or do the work of the Holy Spirit. And yet some people wanted me to play that role.

Oftentimes a woman would come to church and get saved, but her husband wouldn't care about church. He wants to watch the ballgame. The woman would come to church faithfully, and grow in love and faith. But she'd be so desperate to see her husband come to Christ that she would send me a little note saying something like, "My husband is going to be in the 9:30 service. He has not been to church in a year. If you could just say this or that, it will get to him." I understand her concern, but I only take direction from God, not from people when it comes to preaching. I have to say what God puts on my heart to say. I have no choice.

I received a letter from a man one time asking me to please preach a sermon on wives submitting to their husbands. I guess he wanted to teach his wife a lesson! But unless I believe the Holy Spirit wants me to, I can't just preach any sermon that comes to mind.

There is another difference between a pastor and the Holy Spirit. A pastor cannot be in every place at once. There are often four telephone lines lit up at our church with people who want to talk to me. Oftentimes I need to be in five places at one time.

The best thing a church can do for its pastor is to honor him despite his limitations.

PASTORS WHO LORD IT OVER THE FLOCK

Throughout history, the Church has gone back and forth in its opinion of clergy. At one extreme in history were the Nicolaitans.[54] They treated their clergymen like pontiffs or dictators over the church. You could not do anything without checking with the pastor, elder, or overseer. If you wanted to buy a Chevrolet and you went to the overseer, he could say, "No, God wants you to buy a Buick." Jesus said in Revelation 2:6 that He hates the deeds of the Nicolaitans because they lorded it over the laity.

WHEN EVERYBODY IS IN CHARGE...NOBODY IS IN CHARGE

The other extreme is congregationalism where the laity runs the church, determines the vision for the church, and determines who is going to preach. Some congregations have no pastor but choose someone different every week to preach a sermon. The church doesn't grow. There is no soul-winning because when everyone is in charge, no one is in charge—including the Holy Spirit. Having different people preach can be good once in a while, but just as there is a head of the universal Church, Jesus, there has to be a head of the local church. There has to be authority and leadership. That person is neither a dictator nor a paid servant to the laity but is a God-ordained, Spirit-chosen leader to carry out the will of God in that local church.

Some churches bring reproach to the name of Christ and damage their image in their city because of the way they treat their pastor.

I served 24 years in both district and national leadership in my denomination. I have seen this type of thing up close. One church ran off four pastors in eight years. I know the pastors and they are good men. They are successful now at other churches. But this particular church had a deacon who owned a business and had quite a bit of money. He always made sure that the church could not operate without his money.

Whenever the church would begin to grow under a new pastor, he felt threatened and didn't want to lose his power. He would create discontent about the pastor, sowing seeds of doubt in other people's minds. Finally, he would say, "I am afraid if we keep him, I am going to have to withdraw my tithe." The rest of the people, believing that the church could not get along without his money, would get rid of the pastor. When reviewing the problems at this church I said, "I know exactly what the problem is. It's not those pastors. The problem is that deacon. Get him out of the church and the church will succeed."

The pastor is supposed to hear from God, get a vision from God, and share the vision with the people. When the people decide to follow the vision of the Lord, the church will move in the direction of fulfilling that vision.

1 Thessalonians 5:14

WARNINGS AND EXHORTATIONS

Paul continues in verse 14,

> **[14] Now we exhort you, brethren, warn them that are unruly, comfort the feebleminded, support the weak, be patient toward all men.**

"Unruly" has a two-fold meaning.

FIRST, IT IS PEOPLE WHO DON'T RESPECT RULES.

They do whatever they want, disrupting and behaving boorishly no matter the circumstance.

THE SECOND MEANING IN THE GREEK LANGUAGE IS "SLACKERS,"

Someone who is AWOL from the army of God. This is the person who wants the church to serve and feed him spiritually, but he does nothing to add to the church himself. This type of unruly person does not attend prayer meetings to pray for others but when he encounters a crisis, he expects you to stop everything and focus on him. I call them the "won't do's" of the church. They want everything just perfect for themselves but they will not personally contribute even in the smallest way.

Consider this. If you are a Christian, you are a minister ordained by God. We are all ministers of sorts if we are in the family of God. God did not call us just to be Christians so that we could have fire insurance when we die. He called us all to be active members of the Body of Christ. I wrote earlier about how the Body of Christ works like a physical human body, each part doing its work. Even if you are the little finger in the Body of Christ, you are important! Don't go AWOL from the rest of the Body. We need you!

Paul then writes,

> **...comfort the feebleminded, support the weak** (v. 14)

This refers to weak-minded, timid people—those who think they can't do anything. They do not have a spiritual problem, they have a problem with their minds. Maybe someone told them they would never amount to anything or they were too dumb to accomplish anything.

A PICTURE OF A FEEBLE MINDED CHRISTIAN

The picture Paul gives is of a wobbly, weak Christian. It is someone afraid of God's grace and liberty, who has to live by strict rules to feel happy. Feeble-minded Christians make lists of "do's and don'ts" and feel awful when they break one of them. They are devoted to special days and certain traditions so much that these become more important to them than relationships. I have known families that fought with one another because one member would not participate in a certain holiday for some religious reason. That is a weak Christian. Paul said strong Christians do not need special days.

Feeble-minded people go up and down in their emotions. They feel guilty much of the time for breaking their own rules. They might commit themselves to praying an hour a day, then get interrupted by a telephone call and forget to finish, so they feel sick with guilt. They often feel they have failed God. Or they might blame you for being sacrilegious because you had a hot dog and corn on the cob for Thanksgiving, or because you do not pray an hour a day.

Feeble-minded people also are the ones who quit church after an initial wave of enthusiasm and faith. They receive Christ, then face a trial or a little trouble and they get depressed. You do not see them at church for five or six months. Then they come back and feel wonderful again. But soon enough they get depressed or offended again. They think people are giving them dirty looks, or they get bent out of shape because they failed somehow. They don't realize that if you have not failed at one time or another, you are probably not a success! The feeble-minded tend to just quit.

What should be our response to these kinds of people? Should we give them the boot, ask them to leave the church, and tell them to straighten out their act before they come back? No, Paul said we should strengthen and encourage them! That means to try to put strength into them. Even if they blame us and seem wishy-washy and flaky, we have to try to make them stronger.

TRUTH ILLUSTRATED – THE LEGLESS MERCHANT

I read a story about a banker who always tossed a coin in the cup of a legless beggar outside the bank. The beggar always had a few pencils sitting there for sale. The banker would put money in his jar and say, "I expect something in return because you are a merchant. I always expect a good value when I do business with a merchant." He would take one of the legless man's pencils and walk off. He did this every day. One day the beggar was no longer there. The banker wondered what happened to him. While out shopping a few months later, he went into a building. In the foyer was a concession stand with pens, pencils, and office products. Behind the stand was the legless beggar. The beggar said, "I was hoping I would see you again. I want to thank you. I saw myself as nothing but a hopeless beggar. But day after day, you kept telling me I was a merchant and you demanded good value for your investment. You got me to believe that I really could be a merchant. Here I am, doing well."

One day I was griping to God about certain people in our church and I asked, "God, if you ever decide some people should leave our church, can I pick who goes?" Then I read this very passage, which says to comfort the feeble-minded. I realized then that some thoughtless people are simply feeble-minded. They don't have a strong mind. Suddenly I had love for those people because I saw them as feeble-minded, rather than just troublemakers, and God commanded me to comfort and strengthen them. Paul writes,

> **...be patient toward all men. (v. 14)**

Do you want God to be patient with you? I sure want God to be patient with me. He has been patient with me many times. If we want God's patience, we must be patient with all people, including weaker brothers and sisters.

Many times I have cried out to God, "Please don't give up on me!" In those times I am reminded that I likewise should not give up on other people. Let's exercise patience toward one another, and even toward ourselves, as the Holy Spirit continues to build a healthy, happy church and as He changes us, "from glory to glory," into model Christians.

POWER PRINCIPLES:

- **As believers, we are brothers and sisters in Christ. Our calling is to stay unified and accomplish eternal things for God.**
- **We should comfort, strengthen and encourage the feeble-minded among us, being patient with all men.**

LESSON 13

HOW TO REBOOT YOUR LIFE

I Thessalonians 5:15-28

15 See that none render evil for evil unto any man; but ever follow that which is good, both among yourselves, and to all men.

16 Rejoice evermore.

17 Pray without ceasing.

1[8] In every thing give thanks: for this is the will of God in Christ Jesus concerning you.

19 Quench not the Spirit.

20 Despise not prophesyings.

21 Prove all things; hold fast that which is good.

22 Abstain from all appearance of evil.

23 And the very God of peace sanctify you wholly; and I pray God your whole spirit and soul and body be preserved blameless unto the coming of our Lord Jesus Christ.

24 Faithful is he that calleth you, who also will do it.

25 Brethren, pray for us.

26 Greet all the brethren with an holy kiss.

27 I charge you by the Lord that this epistle be read unto all the holy brethren.

28 The grace of our Lord Jesus Christ be with you. Amen.

1 Thessalonians 5:15

Have you ever heard someone say, "I don't get mad, I get even?" What a terrible and immature attitude! St. Paul writes,

> 15 See that none render evil for evil unto any man; but ever follow that which is good, both among yourselves, and to all men.

In other words, do not try to get even with someone who has done you wrong. If you try, you push God right out of the picture.

God knows how to deal with people a whole lot better than you and I do. In Hebrews 10:30 (MSG) we read, "'Vengeance is mine, and I won't overlook a thing'...'God will judge his people.' Nobody's getting by with anything, believe me."

We'll find out in 2 Thessalonians that God delights in bringing trouble to those who cause you trouble. If you want God involved, do not render evil for evil. God will take care of it.

[15]... but ever follow that which is good, both among yourselves, and to all men.

1 Thessalonians 5:16

REBOOT YOUR JOY

Now Paul gives us practical and pithy instructions in verse sixteen:

[16] Rejoice evermore.

Do you know what it means to reboot your computer? It means to restart it. In the same way, "rejoice" means to start your joy up again. If the devil has come against your life in some way and tried to steal your joy, you can restart that joy because the joy of the Lord is your strength.

Nehemiah 8:10 NLT
... Don't be dejected and sad, for the joy of the Lord is your strength!"

TRUTH ILLUSTRATED – JUMP START THE JOY

I remember having all kinds of difficulties one time. I was scheduled to do a radio interview that I did not want to do because of the many other pressing tasks I had. I was driving along, griping all the way down the road. All of a sudden, I remembered this verse in Nehemiah. So, I decided to start praising the Lord. I did not feel joyful when I started. I had to reboot my joy. I began thanking Him in advance for the joy, thanking Him for love, thanking Him for peace, thanking Him for everything I could think of. Soon, I did feel joy and peace come over my soul. I finished the radio interview, got back to the office and all the other things that had bothered me were taken care of. Pouting my way down the highway had done me no good. But rejoicing changed my whole day.

There is an old pop song called, "Don't Worry, Be Happy." That's solid biblical advice!

Mark Twain once said, "Don't talk about your troubles, because eighty percent of the people do not care. The other twenty percent think you deserve them."

Instead, rejoice evermore. Jesus said to rejoice that your names are written in heaven (Luke 10:20). What do you face that God cannot handle? When have you stumbled, do you think God cannot pick you up? God is omnipotent—that is, all-powerful. He is omnipresent—everywhere you will ever go. He knows your situation from beginning to end. Don't you think He is willing and able to make the outcome just perfect on your behalf? So, rejoice evermore!

1 Thessalonians 5:17

REBOOT YOUR PAYERS

And then,

> [17] **Pray without ceasing.**

Don't get the wrong idea. This does not mean praying twenty-four hours a day, seven days a week. It does not mean staying on your knees all the time. Picture someone taking this literally and walking around on their knees, unable to hold a conversation with anyone because they are praying.

No, this means never give up on prayer. Keep your life in an attitude of prayer. As Jude exhorted:

> **Jude 1:20-21 MSG**
> [20-21] **But you, dear friends, carefully build yourselves up in this most holy faith by praying in the Holy Spirit, staying right at the center of God's love, keeping your arms open and outstretched, ready for the mercy of our Master, Jesus Christ. This is the unending life, the real life!**

TRUTH ILLUSTRATED – THANK YOU FOR THE FOOD, GOD

A minister told me this story. He took his children to a restaurant and his six-year-old son asked if he could pray over the food. The boy prayed, "God is good, God is great, thank you for the food. I would thank you even more if Mom got us ice cream for dessert. Amen."

There was laughter from nearby customers, but some woman was overheard saying, "That is what is wrong with the country. Kids today don't even know how to pray. Asking God for ice cream, why I never."

The little boy burst into tears, looked up, and said, "Daddy, did I do it wrong?"

His dad assured him that he had done a terrific job and God was certainly not mad at him. An elderly gentleman approached the table, winked at the boy, and said, "I happen to know that God thought that was a great prayer."

"Really?" the boy asked.

The elderly man said, "Cross my heart," then added in a theatrical whisper, pointing to the woman who had commented, "Too bad she never asked God for ice cream. Ice cream is good for the soul sometimes."[55]

Naturally, at the end of the meal, the dad bought his kids ice cream. His son stared at his for a moment, then picked up his sundae, and without a word walked over and placed it in front of the woman. With a big smile, he told her, "This is for you. Ice cream is good for the soul sometimes, and my soul is good already."

UNTIL YOU PRAY...YOU DON'T UNDERSTAND PRAYER

The late missionary evangelist, Luis Palau[56] said you can read all the manuals on prayer, go to all the prayer meetings, and listen to other people pray. But until you pray yourself, you do not understand prayer. It is like riding a bicycle or swimming. You learn by doing.

Peter Marshall[57] prayed, "Forgive us for thinking that prayer is a waste of time and help us to see that without prayer our work is a waste of time."

It is God's will for us to stay in an attitude of prayer all day long. My wife, Mary Jo tells me that she wakes up in the night sometimes and hears me praying in my sleep. I hope that's true every night!

1 Thessalonians 5:18

REBOOT YOUR THANKS

A healthy, happy church is a rejoicing church made up of rejoicing people, and a praying church made up of praying people. It is also a thankful church.

18 In every thing give thanks: for this is the will of God in Christ Jesus concerning you.

Why do people struggle to know the will of God when it is so plain? The will of God is that we give thanks in everything. Notice he did not say give thanks for everything. You cannot give thanks for things that God did not bring to you like sin, sickness, or disease. But when we face bad things we thank Him in everything.

TRUTH ILLUSTRATED – VOW OF SILENCE

A monk joined a monastery and took a vow of silence. He could say only two words every ten years. After the first ten years, his superior said, "You have been here ten years. What do you have to say?" He said, "Food bad." Another ten years went by and his superior met with him. This time the monk said, "Bed hard." Another ten years went by; his superior met with him and this time the monk said, "I quit." The superior said, "I could have expected this. You have done nothing but complain ever since you got here."

God doesn't like being around people who complain all the time, any more than you probably do.

Back when the children of Israel were wandering in the wilderness, judgment came when they complained. But miracles happened when they were thankful. The Bible says this is the will of God.

Don't wait for your life to become perfect to become thankful. Perfection is not going to come along often in life. There is no perfect man, so ladies: quit trying to make your man perfect. Just thank God you've got one!

Men should realize there is no perfect woman. Thank God for the one you have. There are no perfect jobs or careers. Every job has aspects you will not like. But thank God that you have a job.

When you are tempted to envy someone else, start thanking God for that person. When you see someone else being blessed, thank God that He is blessing them. This opens you up to receive the same kind of blessings.

TRUTH ILLUSTRATED – PASTORAL JEALOUSY

F.B. Meyer, a pastor in London, England, told a story. He was pastoring at the same time Charles Spurgeon and G. Campbell Morgan, two great pastors of the twentieth century, were pastoring. Spurgeon's church was overflowing with people. Morgan's church was overflowing with people. And though F.B. Meyer was an excellent teacher and writer, he could not seem to fill up his church. He was jealous of Spurgeon and Morgan.

One day while he was praying, the Holy Spirit convicted him of this jealousy. He said, "Meyer, I cannot spectacularly use your life until you thank me for blessing those men." From then on, he started thanking God. "Thank You for blessing Spurgeon. Thank You for blessing Morgan. Thank You for bringing them to London to have great churches where people are being saved and growing in their faith." When he started thanking the Lord for those other men, his church started growing and overflowing. It stayed overflowing from that time forward.

1 Thessalonians 5:19

REBOOT YOUR FIRE

Next, Paul writes,

> **[19] Quench not the Spirit.**

The Greek word picture of Verse 19 is that of pouring water over a fire.

Every church has its spiritual firefighters. People say to me, "Oh, Brother Williams, we'd better not let this spiritual excitement and exuberant worship get out of hand. It's like a wildfire. People might get in the flesh."

But I love seeing people young and old dance around and worship God. They are not distracting, they are energizing! But there is always someone standing by wanting to put the fire of the Spirit out. The Bible says God is a consuming fire (Deuteronomy 4:24). Let's not be afraid of His fire.

I've learned that God does things differently than I would. He does not need to be as neat as I am. He does not demand that everything be just the way I think it should be. Rather, Paul warns us to let God move among us and not quench the Spirit.

- **The Holy Spirit teaches us**
- **The Holy Spirit guides us**
- **The Holy Spirit comforts us**
- **The Holy Spirit comes alongside to help us**
- **The Holy Spirit shows us things to come.**

Why would we want to quench Him? I want to be taught, guided, and comforted. Let's enjoy the fire from the Holy Spirit whether it is a cleansing fire or a revival fire.

1 Thessalonians 5:20

> **[20] Despise not prophesyings.**

Prophecy is simply man speaking to man on behalf of God under the inspiration of the Holy Spirit. It can refer to anointed preaching or it can refer to someone speaking in an anointed gift of prophecy.

There are many times when I am preaching and simultaneously speaking a prophetic word.

People think it's in my notes, but it is not. The Holy Spirit speaks to me as I am speaking to others. But some people do not like that. They don't like the Holy Spirit speaking to them that way. They despise prophecy.

Some people despise prophecy because of the people through whom the prophecy comes. They don't like the person's personality, style, tone, or wording, so they reject the prophetic word, figuring, "God wouldn't use a person like that." We must look past the person to the validity of the word. We can't throw out the whole chicken because there are bones in it.

TRUTH ILLUSTRATED - A PROPHETIC WORD

I was in Dallas with a couple of staff members at a time when our church had grown to a certain point and plateaued. We could not seem to get off that plateau. We got together in a hotel room and prayed and prayed.

After about two hours something like a movie came before my eyes. I saw a ship that was caught on a sandbar, expending energy to try to get off the sandbar. The propellers were turning, and sand and mud were stirred up everywhere. A lot of energy was being expended but it was not moving. I knew that ship represented our Mount Hope Church. I saw all these sailors come out on deck and throw package after package overboard, each marked "excess baggage." They were throwing ministries overboard that I thought were valid and good. But as the ship lightened it lifted off the sandbar, the propellers started spinning faster and the ship sped out to sea, moving ahead with purpose. It got back on the move. I told the other guys what I had seen and we knew we had to figure out what the excess baggage was. I told them we would take it one step at a time and let God show us where the excess baggage was.

By the time I got back home I was thinking, "Did I really have that experience, or did I just make it up in my own mind?" Then a man I trusted walked up to me and said, "I don't mean to be intrusive, Pastor, but I had a vision from the Lord the other night about the church. I saw the church as a ship caught on a sandbar ..." And he essentially repeated everything I had seen in the vision. I thanked him, hugged him, ran back to my office, and thanked God for the confirmation.

Then I asked how we would know where the excess baggage was. The Lord said, "Everyone who comes to you and says their ministry is not excess baggage, it is."

That night I shared with the church about the excess baggage and the vision and how we had to get the church on the move. A lady walked up to me and said, "My ministry is not born of the flesh but of the Spirit, but if you want me to, I will stop it." I said, "I do." We lost many people during that time of cutting back ministries, but as soon as it was over the ship took off again. We broke through the plateau and grew by another 250% in a matter of 18 months.

Despise not prophecies, whatever way they may come to you! They can be important to your future. Just remember what Paul says in the next verse.

1 Thessalonians 5:21

The next verse says,

> 21 **Prove all things; hold fast that which is good.**

That means to test and sift all things, examining them for genuineness. In my vernacular, it means, "Don't be a sucker."

Scams are everywhere. I get emails asking for my bank account number so they can transfer money to me because I have won some overseas lottery. Rip-off artists send scam emails like that by the millions. And many people are defrauded because they do not prove all things. There are even organizations posing as ministries to raise money for orphanages that do not exist.

We found that some churches were giving money to an orphanage in Haiti. They went down to see it and sure enough, there was the orphanage with its children and workers. After the church group left they decided to go back and see it one more time—a surprise visit. They drove back to the orphanage and the banner was down. The building was empty. The whole village was part of a scheme to rip off Americans.

You can get yourself into a mess if you do not prove all things. I have seen predatory men go to a singles' meeting, find a girl, and say, "God told me you are the one I am to marry." I have known young Christian girls who have fallen for that. If someone does that to you, slap him right across the face (figuratively, unless necessary literally). Don't fall for schemes by failing to prove them.

TEST IT, SIFT IT, AND PROVE IT.

A lady came to our church service one week. As we were worshiping the Lord she started yelling, "J-e-e-e-e-sus, J-e-e-e-e-sus." I'm a fairly tolerant person and can overlook silliness when people are sincere, but there was a spirit behind this that was taking attention from Jesus Christ. She was doing a lot of weird gyrations and serpentine movements as she screeched the Name of Jesus over and over again. I've learned that that usually means there is a demon involved. I asked the ushers to help this lady out and she kept screeching, "Je-e-e-e-sus" all the way out of the sanctuary.

Our ministry team then cast several demons out of her. It was like in Acts 16:17 when a woman followed Paul and his team saying, "These men are the servants of the most high God, which shew unto us the way of salvation." She was saying the right things but was of the wrong spirit. What did Paul do? He turned around, rebuked the demon, and cast it out of her.

In the same way, we have to test the spirits and prove whether they are of God.

1 Thessalonians 5:22

Reboot your holiness

> [22] **Abstain from all appearance of evil.**

I have heard people say so many times, "We are just living together to save money until we can get married. We are not having sex."

Even if that's true, the appearance of impropriety is a sin.

If you are cohabiting unmarried, you are in sin. The Bible says,

"Let every one that nameth the name of Christ depart from iniquity." (2 Timothy 2:19)

I have known of so-called Christian bands that would go to nightclubs to get ideas for how to make Christian music. Imagine that—going to the devil to get ideas for ways of blessing God.

1 Thessalonians 5:23

Paul's closing remarks now begin,

> [23] **And the very God of peace sanctify you wholly; and I pray God your whole spirit and soul and body be preserved blameless unto the coming of our Lord Jesus Christ.**

The word "sanctify" means setting you apart for God's service.

We know that no man can be perfect, so why worry about being sanctified and becoming more like Jesus? Because sanctification gets us ready for our position in the next life. Your position in the next life will be the same for all eternity.

TRUTH ILLUSTRATED - RECITAL

It's like this. When a six-year-old plays a simple song at a piano recital, the teacher might say, "That was perfect." It was perfect—for a six-year-old. But when she is twenty or thirty years old, she had better play something more complex and interesting. As believers and followers of Jesus Christ, what may have been all right in our third month of knowing Christ is no longer considered "perfect" after we have walked with him for twenty years. He wants to change us into the image of His Son Jesus. That is sanctification, and both the Word of God and the Holy Spirit help us.

1 Thessalonians 5:24

24 Faithful is he that calleth you, who also will do it.

This verse means a lot to me personally.

Mary Jo, now my wife, sent this verse to me painted on a little stone back in 1977 when I started in ministry. She was in Bible School at the time. I did not know how I was going to succeed in the ministry. Then this verse arrived in the mail. She had no idea what was going on in my life. I hung onto that verse as a special gift from God. When I did not know how to do something that God told me to do, I leaned on this verse. God called you, and He'll be faithful to do it when you yield to Him.

1 Thessalonians 5:25-28

Paul closes with these words:

25 Brethren, pray for us.

26 Greet all the brethren with an holy kiss.

27 I charge you by the Lord that this epistle be read unto all the holy brethren.

28 The grace of our Lord Jesus Christ be with you. Amen.

Paul wanted this letter to bless everyone in the church, not just the few who received it.

And now it's time to keep studying how to be a model church and a model Christian by seeing what Paul wrote in 2 Thessalonians. There, too, we will meet a new friend.

POWER PRINCIPLES:

- You can choose to reboot your joy at any time. Remember—the joy of the Lord is your strength!
- Our lives can be characterized by prayer, thankfulness, holiness, fire, and passion for God.

The Thessalonians were grateful that Paul had written them a letter. They missed him. But that one letter did not answer all their questions, so he wrote them again a few months later in a letter we now call II Thessalonians.

HISTORY OF PAUL'S SECOND LETTER TO THE THESSALONIANS

The Church in Thessalonica needed a hand-signed letter from the Apostle Paul for a very good reason. Counterfeit letters were circulating in the church concerning the coming of the Lord and the Day of the Lord, some purporting to be from Paul, himself. They were experiencing much the same thing as a pastor who finds a silly member distributing massive quantities of a book like *101 Reasons Why Jesus Came in 1914*, or some error just as ridiculous, to members in the church. Paul had to clear up the false teaching that had upset the young church.

They were confused. Christians in Thessalonica didn't know if Jesus had returned or even if He would return. They didn't understand the time-line of end time events. Thus, Paul's primary purpose in writing this second letter was to correct the eschatological doctrinal errors. But that's not all. Paul also wanted to commend the believers and encourage them in their faith.

Paul wrote the letter shortly after the first letter, perhaps a year or less, making it's date around A.D. 51.

Paul assures his readers that the Day of the Lord could not arrive until the Church was taken, giving rise on the scene to the man of sin (2:9-10). Some in the church had fallen into the error of thinking the world was already experiencing the Great Tribulation, however Paul instructs them that certain things must occur first.

Not only does the apostle cover eschatological matters of correction, he also covers some very practical matters, not the least being how to deal with lazy Christians and believers who are out of step.

Paul signed the letter in his own handwriting so the believers at Thessalonica would know the letter was not a counterfeit, but had indeed actually been dictated by the great apostle.

2 THESSALONIANS OUTLINE

I. Introduction
   - A. Salutation (1:1)
   - B. Greeting (1:2-3)

II. General Instructions
   - A. How Faith Works (1:1-3)
     1. Faith in Crisis
     2. Launching out in Faith
     3. Dreaming and Speaking by Faith
   - B. How to Succeed and Never Fail (1:1-4)
     1. Love: God's Plan
     2. Love is Encouraging
   - C. How to Endure Hardship (1:4-12)
     1. Law of the Boomerang
     2. The Spirit of Glory
     3. Seeing the Finish Line

III. End Times Instructions
   - A. How to Avoid Deception & Delusion (2:1-12)
     1. Greatest Delusion in History
     2. The End of the Age
     3. Biography of Antichrist
   - B. How Deception Will Increase in the End Times (2:13-17)
     1. Lying wonders and Sham Preachers
     2. Looking for Fruit

IV. Concluding Remarks
   - A. How to Deal with Troublemakers (3:1-15)
     1. Why Order Matters
     2. When a Believer Sins
     3. Signs of True Repentance
   - B. Paul's Closing Blessing (3:16-18)

2 Thessalonians 1

1 Paul, and Silvanus, and Timotheus, unto the church of the Thessalonians in God our Father and the Lord Jesus Christ:

2 Grace unto you, and peace, from God our Father and the Lord Jesus Christ.

3 We are bound to thank God always for you, brethren, as it is meet, because that your faith groweth exceedingly, and the charity of every one of you all toward each other aboundeth;

4 So that we ourselves glory in you in the churches of God for your patience and faith in all your persecutions and tribulations that ye endure:

5 Which is a manifest token of the righteous judgment of God, that ye may be counted worthy of the kingdom of God, for which ye also suffer:

6 Seeing it is a righteous thing with God to recompense tribulation to them that trou[bl]e you;

7 And to you who are troubled rest with us, when the Lord Jesus shall be revealed from heaven with his mighty angels,

8 In flaming fire taking vengeance on them that know not God, and that obey not the Gospel of our Lord Jesus Christ:

9 Who shall be punished with everlasting destruction from the presence of the Lord, and from the glory of his power;

10 When he shall come to be glorified in his saints, and to be admired in all them that believe (because our testimony among you was believed) in that day.

11 Wherefore also we pray always for you, that our God would count you worthy of this calling, and fulfil all the good pleasure of his goodness, and the work of faith with power:

12 That the name of our Lord Jesus Christ may be glorified in you, and ye in him, according to the grace of our God and the Lord Jesus Christ.

LESSON 14

HOW FAITH WORKS

2 Thessalonians 1:1-3

[1] Paul, and Silvanus, and Timotheus, unto the church of the Thessalonians in God our Father and the Lord Jesus Christ:

[2] Grace unto you, and peace, from God our Father and the Lord Jesus Christ.

[3] We are bound to thank God always for you, brethren, as it is meet, because that your faith groweth exceedingly, and the charity of every one of you all toward each other aboundeth;

2 Thessalonians 1:1-3

The Thessalonians were grateful that Paul had written them a letter. They missed him. But that one letter did not answer all their questions, so he wrote them again a few months later in a letter we now call II Thessalonians. He began,

> **[1] Paul, and Silvanus, and Timotheus, unto the church of the Thessalonians in God our Father and the Lord Jesus Christ:**

Right away he assured these believers that they were in God and the Lord Jesus Christ. It's always nice to be reminded and encouraged like that.

> **[2] Grace unto you, and peace, from God our Father and the Lord Jesus Christ.**
>
> **[3] We are bound to thank God always for you, brethren, as it is meet, because that your faith groweth exceedingly, and the charity of every one of you all toward each other aboundeth;**

A TROPICAL GARDEN BURSTING WITH NEW LIFE

Paul, like any pastor, was happy to hear that his flock was growing exceedingly in the faith. The word picture he used in the phrase, "your faith groweth exceedingly" is beautiful. In the Greek language, it brings to mind a lush tropical garden. I love to go to Florida in the winter, even if just for a week or two, because in Michigan all the trees have lost their leaves and everything looks barren and chilly. But in Southern Florida, it is green everywhere you look. Paul said that's what their faith was like—a tropical garden bursting with new life.

Paul was especially pleased because faith is so critical to the Christian walk. Faith is the one and only thing that can take the limits off of your life. It is the miracle ingredient that God planted in you when you came to Jesus. He gave everybody on planet earth just enough faith to bring them to Jesus Christ. And when we come to Christ, He then plants a measure of faith in us that can begin to grow into a lifestyle of ever-expanding possibilities. Faith is what drives any spiritual progress we make. It turns promises into provisions, dreams into realities, fear into freedom.

Faith can bring healing to us physically and mentally. Faith in Christ can set the stage for miracles in our lives. Faith can also bring healing to the deepest hurts, sorrows, and disappointments of the past.

Faith can take a mediocre marriage and make it great. Faith is what can change your life forever for the better.

RIGHT FROM THE LIPS OF JESUS

Matthew 9:22
But Jesus turned him about, and when he saw her, he said, Daughter, be of good comfort; thy faith hath made thee whole. And the woman was made whole from that hour.

Matthew 15:28
Then Jesus answered and said unto her, O woman, great is thy faith: be it unto thee even as thou wilt. And her daughter was made whole from that very hour.

Mark 5:34
And he said unto her, Daughter, thy faith hath made thee whole; go in peace, and be whole of thy plague.

Mark 10:52
And Jesus said unto him, Go thy way; thy faith hath made thee whole. And immediately he received his sight, and followed Jesus in the way.

Luke 8:48
And he said unto her, Daughter, be of good comfort: thy faith hath made thee whole; go in peace.

Luke 17:19
And he said unto him, Arise, go thy way: thy faith hath made thee whole.

THINGS FAITH CAN DO

Hebrews tells us some of the things faith can do:

Hebrews 11:33-35 NLT
33 By faith these people overthrew kingdoms, ruled with justice, and received what God had promised them. They shut the mouths of lions,

34 quenched the flames of fire, and escaped death by the edge of the sword. Their weakness was turned to strength. They became strong in battle and put whole armies to flight.

35 Women received their loved ones back again from death. But others were tortured, refusing to turn from God in order to be set free. They placed their hope in a better life after the resurrection.

- **Faith took weak people and made them into champions!**
- **Faith took ordinary people and helped them accomplish extraordinary things**
- **Through faith they waxed valiant in fight.**
- **Through faith they turned back the armies of the enemy.**
- **Women received their dead raised back to life again by faith.**
- **With faith, all things are possible.**

Jesus once told a man, "If thou canst believe, all things are possible to him that believeth" (Mark 9:23).

Faith is an invisible substance. You can't see it with your physical eye. You can't hear it with your physical ears. But you can hear and see the evidence of faith.

Hebrews 11:1 says that faith is the substance of things hoped for, the evidence of things not seen. One translation reads, "It's the confident assurance that what we hope for is really going to happen."

I love Darby's translation: "Faith is the substantiating of things hoped for." In other words, faith substantiates the things we hope for, the things we dream about.

Through faith, we pull the promises we need from God out of the invisible realm and into the realm of our reality.

Faith can accomplish what all the personality and charisma in the world can never accomplish.

FAITH IS FREE

And the beautiful thing is that faith is as free as the air you breathe. It's as abundant as the universe. Faith is not static. It can grow or it can shrink. Some people talk about faith as if it is a permanent characteristic that cannot change. I hear people say, "Boy, I wish I had your faith," in the same way they might say, "I wish I had your complexion," or "I wish I had your metabolism." But God said He has dealt to every one the measure of faith. Paul said the Thessalonians were growing in faith.

For I say, through the grace given unto me, to every man that is among you, not to think of himself more highly than he ought to think; but to think soberly, according as God hath dealt to every man the measure of faith. (Romans 12:3)

Faith can transcend space and time and all things that limit us. Faith can grow!

FAITH IN CRISIS

The Thessalonians were facing a crisis, an emergency. Their persecution was worsening. They were being ridiculed. They needed their faith to grow.

Verse 5 promises us that all these challenges will eventually come to every new believer. When you come to Christ it doesn't end all your problems. Your faith will be tested to prove that it is genuine, that it is a "manifest token," as Paul wrote in verse 5. When we face an emergency we are forced to decide which road we will travel, the road of fear or the road of faith.

TRUTH ILLUSTRATED – A MIRACLE STOMACH

A woman went in for stomach surgery, but the surgeons made a mistake. They sewed the bottom of her esophagus to the top of her intestine and completely removed her stomach. Afterward, she couldn't figure out why she couldn't eat much of anything. She lived on pickles for a year because that was all she could keep down. Finally, they did an MRI and found she had no stomach. Her food was going right through. She was going to die, but she believed in a miracle-working God. Her faith told her that the One who brought this world into existence could be trusted to create something new in her. So, she went to an evangelistic meeting where Evangelist Billy Burke was ministering.

Billy prayed for her, and on the way home she got hungry. She thought, "If I die, I'll just die. I'm hungry for the first time in the past year, so I'm going to eat. So, she stopped at McDonalds and had a Big Mac and some French Fries. She went to bed and got up the next morning and was hungry again, so she went out to breakfast. Her body gave her no trouble. She had another MRI and doctors discovered a completely new stomach inside of her. God had created it in response to her faith. My wife met and talked with this woman in St. Pete Beach, Florida where we have our winter home.

- **Faith can accomplish what all the money in the world cannot.**
- **Faith can accomplish what all the education in the world cannot.**
- **Faith levels the playing field for all of us.**

RETIRED AT 44

Lee Braxton retired at age 44.[58]

Lee barely had a sixth-grade education, but he met Jesus Christ and received the measure of faith that all new converts receive. Lee had always wanted to work in a bank. He applied for a position there, but they wouldn't even let him be a teller because he didn't have a high school education. But that little measure of faith rose up in him and he decided to start his own bank. He opened up the First Bank of Whiteville, South Carolina, and was the president. Then he built the most luxurious hotel the town had ever seen. Eleven subsequent corporations and businesses later, he was a multi-millionaire. The people of the town loved him for all the jobs he brought, and they made him mayor of the city. At the age of 44 he sold his businesses and gave the rest of his life, free of charge, to work in the ministry and was responsible for much of the global evangelism of the century. He had no education and no money to begin with. But he had that one thing that every one of us possesses. He had that measure of faith.

HOW TO ATTRACT GOD'S FAVOR

Faith attracts incredible favor from God. It is like a magnet drawing angels to come and help you fulfill your dreams.

Faith attracts God!

Your car doesn't impress God. Your home doesn't impress Him. Your good looks and your bank account don't impress Him. But your faith does! Believing what He said and acting on it impresses God. It attracts His attention. When you need a miracle to achieve a dream, to receive a promise, God will assign angels to help you every step of the way when you act in faith.

TRUTH ILLUSTRATED – GOD'S SIMPLE FAVOR

I lost my elite status on my preferred airline a few years ago due to a strike, but I was going up to Canada to do a television broadcast and I didn't want to ride coach. I had only paid for a cheap ticket this time, but I wanted to go first class. As I walked to the check-in counter I said, "God, please give me your favor. I want to go first class. Would you please get me an upgrade, even if I have to buy one?"

There were two agents at the counter. One looked friendly and the other looked grumpy. When it was my turn the grumpy one said, "Next." I stepped up, told her my name, and asked, "Is there any way I can get an upgrade?" She looked at me and asked, "Do you have elite status?" I answered, "No, I lost it during your strike last year, but the airline promised to give it back." She snapped back, "I can't give you an upgrade without you having an elite status."

She punched at the computer a bit, then looked up at me real grouchy, then punched some more, and finally said, "There's only one first-class seat left. I might as well give it to you as to anybody." Oh, the favor of the Lord through faith! I went first-class all the way.

Faith works when we hope for something specific—like a first-class upgrade! Of course, we are not guaranteed first-class upgrades every time, but my story illustrates the importance of being specific about what you are hoping for. Faith goes after something specific, and operates with a clear promise from God's Word.

Faith doesn't help you with obscure goals or dreams. Some people say, "I'm having faith that I will be happy one day." Forget it! That is too vague. Faith needs a specific goal to go after. That is where hope comes in. Faith is the substance of things hoped for. What do you hope for?

- **A restored marriage?**
- **A better career?**
- **More ministry opportunities?**

Hope is the picture or blueprint of what is to come.

I had a continuing vision for twenty years of building a Kingdom class healing center at our church in Lansing. I knew there would be a right time. When God said, "Now is the time," we made blueprints, pictures, and renditions. Then we had to use our faith to take the next step and turn blueprints into reality. We took action and started laying the bricks and now the beautiful first-class healing center is a reality.[59] That's the way faith works. Now we enjoy a multi-million-dollar center where people are led to Jesus, trained to bring God's healing love to our generation. And God saw our faith and gave it to us debt-free. You have to have hope for something specific first.

I had long hoped for a wife when I met Mary Jo, a student of my home Bible Study. She was now in Bible school and while home for a visit she stopped by to see me with her brother, Tim. When I opened the door to greet her, I saw her in a way I had never seen her before. She saw me in a way she had never seen me before.

We wanted to be together all the time. I took her to a baptismal service I was leading down at the Grand River. When she had to go back to Texas to finish school, my long-distance phone bill skyrocketed. Sometimes we talked until 3 a.m. We began to have a picture of our future together. That was our hope. Then we started speaking about it to each other. I asked her to marry me while we were parked at the old Landmark Restaurant in Lansing (now Applebee's). I looked at her and said, "You know what?" and she said, "Yeah, but you're going to have to ask my dad."

I went to her dad and said, "Joe, I'd like to marry your daughter." He grabbed his chest and whispered, "Ruth, get me my heart pills." He was joking. But with his approval, we booked the church, the pastor, the invitations, and all until it became a wonderful reality. That's the way faith works—it goes in the direction of what you hope for.

DREAM BY FAITH AND SPEAK BY FAITH

What do you hope for? God designed you for greatness. He gave you hopes and dreams and that measure of faith to attain the impossible. Take the next step and speak what you hope for. Jesus said if you have faith as a grain of mustard seed, you shall say unto this mountain, "Be thou removed, and be thou cast into the sea; it shall be done." (Matthew 21:21)

What do you do to that mountain? You speak to it. Words are things. They are creative. God exhibited faith to create this universe and He spoke it into existence. We must speak the hope, the picture, the vision that we have. Then use faith as your evidence when there is no physical evidence. Because "faith is being sure of what we hope for and certain of what we do not see." (Hebrews 11:1)

LAUNCH OUT!

Then launch out and take an actual step toward your goal. James 2:26 says "For as the body without the spirit is dead, so faith without works is dead also." You can say, "I've got faith" all day long, but if you don't do anything, it is dead faith which brings you nothing. Your life remains run of the mill, business as usual, same old humdrum.

Real faith reaches out, takes the limits off, and helps you achieve the impossible.

Peter did not need faith to get into the boat. Boats are designed to float on water. But he needed faith to get out of the boat in the middle of the raging sea when Jesus said, "Come" (Matthew 14:29).

David had to take action against a filthy giant named Goliath who kept tormenting the people of God. The whole nation was in fear, but one little guy with authentic faith attracted the attention of God. I don't know how good he was with a slingshot, but I know that faith attracts the attention of angels, and even if his shot was off by a mile, that angel could bring the rock right back in line with Goliath's forehead.[60]

After speaking and acting on your faith, you have to keep going in faith.

The proof that your faith is real comes when you stay with it despite the outward evidence. Hebrews 6:11-12 says, "And we desire that every one of you do shew the same diligence to the full assurance of hope unto the end: That ye be not slothful, but followers of them who through faith and patience inherit the promises."

Encourage yourself with the proper diet. Romans 10:17 says, "So then faith cometh by hearing, and hearing by the word of God." Make sure you hear the right things, because faith comes by hearing. I am always surprised when people complain that audio sermon messages or books cost too much. They balk at paying, say, $40 for an audio set of messages, but they think nothing of signing a $42 credit card bill at a fast-food restaurant. They gorge on physical food but let their faith starve. For my part, I've got an audio Bible message going all the time in my car. Today there are downloads, Podcasts, and Thumb drives. Unless I am meditating with the Lord, I have the Word of God going into me. Why? Because I want to feed my faith so it grows. I have things to achieve for God while I'm here. I've got big dreams and visions. I need my faith to grow, just as the Thessalonians needed their faith to grow in the time of their trial.

Remember, too, that faith is not striving. Faith takes proper rest. It can relax in God when necessary. When you find yourself in the persevering phase when your faith is being proven, learn also to wait on the Lord, as it says in Isaiah 40:31.

One more thing about faith—it commands the best room in your life, the finest suite. Faith will not be relegated to the basement, the closet or the servant's quarters of your life. Faith demands to occupy the finest part of your life. It will not share a room with envy or greed. It will not share a room with jealousy or covetousness. It will especially not share a room with doubt, unbelief, or worry. All those things are soft-colored forms of fear, and fear and faith cannot be present at the same time.

Give faith the best room in your spiritual house; the place of honor.

It is no wonder Paul was happy and thankful that the Thessalonians had exceeding, growing faith. Because faith brings joy, attracts the favor of God, and helps you achieve what is otherwise impossible.

POWER PRINCIPLES:

- God gave everyone the faith to bring them to Christ. We use the measure of faith to accomplish great things for Him.
- Faith means doing, not just believing.
- With faith, anything is possible!

What is it that can put us on the road to success in any endeavor? It is love. In any language, the words "I love you" are the most powerful expression in all of creation.

LESSON 15

HOW TO SUCCEED AND NEVER FAIL

II Thessalonians 1:1-4

[1] Paul, and Silvanus, and Timotheus, unto the church of the Thessalonians in God our Father and the Lord Jesus Christ:

[2] Grace unto you, and peace, from God our Father and the Lord Jesus Christ.

[3] We are bound to thank God always for you, brethren, as it is meet, because that your faith groweth exceedingly, and the charity of every one of you all toward each other aboundeth;

[4] So that we ourselves glory in you in the churches of God for your patience and faith in all your persecutions and tribulations that ye endure:

How would you like to possess a recipe for success that is guaranteed to never fail? There is such a recipe and the key ingredient is love. Paul wrote in I Corinthians 13:8 that love never fails. He said there are three most important things in life—faith, hope, and love, and the greatest of these is love. He also said in Galatians 5:6 that faith works by love. Without love, faith won't operate at an optimum level.

Galatians 5:6b

What is important is faith expressing itself in love.

2 Thessalonians 1:3

Paul started his second letter to the Thessalonians by mentioning love.

[3] We are bound to thank God always for you, brethren, as it is meet, because that your faith groweth exceedingly, and the charity of every one of you all toward each other aboundeth

The word charity is translated as "love." Here's the Amplified Version:

2 Thessalonians 1:3 AMP

We ought and indeed are obligated [as those in debt] to give thanks always to God for you, brethren, as is fitting, because your faith is growing exceedingly and the love of every one of you each toward the others is increasing and abounds.

There is an amazing power in love, or "charity" as it is called here. In fact, a church that exceeds in faith, abounds in love and endures hardships is a church that will not have to market itself because everyone will be talking about it. The Thessalonians were a great example of this. Paul bragged on them wherever he went. Jesus, too, said, "By this shall all men know that ye are my disciples, if ye have love one to another" (John 13:35). Follow love and you will never fail. If you are in business, love your customers and clients. In your ministry, love the people God has entrusted to you.

> **1 Corinthians 13:8 AMP**
> **[8] Love never fails [never fades out or becomes obsolete or comes to an end]...**

Love could keep any church in America from shutting its doors. Every week churches across America and the Western world are closing down. Amidst all the specific reasons, it always boils down to one reason: somewhere there was a failure to genuinely love.

Every business failure, every career failure, every family failure comes down to essentially one thing—lack of love.

We know that the Thessalonians were going through a time of persecution, tribulation, and trouble. Often when we face a personal problem, it is difficult to focus on somebody else and love them. You become so focused on your problem that it's all you can think about.

Paul said these Thessalonians, even though they were having personal difficulties,

- **They were still reaching out in love to each other**
- **They were putting other people's best interests ahead of their own**
- **They were loving God with all their heart, soul, strength and mind**
- **They were loving their neighbors as themselves**

Jesus said all the law is summed up in doing two things. (Matthew 22:38-40) You can come up with 152 other principles of success that may be good, but all true success boils down to one thing—love. (Loving God and loving people.)

> **Matthew 22:37-40 NLT**
> **[37] Jesus replied, "'You must love the Lord your God with all your heart, all your soul, and all your mind.'**
>
> **[38] This is the first and greatest commandment.**
>
> **[39] A second is equally important: 'Love your neighbor as yourself.'**
>
> **[40] The entire law and all the demands of the prophets are based on these two commandments."**

THE POWER OF LOVE

I remember back in 1971 walking into Calvary Chapel in Costa Mesa with some friends who had convinced me to go. I was not a Christian at the time, though I knew the Apostle's Creed, the Nicene Creed, the Lord's Prayer, Genesis 1:1, Psalm 23, and John 3:16. I thought I knew a lot, but I had never experienced a church where there was genuine love until I stumbled into that tent meeting in Costa Mesa, California.[61]

They met in a tent because they had outgrown the little chapel where they had been worshipping. Some folks drove 80 and 90 miles or more to get to that place. There were three or four thousand people when we walked in on that Monday night for a Bible Study with Pastor Chuck Smith. Though I was a stranger, people hugged me and greeted me warmly. I wasn't used to that. I looked around and there were hippies, businessmen, and even a couple of Catholic nuns in their habits, raising their hands and worshipping Jesus in the front row. Everyone seemed to care about each other. I had never encountered anything like that before. That experience led me to give my life to Christ.

Love had won me over. Of course, love must be based on truth. I once saw a billboard that read: "True Christian Community is Love + Truth." If you really love someone, you have to tell them the truth.

The cause of every success is authentic love, and every failure is a love failure.

TRUTH ILLUSTRATED – LOVING CUSTOMERS

I met a man on an airplane who said he worked for a large American Meat Company and he told me how they offered private labeling for stores like Wal-Mart. He said, "I've never worked with anyone like Sam Walton. That man genuinely cared about his customers. When it was winter, he would put the winter clothes on sale, while everybody else was raising their prices. When it was back-to-school season, he lowered the price on notebook paper and school supplies."

He told me that Wal-Mart even checked their own products to make sure they contained what they claimed to contain. For example, they sent vitamins to be independently tested to make sure the ingredients were what they claimed. If they didn't, the man told me that Wal-Mart would discontinue the whole line of products.

Then this man told me, "When we deal with Wal-Mart and we put 15 ounces on the label of a can of meat, there had better be that many ounces or more in the product. If there is just a fraction less than 15 ounces, they remove it from the store."

Why is Wal-Mart the top retailer in the world today? Could it be because the late Sam Walton, the born-again Christian, cared about his customers? He expressed love for his customers by treating them the way he wanted to be treated when he went into a store.

This is true of many businessmen and retailers. JC Penney, another born-again Christian, had the goal to love the customers and to treat them the way he would want his mother or daughter to be treated when they were shopping.

- **Love is God's plan for success**
- **It is guaranteed to never fail**
- **That's why Paul thanked God for the love of every one of the Thessalonians.**

TRUTH ILLUSTRATED – THE OLD MONASTERY

Once upon a time, there was an old monastery that had fallen upon hard times. Over the years policies and regulations caused the atmosphere to grow cold. All that was left were five old monks. They would sit around commiserating about their dying order and how grim things looked. But deep in the woods near the monastery was a hut sometimes used by a prophet as a prayer getaway. The monks said, "The prophet is in the woods again. Maybe the Abbot could get some advice from him about our monastery."

So, the Abbot found the hut of the prophet, and the prophet welcomed him in. The Abbot explained his problem, but the prophet could only commiserate with him. "I know how it is," he said. "The spirit has gone out of people. It's the same in my town. Almost nobody comes to church anymore."

The old Abbot and the prophet wept together, and then the Abbot had to leave. The Abbot asked the prophet one final time, "Are you sure you don't have any advice on how we can revitalize our monastery?"

The prophet responded, "I have no advice. But there is one thing I can tell you. One of you in the monastery is an angel in disguise."

When the Abbot returned to the monastery, he told the other monks, "The prophet gave me a message I wasn't able to understand. It must have been in code. He said that one of us here in the monastery is an angel in disguise."

The weeks passed, and the old monks pondered the significance of the prophet's words. "Is one of us actually an angel?" they asked. "Do you suppose it's Father Abbot? He's been our leader for more than a generation. On the other hand, it might be Brother Thomas, a very holy man. Certainly, it's not Brother Eldridge. He gets so grumpy at times, but come to think of it, he is very often right. Maybe Brother Eldridge is the angel. But certainly not Brother Phillip. Phillip is so passive, a real nobody. But he does have a gift for somehow always being there when you need him. He just appears by your side. Maybe Phillip is the angel."

As they contemplated this, the old monks began to treat one another with extraordinary love and respect, believing that one of them might be an angel. Occasionally people would come to the tiny lawn of the monastery to picnic and to wander along the paths. Soon they sensed an extraordinary feeling of love and respect that seemed to radiate from the monastery. There was something strangely attractive about it now. Something compelled people to come back to picnic, play, and pray. They began to bring their friends. Pretty soon, many of their friends began to have faith in God. Some younger men visited the monastery and talked with the old monks. One young man joined, then another. Within a few years the monastery re-opened its long-defunct ministry training center. Thanks to the prophet's gift, life came back to that town, all because they began to love one another.

THE ROAD TO SUCCESS

What is it that can put us on the road to success in any endeavor? It is love. In any language, the words "I love you" are the most powerful expression in all of creation. An old song says, "You're nobody until somebody loves you." That means everybody is somebody because God loves everybody. As His children, God's number one desire is not only for us to love Him, but to send that love out to others. When people get anywhere near you, they should sense a compelling and magnetic sense of God's love.

WHAT LOVE LOOKS LIKE IN ACTION

A person who has God's love hardly notices when others do wrong. Love doesn't keep a record of wrongs, Paul wrote in 1 Corinthians 13. Rather, love covers a multitude of faults. That is a good thing because none of us is perfect. I have met too many faultfinders who treat life like one long "perfection inspection." They develop a fault-finding nature. They find something wrong with everybody. "I don't like the way the preacher does this. I don't like those green coats the ushers wear. I saw a spot on the church floor. You would think they would keep it a little cleaner. What is wrong with that church?"

Well, those fault-finding nitpickers are not walking in love. They are like modern-day Pharisees.

When you are quick to criticize everybody else, you actually put the brakes on your own faith.

I remember a little lady who started coming to our church, and she loved to pray. I let her come in the back room before service to pray with me and the other intercessors. One of the intercessors was a "woman of faith," and proud of it. Out of ten levels of faith, she was at level eleven, in her own opinion.

I asked the new little lady, "Is there anything I can pray with you about?" She said, "My back has been in a lot of pain." The woman of faith jumped up and criticized harshly, "Well, of course, your back is in pain. You are not going to be healed because you just confessed that your back was in pain. You need to start confessing that there is no pain in your back." I wanted to slap that so-called woman of faith! The Bible says to confess your faults one to another so others can pray for you and agree with you in faith. Refusing to acknowledge pain or weakness is not faith, it is more like Christian Science, which is, in my opinion, based on fantasy.

- **Faith doesn't blame others**
- **Faith works hand in hand with love, which covers people's faults. People are not walking in love when they make a list of others' faults, and keep bringing up things from the past**
- **Love covers a multitude of faults (Proverbs 10:12; Proverbs 17:9; 1 Peter 4:8)**
- **Love tries to make every human being on earth feel loved, accepted, noticed and appreciated**

I want our church and myself to be remembered for the crazy amount of love we have for one another and for the people of our community.

The love of these Thessalonians was tangible, practical, and personal.

Love makes you do things you would never do for money.

TRUTH ILLUSTRATED – A MILLION DOLLARS?

Evangeline Booth, daughter of the founder of the Salvation Army, was down in the slums washing the sores of a pitiful woman. A friend said, "I wouldn't do that for a million dollars." Evangeline looked up at her and said, "Neither would I."

Jesus would not have gone to the cross for a million dollars. That's "chump change" compared to the priceless salvation He purchased for us. "For ye know the grace of our Lord Jesus Christ, that, though he was rich, yet for your sakes he became poor, that ye through his poverty might be rich" (2 Corinthians 8:9).

TRUTH ILLUSTRATED – OLD SPOT

During quail season in Georgia, a journalist met an old farmer hunting with a pointer at his side. Twice the dog ran ahead and pointed. Twice the farmer fired into the open air.

When the journalist saw no birds rise, he asked the farmer for an explanation. The farmer smiled. "I knew there were no birds in that grass," he said. "Spot's nose isn't what it used to be. But he and I have had some wonderful times together. He is still doing the best he can. It would be mighty mean of me to call him a liar at this stage of the game."

A guy went to the Super Bowl and was surprised to see an empty seat in a good section. He sat in it and the woman sitting next to him said, "That was my husband's seat, but he died." The man said, "I can't understand why another member of the family didn't take this seat." She said, "Beats me. They all insisted on being at the funeral."

I hope I am loved more than that!

LOVE IS ENCOURAGING

A man once said, "Flatter me and I may not believe you. Criticize me and I may not like you. Ignore me and I may not forgive you. Encourage me and I'll never forget you."

Sometimes a simple expression of love brings an incredible sense of affirmation and acceptance.

A study was done at UCLA, I believe, several years ago. Researchers found that physical and emotional health improves when people are touched in a meaningful way eight or ten times a day. A meaningful touch, a gentle tap, a stroke, a kiss, or a hug given by a significant person like a husband, a wife, a parent, or a friend can actually increase your levels of emotional and physical health.[62]

That is exactly why I have a big dry-cleaning bill. Women come up to me after a church service and give me hugs and wearing all their makeup, it gets all over my suit. Now I know why some of the old preachers used to preach against makeup. Their dry-cleaning bill was too high!

The former superintendent of my denomination is one of the most demonstrably loving people I know. He always hugs me and kisses my neck when he greets me. I remember seeing him demonstrate the kind of love that overlooks faults toward me one time. I was at a meeting with him and other important people in our denomination, and the discussion was about what we could and could not do in a certain situation because of the secular media. People were saying, "Well, if the press finds this out ..." and "We can't do this because of the press." It was building up until I finally blurted out, "To hell with the press. The only One we have to be concerned about is the Holy Spirit. This is the kingdom of God we're dealing with!"

Just then I got one of those hot flashes you get after you say something you shouldn't have said. All I could think of was Alaska—how they were going to transfer me to Alaska. But the superintendent grabbed my cheek, pinched it, and said, "David, I am so glad you are on this board." Then he hugged me and kissed me on my neck. Love covered what could have been a real disaster!

When people mess up, they tend to feel bad enough on their own. To have someone rub it in their face is cruel. Love is proactive and encouraging.

The Harry S. Truman Library in Independence, Missouri[63], made public 1,300 letters that the late President wrote to his wife, Bess, throughout a half-century. He wrote her a letter every day that they were apart to affirm his love for her. If the President of the United States took time out from dealing with national matters and heads of state to write a letter to his wife, can't you leave a note for yours? Bring home a flower. Leave a note in your husband's lunch pail. Do something to demonstrate the love you have—and I assure you, your love will grow as you give it away.

The years 1984 and 1985 were tough for me. I went to bed at night feeling like I was dying and I almost didn't care if I woke up in the morning. But I couldn't tell people how bad I felt, because I had to be there for them as their pastor. I had to encourage them, though I wanted to die.

Every week people came to my office to tell me everything I did wrong the previous Sunday. Some people implied that I was like the cult leader, Jim Jones, because the church was growing so much. There were always people claiming I said something that I didn't say. Then one day I got a note from a 15-year-old boy that so touched my heart. Here I felt like all the world was against me and that I was never going to amount to anything as a pastor because I didn't know how to deal with certain people. But this note read:

Dear Pastor Dave,

I go to your church. I go to a Christian school near Eaton Rapids. During our Bible time, I am writing you this letter because I appreciate that you took on this job to teach a giant church like this. I prayed for you today during prayer time. I'm not going to complain to you about your message two weeks ago. I'm not going to tell you negative things about you, your sermons, or your family. I'm going to tell you I like all the positive things you do and let you know you are a good and funny preacher that I wouldn't mind listening to seven times a week. Thank you. May God bless you and give you a happy Christian life.

Signed, Chad

Chad will never know what that act of love meant to this preacher at that time.

Love is God's plan for success. It is guaranteed to never fail. We may not demonstrate our love perfectly all the time. But love will cover a multitude of sins. If you want to be a model Christian and be part of a model church, start loving people the way God loves you. It will always put you on the path to success!

POWER PRINCIPLES:

- **Love is the strongest power in the universe. It simply never fails!**
- **The power of love works in every area of life, from business to ministry to personal relationships.**

How do you hang in there when the troubles are so great that they seem to overwhelm you? One way is to keep your eye on the finish line. Jesus went to the cross not because it was pleasant.

LESSON 16

HOW TO ENDURE HARDSHIP

II Thessalonians 1:4-12

[4] So that we ourselves glory in you in the churches of God for your patience and faith in all your persecutions and tribulations that ye endure:

[5] Which is a manifest token of the righteous judgment of God, that ye may be counted worthy of the kingdom of God, for which ye also suffer:

[6] Seeing it is a righteous thing with God to recompense tribulation to them that trouble you;

[7] And to you who are troubled rest with us, when the Lord Jesus shall be revealed from heaven with his mighty angels,

[8] In flaming fire taking vengeance on them that know not God, and that obey not the Gospel of our Lord Jesus Christ:

[9] Who shall be punished with everlasting destruction from the presence of the Lord, and from the glory of his power;

[10] When he shall come to be glorified in his saints, and to be admired in all them that believe (because our testimony among you was believed) in that day.

[11] Wherefore also we pray always for you, that our God would count you worthy of this calling, and fulfil all the good pleasure of his goodness, and the work of faith with power:

[12] That the name of our Lord Jesus Christ may be glorified in you, and ye in him, according to the grace of our God and the Lord Jesus Christ.

Have you ever wondered why, even though you are a believer, you sometimes face hardships? One possible reason is that you are a believer! Hardship and trouble test our faith because tested faith can be a trusted faith. The Thessalonians were experiencing trouble, but they were learning how to endure it. Paul thanked God for their exceeding growing faith, their abounding love, and their endurance.

2 Thessalonians 1:4-6

He wrote,

> [4] So that we ourselves glory in you in the churches of God for your patience and faith in all your persecutions and tribulations that ye endure:

> **5 Which is a manifest token of the righteous judgment of God, that ye may be counted worthy of the kingdom of God, for which ye also suffer:**
>
> **6 Seeing it is a righteous thing with God to recompense tribulation to them that trouble you;**

II Thessalonians is Paul's thanksgiving epistle. He thanked God for their exceeding growing faith, their abounding love, and now for their endurance during times of trouble. We all face trouble sometimes. We go through periods of wilderness, dryness, or temptation. Sometimes the trouble takes the form of relational problems, financial problems, or persecution.

Peter said, that the trial of your faith, being much more precious than of gold that perisheth, though it be tried with fire, might be found unto praise and honour and glory at the appearing of Jesus Christ. (1 Peter 1:7)

Jesus said, "In the world, ye shall have tribulation," but He did not stop there. He said, "but be of good cheer; I have overcome the world" (John 16:33).

Paul told Timothy, "Yea, and all that will live godly in Christ Jesus shall suffer persecution" (II Timothy 3:12).

He told the Philippians to be "not in any way terrified by your adversaries, which is to them a proof of perdition, but to you of salvation, and that from God" (Philippians 1:28).

These verses point to the purpose of hardship. It is intended to make us stronger!

TRUTH ILLUSTRATED – WEIGHT TRAINING

Anyone who trains with weights knows that to develop endurance, you have to have resistance. To build character in your life, you must face opposition and times of testing. That is the one way to become strong in your faith and to move up to the next level of victory and success in God's Kingdom. Lifting weights with your physical muscles breaks down muscle fibers. Then you wait a day or two for the muscle to heal and then you lift weights again. Each time, the muscle breaks down and rebuilds muscle fiber, causing the muscle to grow bigger and stronger. Even elderly people who do resistance training typically gain greater mobility.

We should see hardship as a chance to work out our faith muscle. Don't groan and bellyache about it—welcome it as a faith workout.

TIPS FOR ENDURING HARDSHIP

How do you hang in there when the troubles are so great that they seem to overwhelm you? One way is to keep your eye on the finish line. Jesus went to the cross not because it was pleasant. Rather, for "the joy that was set before him, he endured the cross, despising the shame."[64]

He saw you and me and all believers through history and went to the cross for the joy of knowing that one day we all would be in heaven together having a wonderful time. When you can see the finish line, it is a lot easier to get through the trouble.

TRUTH ILLUSTRATED – SEEING THE GOAL

Florence Chadwick, a swimmer, wanted to swim from Los Angeles to Catalina Island. She set out with a boat going alongside her. When she was just half a mile from Catalina Island, she gave up and signaled the boat to pull her in. It was a foggy day and because she could not see the island, she lost hope. But she was only half a mile away from finishing. She said later that if she had known how close it was, she could have made it the rest of the way.[65]

It is awfully difficult to see the finish line when we're surrounded by trials, tribulations, persecutions, ridicule and criticism. But we can see it by faith. The first key to enduring during times of trouble is to focus on the finish.

TRUTH ILLUSTRATION – TROUBLE WITH DEACONS

There was a time when I thought I could not take any more trouble. I had been a pastor for a little over four years. The church was growing rapidly and we enjoyed hundreds of wonderful members who loved me, yet, it seemed like few in the church leadership wanted me to be their pastor anymore. I found out certain people were even having prayer meetings asking God to get rid of me. I found out that they didn't like that the church had grown ten times bigger in just four years. Someone secretly whispered to me that the older members felt like they were losing control with so many people attending.

A board member came into one board meeting and demanded that I put a "revert clause" on the deed to our church, and then he pointed at me and said, "I don't know, we might have a Jim Jones on our hands." Jim Jones, you may recall was the cult leader, who in the 1970's moved his "church" to South America and gave all his followers poison-laced Kool-Aid. 912 people went into eternity that day.

I felt the pressure every week of having a deacon come to my office to tell me what I did wrong that week. The pressure was enormous for a young pastor. It seemed that those who loved me were not vocal enough, but those who hated me were extremely vocal and working behind the scenes to get rid of me.

When I was almost ready to cave in, I went back to the boiler room, which was my place of prayer back then. I fell on the cement and said, "God, I don't know if I can take it one more day. Maybe you never called me to be a pastor. Maybe I'm supposed to leave." Suddenly the Holy Spirit showed up in that room and gave me a prophetic word: "I have called you as shepherd of this flock. You are to keep your hand to the plow because I am doing something in the Spirit that is like a snowball going down a hill. It is building momentum and growing now. Those who arrogantly get in the way are going to find themselves run over by My supernatural snowball."

Wow! I went to the pulpit that next Sunday as a recharged man because I had gotten a glimpse of the finish line. I said to the congregation, "I have to tell you that if any of you would like to get rid of this pastor, forget it. I am staying. I am a permanent fixture here. If you do not like me, go somewhere else, but I am staying!" It just so happened that in attendance was a board of deacons from a large church that had just lost its pastor and was going to invite me to come and pastor their church. When they heard my words, they simply left.

God gave me the endurance to see that time through.

It always helps to speak faith words out loud.

- **I will endure!**
- **There is no demon in hell that can stop me**
- **I am a child of God**
- **I enjoy the anointing of God**
- **I'm protected by the Blood of Jesus**
- **I have angels watching over me**
- **I speak the Word of God**
- **Whatever comes my way, I am going to get through it.**

TRUTH ILLUSTRATED - GUARDING A PEA PATCH

I have always loved the story of Shammah, a Private in King David's army.[66] His assignment was to guard a pea patch, or lentil field, for the king. Other Privates were assigned to guard it, too, but one day eight hundred Philistines came to take over the pea patch. All the other Privates said, "This is not worth risking my life for," and they ran off. But Shammah said, "I have a mission. I am called by the king to guard this pea patch. It may seem like a small thing to some but it is a big thing to me." He stood there and defended the field against all those Philistines.[67]

When you commit to enduring trouble and what appears to be an impossible situation, God will release supernatural strength upon you as He did with Shammah. Eight hundred Philistines were slain by Shammah alone, with the Lord's supernatural help.

When King David found out what Shammah did, he promoted him up to the rank of General and gave him all kinds of wealth. He was one of the top three people in the whole kingdom because he endured.

Too many people quit before they get a miracle. They say, "I don't have to take this anymore. I give up. I throw in the towel."

But endurance is seeing things to the finish. Trouble is always meant to work for us not against us. Trouble is to prove your faith is genuine. Just like resistance builds muscles, so problems are not hurting us but ultimately helping us.

TRUTH ILLUSTRATED – A MILLION IN ADVERTISING

Dick Mills, a renowned late prophet called me some years ago.[68] He said, "I have a word from the Lord for you. God is going to give you a million dollars of advertising and you are not going to have to pay for it."

I praised God for that, but three weeks later I picked up the local newspaper and there was that article about me that I mentioned earlier in the book. On the front page was a highly unflattering photo and caption about me and our church. But even though the photo wasn't very glamorous, and the article was somewhat negative, our church attendance went up by several hundred the following week! Not only that, the members of our church became more endeared to me, (I think, because they felt sorry for me). I will take a negative report every week if the church grows by several hundred as a result. That article was a blessing in disguise and we got a million dollars' worth of free advertising.

2 Thessalonians 1:6

THE LAW OF THE BOOMERANG

Verse six introduces us to the Law of the Boomerang:

> **6 Seeing it is a righteous thing with God to recompense tribulation to them that trouble you**

The Law of the Boomerang is the inescapable law of sowing and reaping in action. People who deliberately trouble you are in for a rough time because you are God's child. Nobody likes it when people mess with their kids, and God doesn't like it when people mess with His kids.

The boomerang of trouble will come flying back at them. There are plenty of Scriptural examples that demonstrate this.

PHARAOH SOUGHT TO DROWN ALL THE FIRST-BORN JEWISH BOYS.

Instead, Pharaoh's armies were drowned in the Red Sea.

HAMAN, IN THE BOOK OF ESTHER, HATED THE JEWS.

He deceived the king into decreeing that the Jews would be eliminated from the land. But God saved the Jews from that mess and Haman was hanged on the very gallows he built for a Jewish man. He got whacked by the Law of the Boomerang.

JEALOUS OF DANIEL, HIS FELLOW ADVISORS TRIED TO GET RID OF HIM.

His life convicted them because he loved and served the living God. They devised a plan to have Daniel thrown to the lions. But God shut the mouths of the lions, and the king pulled Daniel out and threw the advisors to the lions. All of a sudden, the lions were hungry.

That's the Law of the Boomerang. Those who abuse you, ridicule you, criticize you, find fault with you, and make life tough for you are going to experience it. Just remember that God makes it happen, not you.

TRUTH ILLUSTRATED – REVERSING A CURSE

A great missionary evangelist went into a country and a witch doctor came up to him and said, "I do not like you bringing your religion. I put a curse on you; you will be deaf and dumb." The missionary laughed and said, "My Bible says the curse causeless shall not come. I do not believe you can put a curse on me, but since you believe you can, that curse comes back to you." All of a sudden, the witch doctor went deaf and dumb. He came to the Gospel service to receive Jesus and receive prayer to regain the use of his tongue and ears.

THE SPIRIT OF GLORY RESTING ON YOU!

When I was going through so much trouble, I remember slinking into a Sunday School room and praying. There in that humble children's room, God showed me a verse from Peter that promises when you are having trouble, if you handle it properly, the Spirit of Glory will rest upon you.

> **1 Peter 4:14 AMP**
> **If you are censured and suffer abuse [because you bear] the name of Christ, blessed [are you--happy, fortunate, to be envied, with life-joy, and satisfaction in God's favor and salvation, regardless of your outward condition], because the Spirit of glory, the Spirit of God, is resting upon you. On their part He is blasphemed, but on your part He is glorified.**

When the Spirit of Glory rests upon you, you become the lightest, brightest, most spiritually attractive person in the room. God then spoke to my heart that He had doubled my anointing because I had made it through the trouble. That turned out to be true. I gave altar calls and twice as many people came to Christ. Later the Lord said He had tripled my anointing, and three times more people started coming to the altar to be saved and healed.

When you face trouble and decide in faith to get through it properly, the Law of the Boomerang will go into effect and your light will begin to brighten.

- **You will be a light in other people's darkness**
- **The Spirit of glory will rest upon you**
- **Trouble, when you handle it right, will always work for you, not against you**
- **Trouble will promote you, not destroy you.**

If you can keep this in mind, it will be easier to get through it.

Remember that though a mushroom can pop up overnight, it is easily crushed and is really nothing but liquid. You can't build a house with a mushroom. But though a mighty oak requires years and many storms to become a strong wood; it is cherished for generations in all sorts of building materials because it has become tough and beautiful.

- **Let's allow hardship to do its work**
- **Let's have faith and endurance**
- **Let's see the finish line**
- **Let's be oaks, not mushrooms!**

POWER PRINCIPLES:

- **Hardship has a purpose—to make us stronger**
- **During times of hardship, keep your eye on the finish line**
- **The Law of the Boomerang says God will seriously re-pay those who cause you trouble.**

2 Thessalonians 2

1 Now we beseech you, brethren, by the coming of our Lord Jesus Christ, and by our gathering together unto him,

2 That ye be not soon shaken in mind, or be troubled, neither by spirit, nor by word, nor by letter as from us, as that the day of Christ is at hand.

3 Let no man deceive you by any means: for that day shall not come, except there come a falling away first, and that man of sin be revealed, the son of perdition;

4 Who opposeth and exalteth himself above all that is called God, or that is worshipped; so that he as God sitteth in the temple of God, shewing himself that he is God.

5 Remember ye not, that, when I was yet with you, I told you these things?

6 And now ye know what withholdeth that he might be revealed in his time.

7 For the mystery of iniquity doth already work: only he who now letteth will let, until he be taken out of the way.

8 And then shall that Wicked be revealed, whom the Lord shall consume with the spirit of his mouth, and shall destroy with the brightness of his coming:

9 Even him, whose coming is after the working of Satan with all power and signs and lying wonders,

10 And with all deceivableness of unrighteousness in them that perish; because they received not the love of the truth, that they might be saved.

11 And for this cause God shall send them strong delusion, that they should believe a lie:

12 That they all might be damned who believed not the truth, but had pleasure in unrighteousness.

13 But we are bound to give thanks alway to God for you, brethren beloved of the Lord, because God hath from the beginning chosen you to salvation through sanctification of the Spirit and belief of the truth:

14 Whereunto he called you by our Gospel, to the obtaining of the glory of our Lord Jesus Christ.

15 Therefore, brethren, stand fast, and hold the traditions which ye have been taught, whether by word, or our epistle.

16 Now our Lord Jesus Christ himself, and God, even our Father, which hath loved us, and hath given us everlasting consolation and good hope through grace,

LESSON 17

HOW TO AVOID DECEPTION & DELUSION

II Thessalonians 2:1-12

1 Now we beseech you, brethren, by the coming of our Lord Jesus Christ, and by our gathering together unto him,

2 That ye be not soon shaken in mind, or be troubled, neither by spirit, nor by word, nor by letter as from us, as that the day of Christ is at hand.

3 Let no man deceive you by any means: for that day shall not come, except there come a falling away first, and that man of sin be revealed, the son of perdition;

4 Who opposeth and exalteth himself above all that is called God, or that is worshipped; so that he as God sitteth in the temple of God, shewing himself that he is God.

5 Remember ye not, that, when I was yet with you, I told you these things?

6 And now ye know what withholdeth that he might be revealed in his time.

7 For the mystery of iniquity doth already work: only he who now letteth will let, until he be taken out of the way.

8 And then shall that Wicked be revealed, whom the Lord shall consume with the spirit of his mouth, and shall destroy with the brightness of his coming:

9 Even him, whose coming is after the working of Satan with all power and signs and lying wonders,

10 And with all deceivableness of unrighteousness in them that perish; because they received not the love of the truth, that they might be saved.

11 And for this cause God shall send them strong delusion, that they should believe a lie:

12 That they all might be damned who believed not the truth, but had pleasure in unrighteousness.

Both of Paul's letters to the Thessalonians contain much about eschatology, or end-time events, because, as we have learned, the Thessalonians were troubled by these questions.

THE GREATEST DELUSION IN ALL OF HISTORY

Second Thessalonians, Chapter Two warns about the greatest delusion in all history, which is related to "the son of perdition," the soon-to-be-revealed Antichrist.

2 Thessalonians 2:1-2

You recall that the Thessalonians were facing persecution and were waiting for the coming of the Lord. Some began to wonder if they were already in the time of great tribulation. False teachers and false prophets reinforced this idea that God had changed His plan. Some even claimed Paul had changed his mind about the eschatological calendar. Paul wrote in response,

> **1 Now we beseech you, brethren, by the coming of our Lord Jesus Christ, and by our gathering together unto him,**
>
> **2 That ye be not soon shaken in mind, or be troubled, neither by spirit, nor by word, nor by letter as from us, as that the day of Christ is at hand.**

1982?

A man gave me a prophecy in 1981 that Jesus would come back on October 12, 1982. October 12 came and went and Jesus didn't come. I didn't see that man in church again. I did see him at a local restaurant though, and I wanted to confront him about his false prophecy. He just looked at me and growled.

1988?

Some of the false teachers in Thessalonica had reported a specific date that the Day of the Lord would begin. But date setters are usually up-setters. In my lifetime I have seen plenty of date predictions come and go. Remember the top-seller *88 Reasons Why the Rapture Will Be in 1988?*

When Jesus didn't come in 1988, the author allegedly revised his mathematics and then announced that Jesus would come in 1989 instead. Jesus didn't come in 1989, either.

1994?

A Korean outfit bought full-page ads in the newspaper that read, "Jesus is coming in 1992." There were other prediction crazes in 1994 and beyond. People bought books by the hundreds and thousands and passed them out to fellow church members. So certain that Jesus was coming, some people actually had their dogs and cats put to sleep.

1914?

Most date-setters disappear after they are proven wrong, but some date-setters prove particularly dangerous. Back in the 1800s, there was a pastor who denied the deity of the Lord Jesus Christ. He was the founder of a modern cult. He prophesied that Jesus would return in 1874. When Jesus didn't return in 1874, he revised his prophecy to 1914. Of course, he was dead by then, but another man succeeded him, and when 1914 came and went and Jesus didn't come, this man said He did come, but He came spiritually and was out in the desert waiting to make His appearance.

Interestingly, Jesus warned about this very thing in Matthew 24:26 where he said, "... if they shall say unto you, Behold, he is in the desert; go not forth: behold, he is in the secret chambers; believe it not."

When I was a young Bible Study teacher, a certain woman would call me often, thinking the Rapture had occurred. Any little thing would trigger her phone call. A street cleaner would go down the road and she would wake up thinking the Rapture was taking place. She would call me to see if I was still here. One time she woke up and her husband was gone, so she called me to see if I was still here on Earth. It turned out her husband was just in the kitchen making a sandwich.

Dater-setters were troubling the believers in Thessalonica, claiming they had missed the Rapture, or that God had changed His plans.

Paul said, "I don't want you to be shaken. I don't want you upset. I don't want you to lose your moorings. I want you to remember what I taught you when I was with you."

2 Thessalonians 2:3-4

THREE SIGNS OF THE END OF THE AGE

Paul wrote to this precious church,

> **3 Let no man deceive you by any means: for that day shall not come, except there come a falling away first, and that man of sin be revealed, the son of perdition;**
>
> **4 Who opposeth and exalteth himself above all that is called God, or that is worshipped; so that he as God sitteth in the temple of God, shewing himself that he is God.**

Because believers have waited 2,000 years for Jesus to return, and He hasn't come yet, it is easy for some to say, "Maybe we got it wrong." But Paul said the Day of the Lord, beginning with the Rapture of the Church, then the tribulation, and culminating with the anticipated millennial reign of Christ on the earth, shall not come until three things take place.

First is our gathering unto him, also called the Rapture of the Church.

The doctrine of the Rapture was taught by the early church fathers.[69] Barnabas wrote about it. Early church fathers wrote that the church would be gone when the man of perdition, the antichrist, is revealed.

But in about 325 AD people began to wonder if that was true. A theologian named Ambrose got tired of waiting for the coming of the Lord, so he said maybe they were reading the prophecy wrong and maybe what Paul said about the Rapture was wrong. That in itself should be a red flag. Whenever you begin to question the apostolic authority of Paul, John, Peter, and the others who wrote letters that became part of God's Word, you can be sure the devil is at work. He always tries to chisel away at sound teaching.

Ambrose started changing the meanings of words. He said that wherever the word "Israel" appears, we should insert the word "Church" because the Church is "Spiritual Israel." I don't agree with this and I don't know a sound Bible teacher who does. The Church is not Spiritual Israel. The church is grafted into the Olive Tree, which is literal Israel. We are not the olive tree itself but a branch grafted in.

Then Ambrose started teaching that Bible prophecy is in reality history, and this so-called prophecy was fulfilled in AD 70 at the destruction of Jerusalem and the temple.

He was the first to say that the thousand-year reign of Christ was just a spiritual event, not an actual event.

This was the beginning of a doctrine known as "amillennialism," which teaches there is no literal millennium. This also opened the door to spiritualizing the Scriptures and introducing another strange doctrine: "post-millennialism," which teaches that Jesus can't come until after Christians bring peace to this world and make it ready for Him.

Up until 325 AD the church fathers taught nothing but the catching away of the church before the revelation of the antichrist and before the world would plunge into its Final Seven-year Tribulation. Paul was asking the Thessalonians, "Don't you remember I taught you these things when I was with you?"

Paul was fighting against many rumors.

- **Rumors can cause trouble.**
- **Rumors can drive stock prices down or up.**
- **Rumors can hurt churches.**
- **Rumors can make morale plunge at an otherwise healthy company.**

This is why Paul began to authenticate all of his letters with his own handwriting. He had a secretary write as he dictated it, but the last few lines he would sign in his own unique handwriting so people would know that it was really from him.

Paul said three things have to happen before the Day of the Lord begins.

NUMBER ONE, THERE HAS TO BE OUR GATHERING UNTO HIM (THE RAPTURE).

God will then begin dealing dramatically and directly with the nation Israel for seven full years (the tribulation). What will happen in those seven years is quite shocking. If you read Revelation 6 through 19, you will see what I mean, and it is not pleasant. Death camps will once again be opened everywhere halfway through the seven-year tribulation.

THE SECOND THING WILL BE A FALLING AWAY.

The phrase "falling away" comes from the Greek word "aphistasthai" which means a departure. It is often referred to as departing from the faith. Paul told Timothy in a different letter that in the last days some will "aphistasthai," or depart from the faith, giving heed to seducing spirits and doctrines of devils.

> **1 Timothy 4:1 NLT**
> **1 Now the Holy Spirit tells us clearly that in the last times some will turn away from the true faith; they will follow deceptive spirits and teachings that come from demons.**

He was speaking of a final apostasy. Apostasy means departing from the faith doctrinally or morally. I believe the stage is already being set for the final falling away. The signs are here. Whenever an entire denomination that names the name of Christ can elect an openly, practicing homosexual man as a bishop, the apostasy has begun.

Note: some credible teachers believe that this "departure" that Paul referred to 2 Thessalonians 2:3 "Let no man deceive you by any means: for that day shall not come, except there come a falling away first, and that man of sin be revealed, the son of perdition" could be speaking of the departure of the Church in the Rapture; not a departure from the faith. Interestingly this could be understood both ways. As the false church increasingly departs from the true faith, that could very well be an indicator that the true Church will soon depart for Heaven in the "Great Catching Away."

Many mainline denominations today are filled with doctrinal apostasy. Some even deny the Lord Jesus Christ who bought them. For example, one particular denomination took songs about the Blood of Jesus out of their hymnals because it made people squirm. Yet without the saving, healing, cleansing, delivering, empowering, miracle-working Blood of Jesus, we couldn't make it into heaven. It was the Blood of Jesus applied to our hearts by faith that saved us.

Other groups of so-called Bible scholars deny Jesus spoke the words in the Gospels.

Not many years ago, secret surveys of seminary students found that more than seventy percent of them didn't believe that Jesus Christ actually physically rose from the dead. Many pulpits in America are being populated with people who have already fallen away.

A BIOGRAPHY OF THE ANTICHRIST

THE THIRD THING THAT HAPPENS IS THE MAN OF SIN WILL BE REVEALED.

He is also known as the son of perdition, the antichrist, the wicked one, the king of a fierce countenance, the little horn, the beast of Revelation, the man whose number is 666.

Antichrist is the subject of more prophecies than just about any other figure in the Bible. The antichrist will, with lightning speed, rise to world dominance and power. When the Church is taken from the earth, the first thing on the antichrist's agenda will be to let everybody know that their missing loved ones are safe and will soon return. Also, he will have confirmed a peace covenant between Israel and a third party (likely an Islamic coalition). This is something nobody has been able to successfully do. Not only that, but he will see to it that the Jews rebuild their temple on the Temple Mount.

People are always guessing at who the antichrist is. Some make a profession out of trying to figure it out.

SELECTING THE ANTICHRIST

Martin Luther said the pope was the antichrist. The Catholics returned the favor and said that Martin Luther was the antichrist. There have been suspects throughout history—like Nero, Adolf Hitler, Mussolini, and Stalin.

HENRY KISSINGER?

30 years ago, many people told me they thought the late Henry Kissinger was the Antichrist because they gave a numerical number to his name that came out to 666. Others have suggested that John F. Kennedy was the Antichrist because he received a deadly wound and was going to rise from the dead, shock the world, and take over. He never did.

I've decided I'm not interested in who the Antichrist is because I don't plan to be here when he takes over the world.

The Bible calls the coming Antichrist the "son of perdition." There have been a lot of antichrists throughout history, but only one person in the Bible shared the title of "son of perdition," and that was Judas Iscariot, who allowed himself to be completely sold out to the devil. The coming Antichrist, likewise will be totally committed to his father, Satan.

Whoever the antichrist is, the Jews will see this powerful world leader as their messiah or possibly the forerunner to messiah. The Antichrist may be an apostate Jew. Some believe he will be an apostate Christian who has Jewish roots because Daniel tells us he does not worship the God of his fathers. In other words, he has some religious history.

- **He will bring a new standard of morality, which will not be morality at all. In the early stages of his leadership, he will accept and affirm all lifestyles, in the name of love and peace.**
- **He will claim to be bringing massive prosperity to the world.**
- **His mantra will be "peace and safety [security]."**
- **People will say, "Who is like this man? Nobody can make war with him. He is marvelous; he solved all of our problems. Never has there been so much prosperity in the world. Never has there been a three-year period of total peace. This is marvelous" (See Revelation 13).**

But at the end of three and a half years, he will double-cross the Jews, after their temple is built. He will move his image into the temple and demand to be worshiped as God. That is when the Jews will realize they have been duped, and they will head for the hills. During the seven-year Tribulation, at least 144,000 Jews will come to Christ and become world evangelists and witnesses.

At the same time, the antichrist forces will slaughter two-thirds of all the Jewish people they can find. He and his teams will slaughter anyone who becomes a Christian and is apprehended. While we are enjoying heaven, we will see souls coming up who died during the Great Tribulation. Antichrist forces will have executed them in their re-established death camps. These martyrs will enter heaven by the tens of thousands.

The Antichrist will implement a system of commerce, according to Revelation 13. You won't be allowed to hold a job or buy or sell anything unless you have a mark on your right hand or forehead. The word "mark" means a seal of some kind. It could be a chip. This "mark" could be anything implanted in (or on) your right hand or forehead that can identify you as loyal to this world leader. Unfortunately, anybody who takes that mark will have no hope of heaven. They will share the fate of the Antichrist when Jesus comes.

Revelation 13:16 NLT

16 He required everyone—small and great, rich and poor, free and slave—to be given a mark on the right hand or on the forehead.

17 And no one could buy or sell anything without that mark, which was either the name of the beast or the number representing his name.

TRUTH ILLUSTRATED – THE CHIP IS READY NOW

As I mentioned in a previous lesson, an electronics technology company already has created tiny microchips, smaller than a grain of rice, that can be inserted under your skin. They contain your social security number, your driver's license number, health information, credit card information, and any other information you want on there. Some people are trying to convince parents to have their children receive the chip in their right hand so that if they are ever lost, satellites will be able to track them down. They say it will keep us secure from terrorism.

As long as Christians are here on earth, those kinds of devices will probably not be implemented worldwide. But after we are gone, almost everybody will take a chip, a mark, a seal, or something in their hand or forehead. The antichrist will say it is for security purposes, to stop terrorism and kidnappings. Most everybody will think it's a good idea.

2 Thessalonians 2:5-7

Paul writes in verses 5-7,

5 Remember ye not, that, when I was yet with you, I told you these things?

6 And now ye know what withholdeth that he might be revealed in his time.

7 For the mystery of iniquity doth already work: only he who now letteth will let, until he be taken out of the way.

I believe the Antichrist is alive and active in globalist organizations or governments right now. I believe he is waiting in the wings for the appointed time to rise from obscurity to prominence. The only thing holding him back is the presence of the body of Christ on earth; the Church.

Here is one example of how the church holds back evil. Europe recently drafted a new constitution for the European Union that did not recognize Christianity as a historic or legitimate religion. But Christians, even though there are few in Europe, rose in protest and hindered that new constitution from being implemented. We may not have a lot of power in this world as it relates to governments, but as the salt and light of this world, we are restraining evil from completely taking over. Or rather, the Holy Spirit is restraining evil through us. Only after that restraining force is removed will the antichrist be able to rise in prominence and be revealed to the world. God will let mankind go its own chosen way.

Holy Spirit, though He will be active in sealing and saving people, will no longer restrain evil on the earth.

2 Thessalonians 2:8

Paul then gives an interesting parenthetical phrase,

> **8 And then shall that Wicked be revealed, whom the Lord shall consume with the spirit of his mouth, and shall destroy with the brightness of his coming**

After slaughtering in cold blood two-thirds of the Jewish population, the antichrist will accuse Israel the Jewish people of causing all the world's problems from the beginning. Antisemitism will be on overdrive at that time. Antichrist forces will try to vaporize Israel off the map and will somehow gather the armies of the world in the only place today that could hold the armies of the world, the Valley of Megiddo, just as was predicted by Zechariah.[70]

They will be equipped and prepared to destroy Israel when suddenly a bright light appears in the sky, along with a huge white cloud. Jesus will come with His people from the sky, riding on white horses to judge the earth for forty-five days and to send the antichrist to the lake of fire with the false prophet and all those who have taken the antichrist's mark. There will be some people who survive the tribulation that never took the mark of the "beast" (the antichrist.) They will not have glorified bodies but will enter into the millennial reign of Christ in their human bodies.

2 Thessalonians 2:9-12

A GREAT DELUSION IS ON THE WAY!

Paul continues,

> **9 Even him, whose coming is after the working of Satan with all power and signs and lying wonders,**
>
> **10 And with all deceivableness of unrighteousness in them that perish; because they received not the love of the truth, that they might be saved.**
>
> **11 And for this cause God shall send them strong delusion, that they should believe a lie:**
>
> **12 That they all might be damned who believed not the truth, but had pleasure in unrighteousness.**

Some commentators believe that if you have heard and rejected the Gospel of Jesus Christ and the Rapture occurs, your chances of ever receiving the Gospel are almost impossible because a strong delusion will blot out your ability to understand and believe any legitimate truth.

This delusion will be released on those who love unrighteousness more than they love the truth. I wouldn't want to risk all of eternity by believing a lie. I want to work hard now to make sure I stay ready for that day when we will be caught away to heaven in a moment, in the twinkling of an eye.[71]

POWER PRINCIPLES:

- **The Rapture will remove the Church from the earth before the 7-year Tribulation.**
- **In the end times, there will be a great falling away from the faith. In the Rapture, there will be a great catching away of the people who put their faith in Jesus Christ, His death, and Resurrection.**
- **The antichrist will be a charming, seemingly brilliant man who does amazing things and gains the world's allegiance. Then he will plunge the world into an agonizing time of war, anguish, and slaughter.**
- **Keep your heart and mind ready for that moment when we will be caught away in a glorious instant!**

LESSON 18

HOW DECEPTION WILL INCREASE IN THE END TIMES

2 Thessalonians 2:13-17

[13] But we are bound to give thanks alway to God for you, brethren beloved of the Lord, because God hath from the beginning chosen you to salvation through sanctification of the Spirit and belief of the truth:

[14] Whereunto he called you by our Gospel, to the obtaining of the glory of our Lord Jesus Christ.

[15] Therefore, brethren, stand fast, and hold the traditions which ye have been taught, whether by word, or our epistle.

[16] Now our Lord Jesus Christ himself, and God, even our Father, which hath loved us, and hath given us everlasting consolation and good hope through grace,

[17] Comfort your hearts, and stablish you in every good word and work.

Jesus accurately predicted that the greatest sign of the last days would be deception (Matthew 24:4). There will be many false prophets and false Christs. In this decade alone more than 600 people in this world have claimed to be the Messiah. That's why Paul echoed exactly what Jesus had warned us about:

2 Thessalonians 2:3,7

"Let no man deceive you by any means...
... For the mystery of iniquity doth already work..."

"The mystery of iniquity" is the hidden principle of rebellion against God's authority. God placed certain authorities in the world. There is the authority of government, the authority of parents, the authority of husbands, the authority of pastors, and, so on.

But soon, powerful satanic forces will be released throughout this world with the specific purpose of deceiving masses of people. Those with discernment, those who are knowledgeable of God's Word, will not be fooled. Those who are listening to the Holy Spirit will not be deceived. But many others will be.

LYING WONDERS

The Antichrist and his false prophet will be empowered by Satan to do amazing miracles. Elijah prayed and fire came out of heaven and consumed the offering (I Kings 18). But there have been people in other nations who serve other gods that have been able to somehow demonically conjure fire and fool people into following them. Even in Moses' day, Pharaoh's magicians worked miracles like Moses did, up to a point (Exodus 7). But regardless of how much satanic power the devil gives to somebody, God will always end up winning. That's why Paul gave that parenthetical phrase in verse 8,

> **... the Lord shall consume with the spirit of his mouth, and shall destroy with the brightness of his coming.**

Working miracles is no sign that someone is a man or woman of God. Jesus said,

> **Matthew 7:22-23 AMP**
> **22 Many will say to Me on that day, Lord, Lord, have we not prophesied in Your name and driven out demons in Your name and done many mighty works in Your name?**
>
> **23 And then I will say to them openly (publicly), I never knew you; depart from Me, you who act wickedly [disregarding My commands].**

TRUTH ILLUSTRATED - SHAM PREACHERS

Some people work lying wonders today. I ran into such a preacher on an airplane during a ministry trip. He was a charlatan, an Elmer Gantry, and when I looked into his eyes I saw a deep emptiness. He used to be on television and was introduced as the man with the greatest ministry in the world. The choir would sing "How Great Thou Art" as he walked out on the stage. Sometimes he would dress in a priest's robe. Sometimes he would dress in a tuxedo. People would supposedly cough up cancer because of his healing power. But one man allegedly took the "cancer" coughed up by a woman and had it analyzed. It turned out to be a chicken gizzard. The whole thing was a sham. This preacher was profiteering off people. People thought they were seeing miracles, but they were nothing but lying wonders.

After World War II, spiritism came into prominence, spurred by two sisters who believed you could contact the dead. Many lying wonders happened in the name of spiritism. People who lost loved ones in World War II wanted to contact them. They would go to spiritualist meetings, and even though the leaders talked about Christ and used the Bible, it was antichrist in nature.[72]

Familiar spirits would manifest and begin to say things like, "Hi honey. I'm over on the other side and I'm doing great. I just want you to know that I love you. Take care of the kids." People would feel soothed. But investigations were conducted and it was discovered that nearly all of the so-called paranormal phenomena that happened in spiritualist meetings were lying wonders. People set up devices under the tables to make them levitate, and so on.[73]

So, it is easy to understand how people will fall for the antichrist's tricks. When Jesus isn't the center of someone's life, their life is based on some kind of deception. That leaves them open to further deception. Not only that, but those who love unrighteousness more than they love the truth will experience a strong delusion and will believe a lie. The Holy Spirit gives us divine defense called discernment. Without it, we would be helpless. But with the Holy Spirit protecting you, and a pastor who teaches you the Word of God, you can be kept safe from deception.

WHERE DO PEOPLE GO WHEN THEY DIE APART FROM CHRIST?

2 Thessalonians 2:10-12

Paul goes on,

> **10 And with all deceivableness of unrighteousness in them that perish; because they received not the love of the truth, that they might be saved.**
>
> **11 And for this cause God shall send them strong delusion, that they should believe a lie:**
>
> **12 That they all might be damned who believed not the truth, but had pleasure in unrighteousness.**

What happens when a person dies without Christ? Instantly their spirit descends into a place called "hades" or hell. There are different Greek words for "hell," but all refer to the regions of the dammed. Currently, hell (Hades) is sort of like a holding tank. It is a place of incarcerated spirits of those who lived for themselves rather than Jesus. Demons are screeching there, and reptilian spirit creatures are everywhere in Hades tormenting the residents (those who refused God's only plan to be saved while they we living on Earth). Occupants of Hades feel emaciated, having all the same drives and desires they had in their human bodies, yet none can ever be satisfied again—ever! They experience thirst and hunger forever.

They will want to tell loved ones still living on earth that hell is real, but they will not be able to make any connection with the living. They will abide in total frustration and hopelessness. And they will remain incarcerated there until the second resurrection–the resurrection of the damned.

After the Rapture of the Church, the Seven-year Tribulation on Earth, and the Thousand-Year reign of Christ on Earth,[74] there will be a short rebellion from some of the great, great, great, great-grandchildren of those who survived the Tribulation and never took the Antichrist's "mark." Afterward, it's time for the Great White Throne Judgement. Heaven's

Courts will now be called to session. No Follower of Jesus will ever go to this court. It's strictly for those who have lived for themselves and ignored God and His Word and His Will.

At the end of the thousand-year reign of Christ, the Great White Throne Judgment[75] will occur. There will be what is known as the second resurrection. The spirits of people who did not receive Jesus will be released from Hades. They will reunite with their bodies and be recreated into a body that cannot die. Instantly they will be transported before the Great White Throne Judgment where they will stand naked before God. Their knees will be trembling and not one of their names will be found written in the Lamb's Book of Life.

People like Adolf Hitler will be standing right next to that wonderfully moral person who lived in your neighborhood but never accepted Jesus. Many will make excuses. Many will hope that their name was somehow written in the Book of Life.

Some will say, "I helped with the Boy Scouts, and I donated to the Salvation Army." They will present all the reasons they think they should be allowed into heaven. But they will hear the dreadful words, "I never knew you: depart from me, ye that work iniquity." (Matthew 7:23)

TRANSFERRED FROM HADES TO THE "GARBAGE DUMP"

Their bodies, now reunited with their spirits, with every feeling and memory of life on Earth intact, will be pulled by an irresistible force into what is known as Gehenna, the final hell, the garbage dump of the universe, where the torment will go on forever with no hope, no prayers, and no presence of God.

It makes you happy you're following Christ!

The trouble we face in this life is nothing compared to what some will experience forever. Those who follow Christ will never participate in the Great White Throne Judgment. Rather, we will be at the Judgment Seat of Christ, a completely different judgment for believers. No matter how lousy of a Christian you think you are, being at that judgment means you have made it to the right place.

The Judgment Seat of Christ is not about judging us, whether or not we are saved. God will not name our sins for everybody to hear. Instead, Jesus is going to say, "Thank you for the times you stood up for me. Thank you for the times you confessed Me before others. Thank you for using the gifts that I gave you." Everything we do with the right motivation, He will reward us. Christians who did everything with the wrong motivation will see their works burn up like wood, hay, and stubble. But they will still be saved.

I think about some major "stinkers" throughout history.

- **Martin Luther, the great reformer, had some bad doctrines toward the end of his life.**
- **Charles Finney taught some heresies, too. If he were judged based on his doctrine, Finney would be in hell today. He didn't believe in original sin, yet he won a lot of souls, and he loved Jesus.**
- **Job, from the Bible, had bad theology, and God came down and confronted him for it.**
- **Elijah's theology was a little off, too, and he was a great prophet. Yet he is enjoying heaven right now, and he even came back to earth to visit Jesus in the transfiguration.[76]**

What is important is not that we are perfect in every way, but that we are born again. Jesus said, "Except a man be born again, he cannot see the kingdom of God" (John 3:3). In fact, St. Paul deals with the subject of going easy on believers who differ in certain areas, like dietary matters, and honoring certain days above others. He wrote:

> **4 Who art thou that judgest another man's servant? to his own master he standeth or falleth. Yea, he shall be holden up: for God is able to make him stand.**
>
> **5 One man esteemeth one day above another: another esteemeth every day alike. Let every man be fully persuaded in his own mind.**
>
> **6 He that regardeth the day, regardeth it unto the Lord; and he that regardeth not the day, to the Lord he doth not regard it. He that eateth, eateth to the Lord, for he giveth God thanks; and he that eateth not, to the Lord he eateth not, and giveth God thanks.**
>
> **7 For none of us liveth to himself, and no man dieth to himself.**
>
> **8 For whether we live, we live unto the Lord; and whether we die, we die unto the Lord: whether we live therefore, or die, we are the Lord's. (Romans 14:4-8)**

At the Judgment Seat of Christ,[77] we will receive our rewards and our millennial position. Not so for those who have died without Christ. That is why it is eternally important that we do our best to reach everyone we can and give them the opportunity to be 'born again' (John 3:3, 7; 1 Peter 1:23). Every believer should be a minister and a spreader of the Gospel. Hell will be more horrible than anyone can imagine.

2 Thessalonians 2:13

HOW TO BEAR FRUIT

Paul goes on,

13 But we are bound to give thanks alway to God for you, brethren beloved of the Lord, because God hath from the beginning chosen you to salvation through sanctification of the Spirit and belief of the truth

It makes me feel good to be reminded that God knew me and chose me anyway. As a boy I was never chosen first for anything. When it came to baseball games on the playground, I was the last one chosen, and then they argued about who had to take me. And yet, God in his infinite wisdom said, "Dave Williams, you are a wreck, a mess, and a nut case, but I am choosing you for salvation." He brought about the right conditions for me to grow in Him and brought the right people into my life. I wouldn't be surprised if you could say the same thing.

Many Christians struggle to try to produce fruit, but the better part of producing anything is submitting to Christ as he molds us into His image. I hear people say they are trying hard to be a Christian and produce fruit in their lives. Some preachers urge people to produce fruit, causing them to go out and work in the natural energies of their flesh. But that can only become a work of the flesh, and that never pleases God.

Think about it—have you ever heard of a fruit tree straining and groaning to produce fruit? No, it just has to be itself and it will produce. It has to stay in the ground, take in the rain, receive the sun, get the nutrients from the ground, and the fruit forms naturally. Abide in Jesus and He will abide in you. You will get the nutrients and everything you need to produce fruit. And it will be fruit of the spirit and not a work of the flesh.

14 Whereunto he called you by our Gospel, to the obtaining of the glory of our Lord Jesus Christ.

15 Therefore, brethren, stand fast, and hold the traditions which ye have been taught, whether by word, or our epistle.

Paul is talking about the traditions handed down by the apostles of Holy Communion, water baptism, good sound doctrine, and of gathering together for worship and fellowship.

16 Now our Lord Jesus Christ himself, and God, even our Father, which hath loved us, and hath given us everlasting consolation and good hope through grace,

17 Comfort your hearts, and stablish you in every good word and work.

Again, Paul reminds us that God himself establishes us in every good work.

It's not about striving but resting and working in His grace.

POWER PRINCIPLES:

- **The last days will be full of spiritual confusion, but those who listen only to the Holy Spirit will not be deceived.**
- **God chose you from the beginning of creation!**
- **Abide in Jesus and you will bear fruit.**

2 Thessalonians 3

1 Finally, brethren, pray for us, that the word of the Lord may have free course, and be glorified, even as it is with you:

2 And that we may be delivered from unreasonable and wicked men: for all men have not faith.

3 But the Lord is faithful, who shall stablish you, and keep you from evil.

4 And we have confidence in the Lord touching you, that ye both do and will do the things which we command you.

5 And the Lord direct your hearts into the love of God, and into the patient waiting for Christ.

6 Now we command you, brethren, in the name of our Lord Jesus Christ, that ye withdraw yourselves from every brother that walketh disorderly, and not after the tradition which he received of us.

7 For yourselves know how ye ought to follow us: for we behaved not ourselves disorderly among you;

8 Neither did we eat any man's bread for nought; but wrought with labour and travail night and day, that we might not be chargeable to any of you:

9 Not because we have not power, but to make ourselves an ensample unto you to follow us.

10 For even when we were with you, this we commanded you, that if any would not work, neither should he eat.

11 For we hear that there are some which walk among you disorderly, working not at all, but are busybodies.

12 Now them that are such we command and exhort by our Lord Jesus Christ, that with quietness they work, and eat their own bread.

13 But ye, brethren, be not weary in well doing.

14 And if any man obey not our word by this epistle, note that man, and have no company with him, that he may be ashamed.

15 Yet count him not as an enemy, but admonish him as a brother.

16 Now the Lord of peace himself give you peace always by all means. The Lord be with you all.

17 The salutation of Paul with mine own hand, which is the token in every epistle: so I write.

18 The grace of our Lord Jesus Christ be with you all. Amen.

LESSON 19

HOW TO DEAL WITH TROUBLEMAKERS

2 Thessalonians 3:1-18

1 Finally, brethren, pray for us, that the word of the Lord may have free course, and be glorified, even as it is with you:

2 And that we may be delivered from unreasonable and wicked men: for all men have not faith.

3 But the Lord is faithful, who shall stablish you, and keep you from evil.

4 And we have confidence in the Lord touching you, that ye both do and will do the things which we command you.

5 And the Lord direct your hearts into the love of God, and into the patient waiting for Christ.

6 Now we command you, brethren, in the name of our Lord Jesus Christ, that ye withdraw yourselves from every brother that walketh disorderly, and not after the tradition which he received of us.

7 For yourselves know how ye ought to follow us: for we behaved not ourselves disorderly among you;

8 Neither did we eat any man's bread for nought; but wrought with labour and travail night and day, that we might not be chargeable to any of you:

9 Not because we have not power, but to make ourselves an ensample unto you to follow us.

10 For even when we were with you, this we commanded you, that if any would not work, neither should he eat.

11 For we hear that there are some which walk among you disorderly, working not at all, but are busybodies.

12 Now them that are such we command and exhort by our Lord Jesus Christ, that with quietness they work, and eat their own bread.

13 But ye, brethren, be not weary in well doing.

14 And if any man obey not our word by this epistle, note that man, and have no company with him, that he may be ashamed.

15 Yet count him not as an enemy, but admonish him as a brother.

16 Now the Lord of peace himself give you peace always by all means. The Lord be with you all.

17 The salutation of Paul with mine own hand, which is the token in every epistle: so I write.

18 The grace of our Lord Jesus Christ be with you all. Amen.

DISORDERLY, LAZY, AND GOSSIPING PEOPLE

In this third chapter of the second letter to the Thessalonians, Paul talks about disorderly people, lazy people, and gossipers, and how to deal with them. He moved on from prophetic matters to deal squarely with some of the other problems the Thessalonian church was facing. They were troubled not just by persecutors and false teachers, but by busybodies and couch potatoes who were mooching off everyone else. They weren't helping the church in any definable way.

2 Thessalonians 3:1

Before Paul dealt with the troublemakers, he began this last section of his letter by saying,

1 Finally, brethren ...

This wording was used to transition between the prophetic material in chapter two and the practical concerns he takes up here.

pray for us, that the word of the Lord may have free course, and be glorified, even as it is with you

He asked the believers to pray that the Word of God would go swiftly, like a marathon runner, around the world and be honored wherever it went. Then he wrote about several kinds of people.

THE MAJOR IMPORTANCE OF INTERCESSORS

Intercessors are the most important people in spreading the Gospel because unless an area is soaked with prayer, all the preaching will fall on hard ground. Intercessors are so tremendously important that I will not step into a pulpit anywhere without knowing that I have intercessors in the background praying.

2 Thessalonians 3:2

Secondly, Paul refers to himself and, by extension, to all pastors,

> **2 And that we may be delivered from unreasonable and wicked men: for all men have not faith**

I have a lot of respect and love for pastors, and not just because I was one for 31 years. I know they face unreasonable and wicked people just about every day of their ministries. Somebody is always trying to pull them down. Pastors, evangelists, prophets, missionaries, and soul-winners of all kinds face misunderstandings, rumors, threats, gossip, slander, lies, persecution, twisting of their words, and so on. Jesus encountered all of these things, and He was God incarnate!

I talked with a pastor in California recently who was discouraged and ready to give up his church because he had unreasonable board members. Every pastor should read my book, *The Jezebel Spirit.*[78]

Another resource I'd like to recommend is my book entitled, *Toxic Committees and Venomous Boards.*[79]

Paul, too, requested prayer to be delivered from unreasonable and wicked men. Not all who name the name of Christ walk in the true faith. There are some unreasonable people out there, and some of them are on church boards! Nothing you say is right, nothing you wear is right, nothing you do is right in their opinion. For pastors, the challenge is especially hard because unlike evangelists, missionaries, and teachers, pastors don't get to leave after one or two services. A pastor speaks two or three times a week to the same people and has more opportunities to say something that offends somebody. After a few weeks or months, a new pastor and his people find out that nobody is as wonderful as they seem when they first meet. The glow fades rapidly.

I can understand why Paul asks for prayer. One of the highest things you can do is pray for the man of God. One of the lowest things you can do is gossip about the man of God.

2 Thessalonians 3:3-4

Thank God for these next words:

> **3 But the Lord is faithful, who shall stablish you, and keep you from evil.**
>
> **4 And we have confidence in the Lord touching you, that ye both do and will do the things which we command you.**

Paul now takes up military language to paint a picture of the church as a military institution. He already had described the church as a body, as a family, and now he describes it as a military organization on the earth.

The word "command" from the Greek means a direct order passed down from a superior officer in a military situation.

2 Thessalonians 3:5

Patient Waiting

> **[5]And the Lord direct your hearts into the love of God, and into the patient waiting for Christ.**

Why did Paul mention "patient waiting for Christ?" Probably because some people in the church at Thessalonica became so prophecy-conscious that they started little prophecy clubs and got off track. Some of them became super-duper saints, at least in their own opinion. Every church seems to have people who think they are superior saints. They are the folks who wear an expression of superior knowledge and think they have a deeper insight than anybody else. Ultimately, they always end up getting into some weird thing.

TRUTH ILLUSTRATED – WEIRD PASTOR

Years ago, a pastor told his congregation, "God has shown me when the Lord is coming. We should all sell our houses and go up on a hill with white sheets around us to wait for the Lord." All these people got up on the hill with sheets wrapped around them, waiting for the Lord to come and get them.

Think about it—why would you have to be on a hill? Couldn't the Lord take you from the ground? And why would you have to sell everything because the Lord is coming? What are you going to do with the money anyway? Take it to Heaven with you? Lastly, why wear a white sheet? As you might expect, the Lord did not come for them, even though they thought they were more spiritual than other Christians. I've seen this type of thing happen many times, though not always to that extreme!

That is one of the many things I love about Paul's ministry—he was so practical. Yes, he talked about prophecy, but always in a balanced way. He said to be patient in waiting. Don't become a goofball. You see, some of the Thessalonians were getting lazy and quitting their jobs because they thought the Lord was coming right away. I've seen that happen over the years, too. One guy I knew had a good job, but he quit it because he said he was going to live by faith. That lasted two months until his family went broke and his wife finally said, "If you don't go back to work, I'm going to throw you out the door."

TRUTH ILLUSTRATED – THE LORD SPOKE?

I heard about three Bible school students who didn't show up to the cafeteria to eat with everyone else. Their dean found them staring out the window in their dorm room. He asked what they were doing and they answered, "Waiting for the Lord to speak to us about whether or not we should go and eat." The dean reminded them that as students they were supposed to attend every meal at a certain time. They insisted they were waiting until the Lord told them to eat. He asked if they were hungry. They all said yes. He said that's because the Lord was telling them they should eat. But they insisted on waiting. Finally, the dean said, "The Lord just spoke to me and all three of you are kicked out of school."

It's hard to blame those students. I used to do things like that, too. I wanted so much to hear from the Lord. I would get in my car and say, "Lord, which way should I drive to work this morning?" I almost felt like the Lord answered, "Go the quickest way." After that, I decided that if the Lord wanted me to go a different way, He could tell me. I don't have to wait for Him to tell me every turn.

When I go into Larry's Ice Cream Shop, the Lord doesn't tell me what kind of ice cream to pick. I don't even ask because I'm afraid He'll say, "None." We need to be normal people in touch with a supernatural God, but not trying to be super-spiritual and floating on a higher plane than everyone else.

WHY ORDER MATTERS

In the next verse, Paul started tackling the subject of discipline in the church.

2 Thessalonians 3:6

> **[6] Now we command you, brethren, in the name of our Lord Jesus Christ, that ye withdraw yourselves from every brother that walketh disorderly, and not after the tradition which he received of us.**

The word "disorderly" means "out of step," or "out of harmony."[80]

It is like a military drill team marching in order but with one guy doing his own thing. Imagine that the drill sergeant tells him to get in rank and he replies, "Hey, man, I've got more talent than the rest of these soldiers. I want to show off." He will get to show off—in the brig. He will be disciplined because he is out of step.

I do not want to be part of a church that does not have order and discipline because that church will go in circles and never accomplish anything.

When I teach a class about church government at our Bible school, I draw a big arrow on the board. The arrow represents the church. At the top of the arrow is a pastor with binoculars. He oversees the church and is supposed to get the vision from God. He tells everyone the direction of the vision, what God is saying, what direction the church should move in. Inside that arrow are a bunch of leaders called "steerers". They each have their own little jet ski and they should be aimed in the direction of the vision. That way the big arrow moves in the direction of the vision that God has laid out. But if one of those guys decides to turn his jet ski to the side, the whole big arrow begins to wobble. There is tension and confusion. It could cause the church to get off target and miss the vision completely.

If someone is out of step, they must be disciplined.

2 Thessalonians 3:7-9

> **7 For yourselves know how ye ought to follow us: for we behaved not ourselves disorderly among you;**
>
> **8 Neither did we eat any man's bread for nought ...**

In other words, Paul and his buddies did not go to a restaurant and expect somebody else to pick up the tab just because they were ministers.

> **... but wrought with labour and travail night and day, that we might not be chargeable to any of you:**
>
> **9 Not because we have not power, but to make ourselves an ensample unto you to follow us.**

Paul was saying that there were busybodies, bums, gossipers, and disorderly people in the church. Some of them had quit their jobs and were sponging off other members of the church. They would go to a Bible study and say, "I am currently unemployed and my rent payment is $1,453.72. Would you all pray that that exact amount would come in?" Everyone would feel sorry for them and take up a collection. Paul said that was not the example he and his group set for them.

- **I have learned that successful ministers, in the early years of their ministries must prove whether they are really committed to the ministry.**
- **Sometimes they have to pay their own way in pioneering a new church.**
- **Sometimes they have to take on other employment to support the church until it is up and running.**

I paid my own way for the first two or three years in ministry, and then I lived off my savings for another year before accepting a meager salary so we could get our church established. The church had needs for property and a new facility. I put those needs before my own need to make a living as a pastor. (By the way, I'm not sorry I "sacrificed" all those years ago. God made up for it a hundredfold, over and over again).

That was the example Paul set for the Thessalonians. He went out and started a tent-making business to support himself and the church. He wasn't in the ministry for a handout. Some Bible teachers believe that Paul's tent-making business became nationally known, like Winnebago Industries of his day. Paul probably had many employees, along with his industry's national recognition.

When Paul came to town, there were no hotel suites for him to stay in, nobody to pay the restaurant bill. There were no love offerings for him to receive until much later when the churches had grown significantly. Paul lived an example of hard work and organization. And he expected every member of the church to follow him in it.

DISCIPLINING DISORDERLY BELIEVERS

What about when people in the church don't follow Paul's instructions but instead cause disorder?

Disorderly people are like a little metal sliver in your finger. It may seem like no big deal, but if you leave it in you might get tetanus, an infected finger, and poisons running up your arm. Untreated, it could become gangrenous and cause you to lose your arm or even die. You must deal with problems while they are little slivers because most problems don't go away by themselves. They usually get worse. So, Paul teaches us to deal with a variety of problems.

CONFLICTS BETWEEN BELIEVERS

One problem a church may face is with Christians who have a conflict with each other. Matthew 18:15-18 and Philippians 4:1 3 give us a road map to a solution. If somebody offends you or you have a dispute with another member of the church, you become disorderly the moment you tell somebody else, even your closest relative, about it. You have no scriptural business talking to somebody else about it—yet.

The first step, Jesus said, is to go to the person in private and work it out personally. If it can't be worked out, you take a second person to be an intermediary and witness. That person can try to bring you both to a point of reconciliation. If that doesn't settle the dispute, the third step is to bring it to the church for official action. That is what a board of elders is for. They handle official conflicts and discipline cases.

DOCTRINAL ERROR

> **Romans 16:17-18 CEV**
> **[17] My friends, I beg you to watch out for anyone who causes trouble and divides the church by refusing to do what all of you were taught. Stay away from them!**

> **[18] They want to serve themselves and not Christ the Lord. Their flattery and fancy talk fool people who don't know any better.**

Another matter for discipline is doctrinal error. The Thessalonians faced doctrinal error from false teachers. Our response to such people should be simply to go to the person promoting the error and find out why they are doing this. Perhaps they are ignorant on a certain matter. Perhaps they are trying to gather a following after themselves with some bizarre teaching.

The first doctrinal error I had to deal with as a young pastor was the "seven steps to perfection" a man in our church was promoting, based on supposed revelations he had about the letters to the seven churches in Revelation. He was teaching that there would not be a Rapture, but rather a sudden manifestation of the sons of God. Those who were part of his group were the ones who would suddenly manifest as sons of God, he said, and they would perform amazing miracles. Amputees' arms would grow back. They would take blind eyes out of people and put new eyes in—but only those in his group of 144,000 would be able to do it.

I had to talk to this man to find out if he would recognize the error and repent, or not. If a person repents, they are welcomed back into fellowship. If they don't repent, the Bible says in Romans 16 to mark them and have nothing to do with them.[81] Paul did this with Alexander the Coppersmith, who did him great harm.[82] Once they are marked, that means you don't go to their Bible studies, you don't talk to them, you don't call them on the phone, you don't visit them, you don't feel sorry for them, you have nothing to do with them because they are leading people into error. That is a second level of discipline in a Church, dealing with doctrinal error.

> **[10] A man that is an heretick [trouble-maker] after the first and second admonition reject;**
>
> **[11] Knowing that he that is such is subverted [perverted], and sinneth, being condemned of himself. (Titus 3:10-11)**

If he repents you restore him; if he doesn't you dismiss him.

WHEN A BELIEVER SINS

> **Galatians 6:1**
> **[1]Brethren, if a man be overtaken in a fault, ye which are spiritual, restore such an one in the spirit of meekness; considering thyself, lest thou also be tempted.**

Another time when discipline in the church is necessary is when a believer slips into sin. Christians sometimes are overtaken by sin. They start playing around with sinful behaviors and they get trapped. Galatians 6:1 tells us what to do as fellow believers:

> **...ye which are spiritual, restore such a one in the spirit of meekness ...**

As a member of a local church, you are involved in discipline, as is every person in your church. If somebody finds out that a believer is snared in some sin, you go to that believer and restore him or her.

The Greek word "restore" means to set a broken bone. Sin has a tendency to break things apart in our lives. When bones break, you put them in a cast. They are not healed immediately. So spiritual restoration does not mean a person is totally healed all at once. Restoration is a process.

> **... considering thyself, lest thou also be tempted.**

Set that bone and give it time to heal. Do it in a spirit of meekness, because the Bible says each of us can be tempted. Nobody is immune!

DISCIPLINING TROUBLEMAKERS

Now we come to the type of discipline Paul was writing about to the Thessalonians: discipline for troublemakers.

Titus 3:10-11 helps us define what he means by "troublemaker." That passage talks about heretics, by which it means not someone who is teaching a heresy but one who has a problem and is trying to recruit people to his or her side. This describes a troublemaker. Troublemakers consider their own opinions the most important and they are always trying to get people to side with them. In reality, there shouldn't be any "sides" in a church. To have different sides means you have division in the Body.

Troublemakers are prideful people who think they know best and who try to recruit people to side with them against others.

But:

- **Just because a person has a problem doesn't mean he is a troublemaker**
- **Just because a person has a relational problem with someone else does not mean he is a troublemaker**
- **Just because someone wants to criticize something doesn't mean he is a troublemaker. There are times to address legitimate problems**

It does become troublemaking when someone divides the church into sides and advocates for their position in a prideful way.

I have found that troublemakers usually carry around a lot of emotional baggage that Satan uses to create trouble. They are usually frustrated in their home, marriage, or job, but instead of dealing with it, they take out their frustrations on others in the church.

MY PASTORAL RULE ABOUT TROUBLEMAKERS

I had a rule when I was pastor: If somebody causes trouble in our church once, I warn them. If they cause trouble twice, I warn them again, and if they cause trouble a third time, they are out, dismissed, rejected, and no longer welcome.

Some people say I don't have enough mercy, because I have had to ask people to leave the church. But I want to obey the Scriptures. And the fact is, it is merciful to the rest of the people in the church to get rid of the troublemaker! I am more concerned about the flock of God than I am about one wolf who is trying to cause trouble.

There is one woman who wanted very much to come back to our church. She called just about every month asking if she could come back. The answer was always no. She had demonstrated that she was a perpetual troublemaker. I would warn her, but she would act up again. I would warn her again and thought I was being merciful by letting her stay. But I was actually giving her license to do much worse.

One day she came in, attacked our receptionist, threw papers around and knocked over chairs. The receptionist went to grab the phone and the woman pulled the phone cord out of the wall, socket and all, and then proceeded to attack the secretary. I heard some rustling, came out and saw what was happening and started chasing her. She ran and hid somewhere in the church and I couldn't find her.

We called the police, and the deputy sheriff came by. When I explained what this woman had done, he looked at me, smiled, and said, "You're supposed to be charismatic. Why didn't you just cast the devil out of her?" I wish it were that simple! Sometimes it is but not in this case. I unfortunately had to ask her to leave the church and not come back.

SPIRITUAL BRATS

There is no place in the church leadership for spiritual brats. Maybe if you are a new believer and get a little bratty, you can be corrected and steered right. But I have seen people supposedly thirty years old in the Lord acting like they are three months old. The church is no place for that. Each church is meant to be a mighty spiritual force in its community and the world. It should be an army marching toward its goal with purpose in every step. But you can't do it when someone is marching to the beat of their own drum. We march to the beat of one drum, the drum of the Lord Jesus Christ.

OPEN IMMORALITY

1 Corinthians 5 says that when we know somebody is in open immorality we should mourn as if somebody has died. It is that serious. You should seek to bring them to repentance, and if they don't come to repentance, then you have to dismiss them.

Once again, the rule is: if he repents you restore him; if he doesn't you dismiss him.

But how do you know if a troublemaker has repented? This is tricky.

SIGNS OF GENUINE REPENTANCE AND SPIRITUAL MATURITY

Church Leadership needs to be reminded over and over again: If they repent you restore them. If they don't you dismiss them.

> **2 Corinthians 3:16 AMP**
> **But whenever a person turns [in repentance] to the Lord, the veil is stripped off and taken away.**

According to Paul, there is a veil (a deception) that can only be broken by true repentance.

Speaking to Christians, Jesus said this:

> **Revelation 2:3 AMP**
> **Remember then from what heights you have fallen. Repent (change the inner man to meet God's will) and do the works you did previously [when first you knew the Lord], or else I will visit you and remove your lampstand from its place, unless you change your mind and repent.**

SIGNS OF GENUINE REPENTANCE AND SPIRITUAL MATURITY

1. He will **accept responsibility** for his part in the actions that led to the discipline.
2. He will stay "under the cover" of spiritual authority, trusting God to restore.
3. He will refuse to talk about his real or imagined "hurt" with others because his highest desire is to protect God's work and God's people.
4. He will express an attitude of repentance, not blaming others for his current condition.

5. He will commit to staying pure in words and actions throughout the process.
6. His faith and trust will be directed toward God.
7. He will not try to "infect" others with his personal justifications, blame, reasons, etc.

SYMPTOMS OF NO GENUINE REPENTANCE

1. He will seek to infect others with his feelings of "hurt," but won't care because his personal issues are more important than protecting others or protecting God's work.
2. He will defend himself under the guise of "defending my integrity, character, and credibility," while casting doubt over the integrity, character, and credibility of those involved in his discipline, whether it be his employer, supervisor, colleagues, or those who witnessed his behavior that led to the discipline.
3. He will begin to re-write history with his personal spin, distorting the facts, not offering the entire truth in order to convince others of his righteous cause.
4. He will begin to accuse others, blame others, or criticize others with the hopes of elevating himself in the eyes of those he is trying to persuade. He feels that if he points out the faults and inconsistencies in those involved in bringing about his discipline, he can erode their credibility, and build his own. He will say the whole situation wasn't handled right. This is an immature attempt, again, to undermine those he perceives to be his "enemies." This tactic is called the "diversionary tactic." He employs this tactic with the hopes of diverting attention from his behavior and focusing on other's faults.
5. He will distort the truth and mischaracterize the words and actions of others, again attempting to hack away at the integrity and honesty of witnesses to discredit the facts or the truth. At this stage his "truth" will always have an emotional spin, will be partial truth at best, important facts will be omitted, or new embellished or sensationalized facts will be added. All the while, he may not even realize what is happening to him. He may refuse to believe that self-deception is setting him up for darkness. Because of his hatred toward those who "caused this to happen" to him, he has no light from God at all. Only darkness can

guide him, direct him, and lead him stumbling along.[83]

6. He will attempt to gain sympathy from anyone who will listen to his story. He may assure the listener that he is doing fine and trusting God, "but my wife is really hurting," or "My 80-year mother is taking it hard, and she has a bad heart as it is," or, "my kids are really hurt over this." He tries to impose his "hurt" vicariously onto weaker individuals in order to gain sympathy for himself or his family and to encourage ire toward the ones involved in bringing about his discipline. He will say things like this: "You know, I really love Bob, my boss, but …" He will try to present himself as being spiritually mature while casting shadows over the integrity of those who witnessed his behavior or "judged him guilty." This is all part of the plan to gain support from those who offer a listening, sympathetic ear. Usually, the listener will not realize they are being reeled into his darkness like a hooked fish, inch by inch.[84]
7. He will recount events from a time when he was walking in the truth and use them to try to confirm his innocence. "18 years of my life, I've given to my boss," or "12 years of love and devotion, and this is how they repay me."[85] Again, it's a tactic of darkness to hide the current facts behind the facts of yesterday. He may pretend to be sorry and try to negotiate to alter his discipline or change the terms already laid out.
8. He will rehearse his version of the "truth," re-writing the clear facts and further distorting reality. He may, in a false humility say he is praying for those who made him a victim. This causes his deception to grow deeper into his soul until he actually believes his personal purity and re-written "truth." This is when self-deception has taken root. When this stage is reached, further deception is attracted. Deception attracts deception, and deep darkness ensues rapidly. He may express a pseudo sorrow for "the misunderstanding," or "the problem," but will not accept personal responsibility in the form of genuine confession and repentance.
9. Now everything he hears, sees or reads will, in his mind, point out his own righteousness and the unrighteous injustice done to him. He may show others magazine articles or books that appear to affirm his innocence and others' guilt at least in his thinking. The tables are turned in his mind because of the dark deceptions now controlling; good becomes bad, bad becomes good, truth becomes a lie, lies become the truth, shame becomes glory, and glory becomes shame.[86] When a person is walking in deception, everything becomes twisted in his mind.

10. He cannot now repent because darkness is dominating his soul. He cannot accept the fact that his choices in words, attitude, or behavior brought him to this point. His pride and arrogance, along with the darkness will lead him into self-exaltation, self-innocence, self-glorification, and self-absorption. He cannot be satisfied for more than a few minutes without once again rehearsing his accusations, his bitterness, exalting himself in some way or de-elevating others.

Truth is no longer absolute to the person when he has reached this stage. His "truth" is subjective, depending on feelings, imagination, or the support he receives from others, which in his darkened mind, he believes, is a form of vindication or approval of some sort.

At this stage, all absolutes are gone. He may begin to pretend he is a prophet or apostle, using subjective dreams or prophesies to pronounce God's judgment on those who "caused this to happen" to him.

He begins to use God as his justification now, saying, "God showed me ..." However, he'll not be able to find anyone credible to confirm his "words," "dreams," or "prophetic announcements." He must perpetuate his momentum by finding undiscerning people to believe his subjective "truth."

Every church, like a body, must have a healthy immune system.

> **"If they repent you restore them; if they don't you dismiss them"**

2 Thessalonians 3:10-11

LAZY CHRISTIANS

Finally, we get to the case of lazy church members. Paul wrote in verse ten,

> **[10] For even when we were with you, this we commanded you, that if any would not work, neither should he eat.**
>
> **[11] For we hear that there are some which walk among you disorderly, working not at all, but are busybodies.**

Work is part of man's life. It was part of life before the fall of man in the Garden of Eden. Adam had to tend to the garden and name the animals. Only after the fall did work become toil. That was when people started sweating and "work" became a dirty word. But we were made to work. Everyone who can work should work. When you work it helps mold your personality.

Lazy people end up with warped personalities. Always!

TRUTH ILLUSTRATED – A UNIQUE STYLE OF LAZINESS

I read a bizarre story about a 53-year-old veteran who bilked the U.S. Government out of $700,000 over twenty years by faking paralysis. Every time he had to go to the veteran's hospital, he would tie his hands and legs up for two weeks beforehand so they would temporarily atrophy and not move while he was being checked. It seems like more work to be lazy!

I hear people say, "I was just too lazy to stop and get that." "Lazy" is an ugly word even used casually. It shouldn't even be in your vocabulary. It is no virtue to be lazy. Again, Laziness is no virtue!

I was standing in Ace Hardware the other day and the man in front of me said, "I should have gotten the pipe dope, but I was too lazy to go back and get it." How lazy can you get? I felt like saying, "Do you want me to go back and get it? It will only take me thirty seconds."

Those who will not work should not even eat, the Bible says (II Thessalonians 3:10).

TRUTH ILLUSTRATED – A BEGGARS ORGANIZATION

In some states, I discovered, there are actually organized "homeless businesses." The homeless men gather in the morning, and the "boss" assigns them to different corners of the city. Standing on the corners, panhandling with cardboard signs, they allegedly "earn" $150 - $400 a day. I watched one day as a guy came and relieved another guy, as if they were working shifts. I couldn't believe my eyes until I found out they had it all organized.[87]

2 Thessalonians 3:12-18

Paul writes,

> **12 Now them that are such we command and exhort by our Lord Jesus Christ, that with quietness they work, and eat their own bread.**
>
> **13 But ye, brethren, be not weary in well doing.**

When lazy people mooch off of others it gets weary for those who are trying to do the right thing.

> **14 And if any man obey not our word by this epistle, note that man, and have no company with him, that he may be ashamed.**

If you have a lazy bum coming to your Bible study or prayer meeting and always mooching off everybody else, tell him not to come back! Tell him you don't want to fellowship with him until he gets a job. But Paul knew that there was a natural tendency to go to extremes and start treating the person with disrespect. He writes verse 15,

> **[15] Yet count him not as an enemy, but admonish him as a brother.**

Now Paul gives a three-fold blessing when we follow his scriptural instructions:

> **[16] Now the Lord of peace himself give you peace always by all means ...**

THERE IS BLESSING NUMBER ONE: PEACE.

In a time of tension and confusion, a busy season, God gives you peace deep on the inside.

> **... The Lord be with you all**

THAT'S THE SECOND BLESSING: PRESENCE.

With His presence, you can do anything He asks you to do.

> **[17] The salutation of Paul with mine own hand, which is the token in every epistle: so I write**

Paul put his own seal and signature on the letter because there were counterfeit letters going around saying they were from Paul.

THEN HE GAVE THE THIRD BLESSING - GRACE:

> **[18] The grace of our Lord Jesus Christ be with you all. Amen.**

What a wonderful way to end! He told this model church to rely again on God's grace. He took them full circle, greeting them with a reminder of God's grace in the beginning, and now ending with the same reminder.

POWER PRINCIPLES:

- **A disorderly church is an ineffective church**
- **There are biblical ways to handle conflicts within a church. Let's stick to them!**
- **God expects us to work effectively**

CONCLUSION

You have blessed me by reading my commentary on 1 and 2 Thessalonians. Thank you for joining me in this "Blue-Collar Bible Study." I trust you are lifting up the Lord Jesus in your words and your life.

I hope you have felt as blessed and enriched in reading this Common Man's Commentary as I have in researching and writing it. I believe the principles in Paul's two letters can change the way ordinary people live. I know they have changed my life, and continue to change my life as I read and understand more about how the Thessalonians became model Christians and a model church.

I look forward to having you along for the next book in the Common Man's Commentary series. Be blessed!

It would be a blessing to me if you would send me a quick e-mail to let me know your thoughts on the Common Man's Commentary Series. I look forward to hearing from you.

Dr. Dave Williams

Dave@DaveWilliams.com

The American Center for Pacesetting Leadership

P O Box 80825

Lansing, MI 48908-0825

ENDNOTES

1. I Peter 2:5 NLT And you are living stones that God is building into his spiritual temple. What's more, you are his holy priests. Through the mediation of Jesus Christ, you offer spiritual sacrifices that please God.
2. Angelus Temple, 1100 Glendale Blvd, Los Angeles, CA 90026-3203
3. Colossians 3:23-24
4. D. L. Moody (1837 - 1899) U.S. Evangelist
5. Romans 11:26: "And so all Israel shall be saved: as it is written, There shall come out of Sion the Deliverer, and shall turn away ungodliness from Jacob"
6. Isaiah 55:11
7. Mark 13:31; Luke 16:17
8. Psalm 141:3
9. https://www.christianstudylibrary.org/article/preaching-word-power-holy-spirit
10. Acts 16
11. Acts 5
12. Vine's Complete Expository Dictionary of Old and New Testament Words, Thomas Nelson, Inc., Nashville, 1996
13. Proverbs 18:16
14. Colossians 1:6
15. Vine's Complete Expository Dictionary of Old and New Testament Words, Thomas Nelson, Inc., Nashville, 1996
16. Time, Inc. Article, "Are Microchip Tags Safe?" By Siobhan Morrissey Thursday, Oct. 18, 2007 / Knight Ridder/Tribune Business News, July, 2003
17. I Corinthians 15:51-57; I Thessalonians 4:13-18
18. Revelation 19:9
19. Matthew 24:21; Romans 1:18; Revelation 14:10: Revelation 15:7
20. Raschke, Wendy J., ed. The Archaeology of the Olympics: the Olympics and Other Festivals in Antiquity. Madison, Wisconsin: Wisconsin University Press, 1987.
21. Acts 16:24-26
22. False Predictions, http://www.creativeyouthideas.com, Posted by Ken Sapp on December 31, 2006
23. Vine's Complete Expository Dictionary of Old and New Testament Words, Thomas Nelson, Inc., Nashville, 1996
24. Matthew 25:21-23
25. Blog Critics Magazine Sports, Did a Woman Cheat to Win the Boston Marathon? Published November 16, 2006, http://blogcritics.org
26. http://www.morethandreams.tv/dreamsofjesus.html
27. Vine's Complete Expository Dictionary of Old and New Testament Words, Thomas Nelson, Inc., Nashville, 1996
28. For example, our Gilead Healing Center in Lansing, Michigan. It's known as "The Place of Another Chance."
29. Lansing State Journal, "Showtime in the Pulpit," by Mark Nixon, October 1, 1990
30. A Current Affair, 1995, Rebroadcast May 13, 1996
31. Demosthenes (384–322 BC) was a prominent Greek statesman and orator of ancient Athens
32. Vine's Complete Expository Dictionary of Old and New Testament Words, Thomas Nelson, Inc., Nashville, 1996
33. The Decline and Fall of the Roman Empire, Edward Gibbon, Henry Hart Milman, Publ: P. F. Collier & Son, 1899
34. TIME, Sunday, Jun. 24, 2001 "Porn Goes Mainstream" By Joel Stein, http://www.time.com
35. 1 Corinthians 12:13
36. Exodus 18:13-27; Numbers 11:10-17
37. Acts 6:1-7
38. Matthew 24:21
39. 2 Corinthians 5:8
40. Zechariah 12:10-12
41. Revelation 19:15. 21
42. Revelation 19:20; 20:10
43. Zechariah 14:4

44. Revelation 20:2, 3
45. 2 Peter 3:13; Revelation 21:1
46. Ante-Nicene Fathers: 10 Volumes, Alexander Roberts (Editor), James Donaldson (Editor), Philip Schaff (Editor), Henry Wace (Editor) Hendrickson Publishers (June 1, 1994)
47. http://www.september11news.com/
48. 88 Reasons Why The Rapture Will Be in 1988: The Feast of Trumpets (Rosh Hash-Ana) September 11-12-13 - Edgar C. Whisenant, Whisenant/World Bible Society (1988)
49. 2 Peter 3:10
50. 1 Thessalonians 5:3
51. Revelation 13; Daniel 7:8-11,20-21, 24-25; 8:8-14; 19-22; 11:21-22; 31-32; 36-39; 12:11-12; Matthew 24:15
52. Matthew 6:33
53. "The Dead Do Tell Tales at Vesuvius," National Geographic magazine, June 1970
54. Revelation 2:6; 14-15
55. (I know, I know, my doctor friends will say, "But ice cream is not good for your body!")
56. Luis Palau, Jr. is an international Christian evangelist living in the Portland area in Oregon, United States. He was born in Argentina, and began preaching at age 18.
57. The Reverend Dr. Peter Marshall was a Scottish-American preacher and twice served as Chaplain of the United States Senate. He is remembered most popularly from the biography *A Man Called Peter*
58. Lee Braxton was Vice-President of the Full Gospel Business Men's Fellowship International; Mayor of Whiteville, North Carolina; Chairman of the Board, of First National Bank; President of Braxton Enterprises; Vice-President of Radio Station WENC; President of Citizens Auto Finance Company; Owner Columbus Finance Company; Vice-President Braxton-Warren Company; President Braxton Motor Sales, Inc. President Braxton Auto Parts, Inc.; Chairman Public Library Board; Chairman Columbus County Development Committee; Member Legislative Committee, "North Carolina League of Municipalities; Member Executive Committee, 279th District Rotary International; National Director Oral Roberts Coast-to-Coast Radio Broadcast; Director Whiteville Merchants Association and Chamber of Commerce; Director North Carolina Merchants Association. http://www.fgbmfi.org/history.htm
59. Gilead Healing Center, 306 S. Creyts Road, Lansing, Michigan 48917
60. I Samuel 17
61. Calvary Chapel of Costa Mesa, 3800 S Fairview St, Santa Ana, CA 92704, www.calvarychapelcostamesa.com
62. UCLA Imaging Study Reveals How Active Empathy Charges Emotions; Physical Mimicry Of Others Jump-starts Key Brain Activity Science Daily (Apr. 8, 2003)
63. The Harry S. Truman Library and Museum 500 W. US Hwy. 24. Independence MO 64050 truman.library@nara.gov
64. Hebrews 12:2
65. Florence May Chadwick (November 9, 1918 – March 15, 1995) was an American swimmer who was the first woman to swim the English Channel in both directions. http://en.wikipedia.org/wiki/Florence_Chadwick
66. 2 Samuel 23
67. 2 Samuel 23
68. http://www.dmm.org
69. Ante-Nicene Fathers: 10 Volumes, Alexander Roberts (Editor), James Donaldson (Editor), Philip Schaff (Editor), Henry Wace (Editor) Hendrickson Publishers (June 1, 1994)
70. Zechariah 12:11
71. 1 Corinthians 15:51-55
72. Spiritism is a kind of the Occult: Divination attempts to foretell the future, Magic to change it, Spiritism tries to communicate with the dead to receive information and help from them. Spiritualism, or Spiritism, uses Christian rites and prayers, misleading some ignorant attendants, because often their meetings may look like Christian services.
73. www.theparisreview.org/blog/2016/11/04/in-the-joints-of-their-toes/ https://www.history.com/news/ghost-hoax-spiritualism-fox-sisters https://adriansalamon.co.uk/blog/the-truth-behind-psychic-mediums-a-magicians-perspective/
74. Revelation 20:4-7
75. Revelation 20:11
76. Matthew 17:1-8; Mark 9:2-8; Luke 8:28-36; 2 Peter 1:16-18
77. Judgment Seat of Christ: Romans 14:10: 2 Corinthians 5:10
78. Jezebel Spirit, David R. Williams, Decapolis Publishing, 428 S. Creyts Rd. Lansing, Michigan 48917
79. https://davewilliams.com/product/toxic-comittees-and-venomous-boards-book/
80. Vine's Complete Expository Dictionary of Old and New Testament Words, Thomas Nelson, Inc., Nashville, 1996

81. Now I beseech you, brethren, mark them which cause divisions and offences contrary to the doctrine which ye have learned; and avoid them. (Romans 16:17)
82. 2 Timothy 4:14
83. I John 2:9-11
84. James 3:14-16
85. Ezekiel 18:19-24
86. Romans 1:25
87. Virtually every city of any size has an established population of professional panhandlers, most of them doing well in that lifestyle and often surprisingly are very well organized. Panhandling http://www.miamiherald.com/136/story/410762.html Brother Can You Spare $4.6 Million? Written by Dave Nalle, Published August 24, 2005 http://blogcritics.org/archives/2005/08/24/0203012.

BIBLIOGRAPHY

Best, Ernest. Commentary on the First and Second Epistles to the Thessalonians. Reprinted with additional bibliography. Bruce, F.F. 1 and 2 Thessalonians. Word Biblical Commentary, 45. Waco: Word Books, Publisher, 1982.

Ellicott, Charles John. Commentary on the Epistles of St. Paul to the Thessalonians. Grand Rapids: Zondervan Publishing House, n.d. Frame, James Everett. A Critical and Exegetical Commentary on the Epistles of St. Paul to the Thessalonians. Edinburgh: T. &T. Clark, 1912.

Gaventa, Beverly Roberts. 1 & 2 Thessalonians, in Interpretation Commentary. Westminster/John Knox Press, 1998.

Harper's New Testament Commentaries. New York: Harper & Row, Publishers, 1977.

Hiebert, D. Edmond. The Thessalonian Epistles. Chicago: Moody Press, 1971.

Hogg, C. F. and Vine, W. E. The Epistles of Paul the Apostle to the Thessalonians. Glasgow: Pickering and Inglis, 1929.

Holmes, Michael W. 1 & 2 Thessalonians; from Biblical Text to Contemporary Life. NIV Application Commentary, ed. Terry Muck. Grand Rapids: Zondervan, 1998.

Jensen, Irving L. 1 and 2 Thessalonians: A Self-Study Guide. Chicago: Moody Press, 1999. Lenski, R. C. H. Interpretation of St. Paul's Epistles to the Colossians, to the Thessalonians, to Timothy, to Titus and to Philemon. Columbus: The Wartburg Press, 1937.

Lightfoot, J. B. Notes on the Epistles of St. Paul. Grand Rapids: Zondervan Publishing Company, n.d. Martin, D. Michael. 1 & 2 Thessalonians, in the New American Commentary. Nashville: Broadman/Holman, 1995.

Marshall, I. Howard. 1 and 2 Thessalonians. New Century Bible Commentary. Grand Rapids: Eerdmans Publishing Company, 1983.

Milligan, George. St. Paul's Epistles to the Thessalonians. London: Macmillan, 1908.

Reprint, Minneapolis: Klock and Klock Christian Publishers, 1980.

Morris, Leon. The First and Second Epistles to the Thessalonians. New International Commentary on the New Testament. Grand Rapids: Eerdmans, 1959.

Morris, Leon The Epistles of Paul to the Thessalonians. The Tyndale New Testament Commentaries. Grand Rapids: Wm. B. Eerdmans Publishing Company, 1956.

Richard, Earl. 1 & 2 Thessalonians, Vol. 11 in Sacra Pagina series. np: Michael Glazier, 1997.

Ryrie, Charles Caldwell. First and Second Thessalonians. Chicago: Moody Press, 1959.

Stott, John R. 1 and 2 Thessalonians: Living in the End Times InterVarsity Press, 1999.

Thomas, Robert L. "1,2 Thessalonians." In The Expositor's Bible Commentary. 11. Edited by Frank Gaebelein. Grand Rapids: Zondervan Publishing House, 1978.

Walvoord, John F. The Thessalonian Epistles. Findlay, OH: Dunham Publishing Company, 1955.

Williams, David, and Gasque, Ward. 1 & 2 Thessalonians, in the New International Biblical Commentary. Hendrickson, 1995.

Woolsey, Warren. 1 and 2 Thessalonians: A Bible Commentary in the Wesleyan Tradition Wesley Press, 1997.

ABOUT THE AUTHOR

ABOUT DAVE WILLIAMS, "AMERICA'S PACESETTING LIFE COACH" ™

Dr. Dave Williams is a teacher, speaker, author, and trainer. He teaches and trains on the pacesetting life with an uncommon prophetic edge.

COACHING PASTORS AND BUSINESS LEADERS

Dave Williams is affectionately called, "America's Pacesetting Life Coach"™

Dr. Dave Williams teaches and trains with an uncommon prophetic edge on how to live the pacesetting life. He serves as a trainer and coach to church leaders, business leaders, entrepreneurs, and high-achievers from all walks of life who want to discover the key to attaining God's best for their lives.

His relentless three-pronged approach—spiritual, attitudinal, and practical—has helped transform individuals, businesses, churches, and pastors into respected and influential executives and leaders. He knows how to help people cultivate their inherent gifts, enhance their professional and ministerial performance, and create the kind of value that attracts real success.

Dave tenaciously guides leaders in how to stay connected with the Great Commission. Best-selling Author, Dave has authored over 60 books, with over 3.5 million copies sold of his platinum bestselling *New Life...Start of Something Wonderful,* which is now published in eight different languages.

AWARDS:

- **The LeBrocq Award for Church Planting**
- **The Illumination Award for his book, *The Art of Pacesetting Leadership***
- **Degrees: D. Min., D.D. (Hon). DSL (Hon), ThM**

- Key to the City presented by the Honorable Mayor Terry McCain
- Certificate from the Michigan State Legislation for having the most significant "religious" influence in the state
- Berean Medal of Honor
- Dozen's of National and State Awards for Missions Participation

PACESETTING LIFE™ SEMINARS

Dave's Pacesetting Life™ Seminars are times of authentic impartation:

- The Pacesetting Life ™ Faith Goals Seminar and Retreats
- The Pacesetting Life ™ Speaker's Seminar: Turning Ordinary Talks into Heavenly Impartations
- The Pacesetting Life ™ Leader's Seminar: 44 Big Mistakes Leaders Make and How to Avoid Them
- The Pacesetting Life ™ High Achievers Seminar
- The Pacesetting Life ™ Holy Spirit Seminar
- The Pacesetting Life's ™ Art of Pacesetting Leadership—Authentic vs. Synthetic Leadership
- The Pacesetting Life's™ Art and Science of Authentic Wealth...by Covenant!

Dave believes that only a handful of God's people will choose to grab hold of this revelation and actually enter a "ministry of wealth" connected with missions and the Great Commission. This is also known as the Club 52 ® Intensive. (See www.DaveWilliams.com for a more detailed list of pacesetting seminars)

GENERAL BIO

Dave is a popular speaker at rallies, minister's conferences, churches, business training sessions, colleges, and Bible Schools. He hosted the "Pacesetter's Path" telecast for 19 years, seen worldwide over four satellite systems and over a syndicated television network. Dave was awarded honorary doctorates from Canada School of Graduate Theological Studies, and Faith Theological Seminary.

THE PASTORAL MINISTRY

Dave Williams served as pastor of Mount Hope Church in Lansing, Michigan, for more than thirty years. During that time,

He trained thousands of ministers and leaders through:

- **Mount Hope Bible Training Institute**
- **Dave Williams' Church Planter's School,**
- **Dave Williams' School for Pacesetting Church Leaders.**
- **Online Courses with students on every continent**
- **Accredited Bible College Curriculums (*Pacesetting Leadership / How to Help Your Pastor Succeed*)**

With the help of his staff and ministry partners, Dave established a 72-acre campus:

- **Worship Center**
- **Training Institute**
- **Children's Center**
- **Global Prayer Center**
- **Valley of Blessing**
- **Gilead Healing Center**
- **Care Facilities**
- **Event Center**
- **Café**
- **Fitness Center**
- **World Evangelism Headquarters**
- **Global Communications Center**
- **A State-Of-The-Art Office Complex**

Church planting and world evangelistic missions were a priority focus under Dave's pastoral leadership:

- **43 new Mount Hope Churches were planted in the United States**
- **Over 300 churches planted in West Africa**
- **200 affiliate churches in Asia, South Africa, and Zimbabwe**

Under Dave's leadership, the church gave over $40 million to global missions by the year 2012, and enjoyed a combined membership of over 100,000.

Dave's Pacesetting Leadership Training™ Courses are used in churches, Campus Ministries, and Missions worldwide.

Today, Dave serves as the global "ambassador" and "bishop" for the Mount Hope Global Church Network and leads Dave Williams Ministries, Strategic Global Mission, and Club 52 (for business people and entrepreneurs).

Dave served as a national general presbyter for the Assemblies of God, assistant district superintendent, executive presbyter, regent for North Central University, and an official global missions board member in Springfield.

Dave and his wife, Mary Jo, have offices and homes in Michigan and Florida.

www.DaveWilliams.com

P O Box 80825 Lansing, MI 48908-0825

FAITH BUILDING PRODUCTS

CREATING YOUR NEW REALITY
(8 MESSAGE MP3 DOWNLOAD)

How to transform the invisible to the visible and get what you want from life. The Master Key to Inexhaustible Resources. What do you want from life? Are you settling for whatever comes, struggling to move forward in your own strength? Learn how your thoughts create what you become, with God's help + faith, you can create a new reality!

A New Dimension of Breakthrough Learn how to transform the invisible to the visible and get what you want from life. Come to a new dimension and declare breakthrough and wealth in every area of your life.

You are destined for success! If it's 80 degrees and too hot, what do you do? Do you go downstairs, switch off the furnace breaker and open the windows? No! You change the thermostat. And that's what I want to share with you over this series. Reset your thermostat and relearn and reprogram the correct thinking. Words create an environment for increase or decrease. Topics include:

- **Words Create: Thoughts attract, words create, and actions multiply!**
- **What do You Want? When you know what you want you start attracting it! To get what you want, keep a list of goals in front of you to sharpen your focus.**
- **Your Outer World: Shaped by Your Inner World What you have on the outside comes from what you think about, dream about, and concern yourself with.**
- **Setting the Direction of Your Future: Fruit is the result of a root. Planning for the future is vital to producing the things you desire These eight insightful messages will show you how to tap into God's reality to overcome your present circumstances. You can live and walk in victory.**

DAVEWILLIAMS.COM/STORE

FILLED
(MP3 DOWNLOAD)

If you believe Jesus is your Savior, you have access to the mightiest power in the universe. You can share in God's overflowing joy and peace; you can access God's power and presence in a very personal and intimate way. You can be filled with God's Holy Spirit. Get ready for an experience that will change your spiritual life forever!

In this audio presentation, Dr. Dave Williams leads you into an understanding of how to have a relationship and be filled with the Holy Spirit. He reveals:

- **False beliefs people hold concerning the Holy Spirit**
- **The three dimensions of your relationship to the Holy Spirit**
- **The benefits of a relationship with the Holy Spirit**
- **How you can be filled with the Holy Spirit**
- **Do You Want the Anointing of Power?**

Do you really want an anointing of power for your life and ministry? A deep, fruitful relationship with the Holy Spirit? Do you want gifts of the Holy Spirit to flow through your life? Do you really want to come into the third-dimensional relationship with the Holy Spirit? If so, ask God to fill you with His Spirit. Are you ready for the adventure? Are you ready for the third-dimensional relationship with the Holy Spirit? Then receive the gift now.

WEALTH 101
(5 SESSION MP3 DOWNLOAD)

Most people try to increase their income without changing their concept of wealth. As a result they continue to find themselves struggling to pay bills, meet mortgage payments, and provide for emergencies. They need a revelation from God. This series is a divine revelation that can bring you into the place the Psalmist called the wealthy place. 1: Using Your Faith for Miracle Wealth Seeds 2: How Jesus Provided for your Wealth 3: God's Perfect Plan for Your wealth 4: Gaining Increase and Multiplication in your Wealth 5: Immutable Principles of wealth You are an uncommon individual with your life aimed at the wealthy place. Join Dr. Dave Williams now as he unfolds the secret of launching your life into the place of greater wealth than you have previously imagined!

DAVEWILLIAMS.COM/STORE

WHAT'S DIFFERENT ABOUT MILLIONAIRES?
(2 SESSION MP3 DOWNLOAD)

What do you believe about wealth? Is it only for a few who are born with it? Do you believe it is your destiny to be wealthy? Your attitude toward money, debt, investing, and financial planning will make or break your monetary worth. This CD set will share the unique viewpoint the very wealthy have toward money.

1. **What's Different about Millionaires: How do the wealthy view money, credit, consumer debt, and investing?**

What part does Christian faith play in your financial success? What do you need to change in your attitudes toward money that will launch you into the wealthy place?

2. **Principles of Wealth: Do you believe God has called you to be wealthy?**

Under Principles of Wealth: God wants to prosper you so that you can enjoy the desires of your heart and also give generously into His Kingdom.

LEARN GOD'S FOOLPROOF PRINCIPLES TO WEALTH.

Club 52 started with a vision: "Millionaires with a Mission." You can be ordinary or you can be extraordinary. It's your choice. Learn why only a handful of God's people experience the power to get wealth and how to recognize a poverty spirit ... or scarcity mentality. The opportunities are greater now than ever before.

YOUR SPECTACULAR MIND
(2 MESSAGE MP3 DOWNLOAD)

Unleash your God-given potential Did you know your inner reality creates your outer reality? The thoughts of your mind must be set for God's success and victory, or nothing you do will make a difference. Now all glory to God, who is able, through his mighty power at work within us, to accomplish infinitely more than we might ask or think. —Ephesians 3:20 (NLT) In this two CD set, Dave Williams unlocks the mysteries of the mind, and gives you plans and strategies for developing your mind—an awesome gift from God. You will discover how to transform weakness to strength and failure to fruitfulness by learning to think like God thinks.

DAVEWILLIAMS.COM/STORE

8 PRINCIPLES OF WEALTH
(2 MESSAGE MP3 DOWNLOAD)

No believer has a money problem! Money problems are most likely the result of lack of knowledge, lack of obedience, lack of desire, or making excuses. You might also have wrong ideas of how God views wealth. The truth is, poverty does not bring glory to God. Your prosperity does bring God glory. He wants you to be wealthy so you can advance his kingdom on earth. And, best of all, God has a foolproof plan for outrageous wealth in your life.

42 THINGS PACESETTING PASTORS KNOW AND DO THAT OTHERS DON'T
(3 MESSAGE MP3 DOWNLOAD)

Leadership principles every pastor should know. Leading a church is one of the most challenging jobs in the world! Satan constantly seeks to confound and destroy the church. There are stumbling blocks, roadblocks, and block heads that seek to destroy the church's effectiveness and frustrate its success. These three messages share valuable insights into overcoming the problems pastors face. You will learn what to do when there is a whole lot of shaking going on in your church. You will learn how to become a highly effective pastor, and what to do when things aren't going according to God's plan and purpose. Your skill as a leader directly affects your ability to run your race—these messages will help you run and win!

HEART-TO-HEART TALKS WITH YOUNG PASTORS
(12 SESSION MP3 DOWNLOAD)

Some of the most important issues for young pastors and how to address them. After over 30 years as pastor of Mount Hope Church, and now serving as a Global Ambassador, Dave Williams talks heart-to-heart to young and new pastors. Download includes the following sessions:

1. **The Deadly Danger of the Second Word: There are two voices—only one will lead you and protect you**

DAVEWILLIAMS.COM/STORE

2. **Surprising Church Trends Now: Why knowing the trends can help you plan for growth**
3. **Dealing with Foolish Committees and Constant Critics: Prophetic words I gave my successor & why they apply to you**
4. **Why Many Are Called but Few Are Chosen: Things I wish I had learned sooner**
5. **Dealing with Deceivers & Properly Advertising Your Church**
6. **Handling Ministry Distress**
7. **Engaging the Prophetic Realm: Taking time for margins in life and intimacy with the Holy Spirit**
8. **How to Give a Powerful Altar Call: Top secrets of the greatest soul-winners.**
9. **Connecting Your Life and Church to What's on God's Heart**
10. **Dealing with Sin in the Ministry: How to Organize the local church**
11. **Stages of Church Growth and Avoiding the Landmines: Sifting and Pruning**
12. **Discipline in the Church & Recognizing True Repentance**

CRASH COURSE IN INTERCESSORY PRAYER
(3 SESSION MP3 DOWNLOAD)

God is looking for a few good men and women! He needs powerful prayer warriors to join his elite team of intercessors. Prayer moves mountains, changes circumstances, and touches God's heart. These messages, by Dr. Dave Williams will help you develop your prayer "muscles" so your prayers bring down blessings from heaven and destroy every snare of the enemy! Become a more powerful, anointed intercessor!

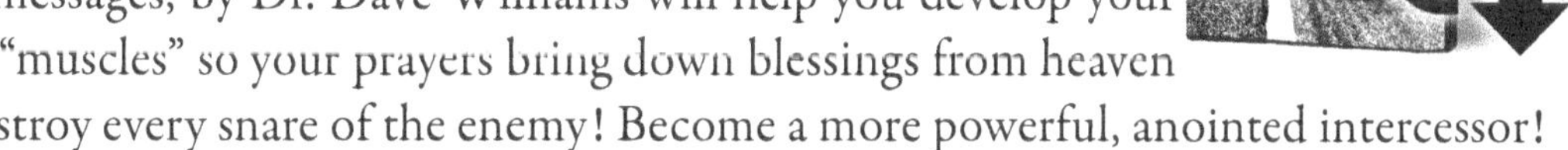

HOW TO FAST FORWARD YOUR LIFE AND MINISTRY THROUGH MISSIONS
(1 SESSION MP3 DOWNLOAD)

When you walk in obedience to God, he will advance every area of your life. In this message, recorded live at Harvest Church in Elk Grove, California, Dr. Dave Williams shares his amazing testimony of how his commitment to world missions put his life and ministry on "Fast Forward" Dave's knowledge and faith grew, he came to believe that knowing what is right is not the same as doing what is right. Doctrine is meant to be experienced; "head" knowledge is not enough, actions are what count. When you walk in obedience to God, he will advance every area of your life. One of the most powerful principles that will put every believer's life on "Fast Forward" is planting financial seeds in God's Kingdom through missions giving. Listen and learn how participating in this important Kingdom principle can make your life more successful.

YOGA CRAZE IN THE LAST DAYS
(AMAZON & KINDLE)

Jesus warned us of a coming Day in which deception would run rampant in the world. He warned that this Age of Deception would usher in a period known as "The Great Tribulation," where the world would be drawn into worshipping a false Messiah known as the Anti-christ. St. Paul said many would come under a strong delusion in the last days.

Yoga Craze in the Last Days will walk you through the truth about this ancient practice called "Yoga" and why so many are running to Yoga studios today. What is the weird appeal of Yoga? You'll discover the truth as you read this well- researched book.

24 REASONS TO AVOID YOGA: IF YOU ARE A CHRISTIAN
(AMAZON & KINDLE)

For those who want to warn others about Yoga in a succinct manner, we've produced a book with excerpts and commentary on the comprehensive book, ***Yoga Craze in the Last Days.*** Dr. Dave Williams takes you on a journey he never wanted to take—a journey into the world of deception and delusion. Most Christians have no idea what Yoga really is, and what it can do to their lives and family.

ON LINE COURSES: JOIN THOUSANDS OF PACESETTERS WORLDWIDE

THE ART OF PACESETTING LEADERSHIP
(BOOK, DVD COURSE, ONLINE COURSE)

Keys to Gaining The Leading Advantage

Dave Williams is recognized as one of America's foremost authorities on leadership. In this course, you will learn the proven principles of leadership that will launch your life, ministry, business, or job to higher levels of success. Join him on a journey of discovery as he shares the secrets of developing the heart of an authentic leader.

Embark on one of the greatest endeavors of your life—becoming a pacesetting leader in whatever you are called to do. The principles in this course will advance your life, to greater levels of achievement as you begin to experience and practice the art of pacesetting leadership. These principles have transformed lives, businesses, and ministries for several decades—and they will transform your life and your calling as you put them into action.

The Art of Pacesetting Leadership (Book)

- 37 Power packed chapters
- 313 pages of step-by-step pacesetting principles

Leadership Course

- 16 sessions on DVD
- 16 audio recordings
- Hardcover book
- Student manual
- Moderator's manual

ONLINE Course

- 16 Video Sessions
- Student Workbook Download
- The Art of Pacesetting Leadership Ebook
- MP3 Session Downloads
- Devotional Reflections

DAVEWILLIAMS.COM/PLONLINE

Made in USA - Kendallville, IN
67571_9781629850726
03.18.2025 2008